Praise for *Notes from Cyberground*

"The best part of waking up is not coffee in your cup but finding on Facebook one of Mikhail Iossel's bracingly brilliant mini-editorials."
—Joel Conarroe, President Emeritus of the John Simon Guggenheim Foundation and PEN American Center

"Mikhail Iossel is tracking in real time as we move through this dark stage of American history. He is such a worthy guide here—his point of view a needed cocktail of rage, knowledge, unique personal experience, and hard-won humor."
—Aimee Bender, author of
The Particular Sadness of Lemon Cake

"Mikhail Iossel's intelligent and impassioned essays are less about the current administration than they are urgent reminders that American democracy, despite its imperfections, still carries a basic decency, a sense of humanity, at its center. Iossel is the realist who offers hope."
—Whitney Otto, author of
How to Make an American Quilt

"Mikhail Iossel's micro-editorials on contemporary American politics have been like tiny little lifeboats on this Trumpian sea of trash. The resulting book—scathing, hilarious, so deeply smart—should be read by everyone who still values decency and democracy."
—Robin Romm,
author of *The Mercy Papers*

T0162457

NOTES FROM CYBERGROUND

TRUMPLAND AND MY OLD SOVIET FEELING

NOTES FROM CYBERGROUND

TRUMPLAND AND MY OLD SOVIET FEELING

MIKHAIL IOSSEL

New Europe Books

Williamstown, Massachusetts

Published by New Europe Books, 2018
Williamstown, Massachusetts
www.NewEuropeBooks.com
Copyright © by Mikhail Iossel
Cover design by Kurt Stengel
Cover photo by Mikhail Iossel
Interior design by Knowledge Publishing

Most of the pieces in this book appeared originally on the timeline of the author's personal Facebook page. Portions of the book appeared previously or subsequent to Facebook posting in NewYorker.com, *Foreign Policy,* SoundrelTime.com, the *Odessa Review,* and elsewhere.

978-0-9995416-0-9

Cataloging-in-publication data is available from the Library of Congress.

First edition, 2018

10 9 8 7 6 5 4 3 2 1

In memory of my father,

Yuri Iossel

A Four-Post Preface

June 4, 2017
Why do I keep talking about Trump in my Facebook posts? Because by the very fact of his occupying the White House, he grossly violates my belief in the basic moral underpinnings of the American system of values. Partly, it must be an emigré kind of thing.

June 16, 2017
Mikhail, your friends have liked your posts 588,934,786,452 times!

We're glad you're sharing your life with the people you care about on Facebook, even though they don't necessarily care about you or even have the foggiest idea of your existence and we don't really know for certain whether your care about them or not and despite the fact that we at Facebook do believe you could be spending your time more productively, doing something more useful for yourself and the rest of the humanity, such as gazing mutely at the sky while sitting on the shore of a majestically flowing river and periodically writing down your thoughts concerning the impermanent nature of life on small pieces of paper, and then folding those pieces of paper into miniature paper boats and tossing the latter into said river. Congratulations, Mikhail, on wasting the time of your life on our social-networking platform with such mystifying consistency!

[Editor's note: This post saw one hundred and twelve likes and three shares. One of seventeen comments: "Your presence online has made the life of this stranger richer in a beautiful ubiquitous way."]

July 2, 2017

I understand all too well that to many people, it feels like a total waste of time—talking about Trump, posting comments about his pathetic criminal authoritarian persona, denouncing him and his boundless sleaziness, mocking him in his extreme moronic ignorance, resisting by any expressive means possible the very outlandishly insulting phenomenon of his being the (illegitimate, most likely) occupant of the White House. One doesn't want to think about Trump's fetid self, the very thought of him makes one feel queasy, one wants to shut out of one's mind the sheer reality of his tawdry existence and keep living one's life as if it had nothing to do with him. That's perfectly natural and relatable . . . and that's just how we lived back in the Soviet Union, too: by pretending that the degenerates ruling our lives—the doddering, disoriented, incoherent Brezhnev and the coldly calculating and uncommonly vicious Andropov and the perfectly brainless and barely breathing Chernenko and all the rest of them, with their many-million-strong army of KGB rats and snitches—had nothing to do with us and the daily grind and steady routine of our lives: not any more than the eternal darkness and brittle snow and piercing damp cold of Leningrad winters or the smog-ridden viscous heat of Moscow summers did. They were an unalterable given, those vile rulers of our reality, and our reality was arranged according to their insane specifications; and everyone knew that it was perfectly pointless and even, potentially, quite recklessly dangerous to dwell too much on that circumstance, let alone to make negative oral or written pronouncements with regard to it. And it just wasn't cool, either—talking about that surreal reality of our reality: to hell with it and with the lot of them, those Kremlin-bound vermin aren't worthy of our wasting the irreplaceable time of our lives on them; sure, they can exercise full control over our physical selves, but not over our immortal souls, and so on. Well, you know. That's how it was in good old USSR.

To be sure, we are nowhere near that point of no return yet in the US—and almost certainly, thank goodness, we will never get to that point here: the democratic system of checks and balances is stronger than any two-bit dictator-loving criminal authoritarian grifter; it is working, resisting, and, so far, successfully rebuffing Trump's repeated encroachments upon the nation's territories of freedom. Trump may be a rolling train wreck, the worst catastrophe to befall the institution of American democracy since the Civil War, the greatest political calamity in the country's modern history—but he too will pass, and will be gone before too long, and the old sands of time will bury the obscene braying sound of his voice; America will survive him and will move on, gradually defeating the stubborn virus of Trumpism in its bloodstream.

Still, it is important to recognize the distinctly totalitarian nature of the chaos, the foul entropy that is Trump's natural existential milieu, and in which he endeavors to immerse all of us on a constant basis, ceaselessly, tirelessly. He pushes himself shamelessly into our lives around the clock, forces us to think of him ten million times more than he deserves; his unarticulated goal is to exhaust us, to force us to give up and accept as an ironclad given his filthy rule, his gross self in the White House and whatever the hell he may intend to do further to enrich himself and his cronies and to humiliate America and all of us more still. An empty shell of a man, whose own life has never had any human meaning, he now is laying a grotesquely oversized claim on the time of our lives, in the hope that we'll give up and accept the inevitability of his reality.

One shouldn't accept it. One shouldn't get tired. One shouldn't get lulled into sleep. One shouldn't allow him, his role model Putin, and the small-minded America he represents to dictate the rules of our lives.

One should not give him the gratification of being taken for granted. That way lies tyranny.

October 8, 2017

What we talk about when we talk about Trump: not Trump. Trump is just a novelty act, if admittedly an uncommonly ugly one: beyond the initial shock, what's there left to talk about?

Ourselves, ultimately, and our own sense of what's right and wrong, good and evil, decent and indecent, acceptable and unacceptable in the world as we hope we know it.

CONTENTS

Mikhail Iossel
November 2016

November 8, 2016
Election Day.

Well,
America . . . Do the right thing today.

November 8, 2016
Dixville Notch (NH) just voted, all eight of its voters:
Clinton 50%
Trump 25%
Johnson 12.5%
Romney 12.5%
Romney?

November 9, 2016
America has proven unable to resist the virus of fascism currently abroad in the Western world. Let's hope its political institutions will turn out to be resilient enough to conquer it from within over the next four years.

Difficult times are ahead, but America must hang in there.

This is how we used to live back in the Soviet Union: rely upon the people you love, upon your circle of close friends, don't talk about politics with strangers, assume that people you don't know may well be, and likely are, possessed by the hateful totalitarian Soviet mindset; try not to watch much of anything other than sports or non political movies and art concerts on television; read books, write, have drinks with friends, look at the sky, dream of a better tomorrow. Hang in there. You still have the potent option of the free elections we did not have back there. This is not the end of the world, even if it may feel that way right now. America is stronger than its temporary madness. In the end, we'll be all right.

November 9, 2016

You can tell children, who may be scared and confused now, that sometimes bad things happen in life, sometimes bad guys win and good people lose, sometimes America decides to take a break from being great and to do something really ugly and stupid instead, hurting its own future pretty badly and embarrassing itself in the eyes of the world—but that in America, for as long as it still is a democracy, where the constant, ceaseless war between the past and the present can only be refought at the ballot box, good people always have a chance to make a strong comeback and defeat the bad guys.

In the Soviet Union of my childhood and youth, parents could not talk about any such "political" stuff with their children. They could not say to their children what they thought of the narrow confederacy of senescent evil dunces running their country gradually into the ground. That would have been foolish and pointless, and they knew, too, that with a high degree of likelihood their children might repeat their dangerous, seditious words at school, with predictable immediate and dire consequences for them and their children. So they kept silent. Only in the middle of the night, surreptitiously, did they attempt listening to the KGB frequencies-suppressed "enemy voices" in Russian (Voice of America, BBC, Deutsche Welle) on their portable short-wave radios.

But this still is America. It still is neither the old Soviet Union nor the totalitarian Russia of today, whose wily and amoral ruler the new American president-elect, that spoiled man-child, so wistfully and openly admires. One can be truthful and open with one's children or anyone else in America, with no fear of political repercussions . . . for now, anyway.

There is no reason to pretend this is not a true tragedy. It is a tragedy. But we will be all right, in the end. America will come through this with its democratic institutions intact, as it did weather the previous, equally and even more desperate calamities in its past. But for now, indeed, we may want to have that talk with our children. We also may want to reach out to those among us whose lives may be more directly and severely impacted than ours by the emboldened multitudes of Trump's triumphantly loud moral nonmajority: those who do not look or sound like Trump or the bulk of his supporters, who do not share his core electorate's faith (while Trump himself, of course, is no more religious than that dead orange animal on top of his head), or their "traditional" values, or their xenophobia, or their homophobia, or their bigotry, or their racism and anti-Semitism, or their misogyny, or their sickening, mad attachment to firearms. . . . We must let each other know we are all in this together now.

November 9, 2016

America is having a peaceful transition of power to someone who does not believe in the US Constitution.

November 9, 2016

Tonight is the seventy-eighth anniversary of Kristallnacht—
The Night of the Broken Glass—when all across Germany,
200 synagogues were destroyed, more than 8,000 Jewish shops
were looted, and tens of thousands of Jews were relocated to
concentration camps.

Today also is the twenty-seventh anniversary of the Berlin
Wall coming down.

Massive protests have broken out tonight in a number of
large American cities—the first night after the election as the
forty-fifth US president of the all-time favorite candidate of
white supremacists and anti-Semites, whose primary campaign
promise was to build a giant wall between the US and Mexico
(and to have the Mexican government pay for it): the candidate
of the Wall.

November 9, 2016

Several people have told me today they were feeling physically
unwell, ill, heartbroken to the point of fearing they might be
having a heart attack. This reaction is qualitatively different
from those normally experienced after one's candidate's
electoral loss, when one would merely be feeling angry or sad,
if sometimes very deeply and intensely so. This time around,
it is the psychosomatic manifestation of the fear of the future,
for oneself and one's loved ones, under the presidency of
an obviously unqualified, entirely unpredictable, emotionally
unstable, intellectually incurious, remarkably vulgar and
offensive and demonstrably deplorable, indecent man. It is the
fear for one's country, fear at the thought of not knowing or
recognizing it anymore, no longer understanding the hearts
and minds of a good half of one's fellow citizens; the gnawing
fear that the country might be going or have already gone

mad; that this is how great civilizations undermine and destroy themselves, fall into decline, hasten their own sunset.

One must take care of oneself and one's friends and family now, in the days, weeks, and months ahead. If withdrawing into the quiet of one's own inner being or the tight circle of one's family and close friends agrees with one, brings one comfort, then that's what must be done. If, on the other hand, reaching out to as many other like-minded people as possible, finding strength in numbers and in the clarity of direct political action is what sustains one, then that's one's path to reclaiming the narrative of one's world.

Whatever it takes. Peace and strength.

November 10, 2016

. . . from the classiest president of my lifetime to the most vulgar and mendacious and altogether sinisterly ridiculous one in modern American history

November 10, 2016

It's true: America will never be the same again. It choked on the bilious ignorance and hatefulness of nearly half of its electorate.

November 11, 2016

It is important to keep reminding yourself that more Americans voted for Hillary Clinton than for Donald Trump; that no part of America can have a claim on being the "real" America and no American is more or less of an American than any other American; that this is a country of laws and not of vile bigots and bullies; that there is ultimate strength in numbers of good people out there, and that, conversely, the overall number of unequivocally and irredeemably bad people among us, ones once and for all lost to the voice of reason, is surprisingly limited and indeed quite smaller than one might expect or imagine; that America will never become a fascist state, or even one like Putin's Russia or the old Soviet Union, because it just won't, this is America, love trumps Trump; and that . . . that if you suddenly notice one or two of them instantly identifiable KGB goons trailing behind you everywhere, seemingly with no concrete purpose other than in order to psych you out and cause you to start feeling paranoid, don't try to shake them off in some amateurish manner (that would accomplish nothing except making them additionally mad at you, which probably would not be the kind of development beneficial to your general well-being), but rather immediately try to locate the nearest phone booth, duck into it, a handful of fifteen-kopeck coins jangling in your pocket (never leave home without a few of those), and start dialing a bunch of random numbers, one after another, with an agitated and alarmed expression on your face, and then pretending to have an actual meaningful exchange of quick replicas with whomever might pick up on the other end of the line, but in reality just spouting into the receiver some extemporaneous nonsequiturs ("My cat is an alcoholic and in love with a married doberman, please advise," or some such) before hanging up abruptly and dialing again, and then again, and then once more, thus potentially creating the impression in your none-too-bright minders' minds that you are informing of your being harassed by the KGB the whole lot of your no-good friends-in-samizdat and maybe even some foreign journalists in Moscow, who the hell could tell, and communicating to everyone your exact location, in hopes of . . . oops, but I seem to have digressed a bit how did that happen and where was I? . . .

Ah, Trump. Right. Trump. The resistible rise of Donald Trump. He obviously is a massive national embarrassment, no doubt about it. Frightening, ominous times, and more difficult months and years ahead—but still, not the end of the world. Trumps come and Trumps go, but the earth—well, it abideth forever.

November 11, 2016

America is not Russia, Trump is nothing like Putin, fighting back is essential, America will overcome Trump.

November 11, 2016

When someone says to you, referring to Trump, "Sure, he's a racist, but . . ."—stop talking to that person at once, I would suggest. That person does not believe racism by itself is a good enough reason not to vote for someone as president. That's all you need to know about that person. There is nothing for you to talk about with him or her.

And when, similarly, someone says to you, again referring to Trump, "Sure, he behaves like a jerk toward women, humiliates them in any number of ways, and, yes, assaults them on occasion, and, sure, he never paid any taxes and probably owes a lot of money to the Russians, admires that shirtless sonofabitch Putin and is basically in Putin's pocket, quite likely, but . . ."—say no more to that person, either, my advice would be. You don't need to hear the end of that sentence. Just walk away quietly.

November 11, 2016

. . . newly discovered old photo. My father and I, New York, 1994.

What would he make of Trump? Even not being able to understand any of Trump's speeches, he would've loathed the guy on aesthetic grounds alone, I am sure. Too much recognizable nazified "Sovietness."

November 13, 2016

A Russian immigrant in Canada, a corpulent friendly-faced man in his late-thirties, jovially inebriated, carries on with his mouth full at the other end of the long party table, his Russian tinged with fragrant Southern softness: "We need our own Trump here. . . . Look, a dame can't be president of a great country, that's just my opinion. . . . OK, here's one to the general joy of being! Ahh, good! The meat's great, by the way, cooked to perfection, congratulations. . . . We need our own Trump here. That was funny when he said about Hillary, 'Hey, if she can't even get into a car on her own, how's she going to freaking govern, who's gonna be afraid of her? And if she can't satisfy her husband, how's she gonna satisfy America?' That was really funny. Seriously, you just take one quick look at her face and you know right away she's a liar and a criminal, she should be in jail, absolutely. . . . OK, let's have one for the most useful physical exercise there is for the arms: raising one's shot glass repeatedly! Ahh, that's what I'm talking about. . . . Honey, this salad is spectacular, yes, this one, with fruit in it, you should ask her for the recipe. . . . Like I said, we need our own Trump here. Way too many illegals and Muslims everywhere. Blacks had their guy running America, OK, fine, wonderful, now it's white people's turn again, back to reality. . . . Yeah, we need our own Trump here. . . . Excellent Olivier salad, if you don't mind me saying so! OK, all right, here, like, here's to happy coincidences, due to one of which, incidentally, each one of us got, you know, to get born! No mean feat! Ahh, simply wonderful. . . . OK, and when they say he, like, Trump, that he grabs women out of nowhere and stuff—what's the English word they use, 'grouper'?—I say, look, he's just a normal red-blooded guy, what do you want, why be such damn prudes, it's all freaking political correctness. . . . What? What, honey? What the hell did you just elbow me for? It's not like I'm saying something stupid, like, remotely objectionable to any rational people in their right mind, if they're honest with themselves. . . . What? What's that look supposed to mean? Don't silence me! I'm a free citizen of a free country! Well, anyway, we need our own Trump here, that's all I have to say to you . . . Let's have now one for the eternal mutual understanding between us, without which no simple human happiness is possible! Ahh, fabulous, I could just die and go to heaven right now. . . . Oh, look, my favorite cabbage pie! But that salad, honey, that fruit salad! You totally should write down the recipe. . . . OK, where was I? We need our own Trump here."

November 15, 2016
Question to any hypothetical history buffs out there:
When was the last time the KKK celebrated the election of a US president, as it is doing now?

November 16, 2016
People will not stop feeling angry. Their anguish will not subside. The rule of a fascist demagogue, no matter how un–self-aware, cannot possibly be come to terms with. There are no paths leading from the depths of contempt to the plain of acceptance. His success would be a stark failure for America.

What will happen next? In the short term, the giant sandstorm of his insanity will continue to overwhelm everyone, buffeting people's minds from every single direction with a host of patently unanswerable questions, such as, for instance: Just how unimaginable is the scope of his conflicts of interests and shady financial obligations in different parts of the world, including a number of countries with openly authoritarian regimes? Could he and his close advisers and associates actually be trusted not to share with Vladimir Putin or some other tinhorn totalitarian any vital secret information concerning America's strategic interests abroad? Is this improbable man, this garden-variety vulgarian, this raging narcissist wholly incapable of introspection or sympathy for others and at once completely shameless and infinitely clueless, someone made of nothing but gaping wants, whose entire life has been one unending barbaric yawp for attention, really, seriously to be our new president? When will we be allowed to wake up from this nightmare already? Etc.

However, sooner or later and before too long, I believe the sheer entropy of his turbulent being, the ultimate chaos of his willfully unexamined existence, will catch up with him, leading to his downfall. He seems to know this, too. You could see it in his gloomy hooded eyes and his uncharacteristically timid demeanor during the sole network-TV interview he's granted so far since the election. He is hiding from the press in New York, seemingly unable to resign himself to the realization that he no longer is in full control of his life. Yesterday he tried to insist on coming to his first briefing at the CIA with his son-in-law. Ivanka's husband! That kid! What's happening to him? He is scared. He is a shallow man, admittedly, but he is no fool. He knows he's gotten himself into a pickle: something much too difficult and immense for him to handle. He knows he's boxed himself into a corner, and it only is a matter of time before he says or does, right in front of a battery of hostile cameras, something so outrageous, so stupid, so beyond the pale of minimally acceptable presidential behavior, that . . . that . . . They already hate him with a passion—the media, along with the majority of Americans. How unfair is that! Sad! This no longer feels like fun. Some victory! He was not bargaining for *this* when setting out on his excellent brand-boosting presidential adventure all those fifteen months ago. Winning by losing your freedom? Thanks but no thanks! He wants to go home, to his beautiful golden penthouse high up in the shimmering New York sky. Could someone else—Mike, you?—please be president for him, or at least do all the heavy lifting? His attention span is not that great. He really shouldn't be president. He wanted the title, not the job, much in the same abstract way he wanted the Purple Heart without having been wounded first, much less killed, God forbid, in Vietnam . . . where, sadly, he could not go, five times in a row, because of those accursed bone heel spurs, God damn them to hell. . . . He had to stay where he was, as a result—right where he belonged, in Manhattan, fighting his own, personal little Vietnam war, doing his level best not to catch a VD amid all that patriotic partying. . . .

And now what's he supposed to do?

November 16, 2016

One still is walking around as though in a shimmering cloud of irreality: Is this actually happening? Did we actually just elect this idiot for four long years?

We didn't. They did.

November 16, 2016

T–p[1] represents a recognizable psychological type: he has no ideological principles or political stances, his attention span is extremely short, and all he cares about is winning. Once having won, however, he quickly loses interest in the object of his pursuit—be it a business deal or sexual conquest—and moves on to something else. This pattern of his behavior is substantiated by the accounts of those who know him well. His natural inner state is one of chaos and perennial gnawing hunger; filled with emptiness, he abhors introspection. I wouldn't be surprised if in short order he were to lose all interest in this whole presidency thing, too. Granted, in this instance the situation is complicated by the presence in it of his most potent and essential psychological nutrient: people's attention. However, the bulk of the attention he will be getting from his fellow Americans from now on, as failure-bound President Chaos, will be one of starkly negative quality: unabated loathing mixed with ever-growing contempt. He cannot be forgiven for what he has done and said in the course of his presidential

---

[1] Here and in some other instances the author declined to spell T–p's name in full. As time passed, he increasingly did.

campaign—and he won't be. How well would he be likely to handle the hatred and ridicule coming at him from every single quarter of society at once? Not well at all, my guess would be, based on his pathetic ongoing anti–*New York Times* Twitter crusade. He might well become the veritable Tasmanian devil of blind lashing-out, spinning himself into an unsustainable frenzy of Twitter-fury, until he just unravels completely.

November 17, 2016

"It's not a question of pessimism or optimism . . . It's just that ninety-nine out of a hundred people don't have any brains."

—Chekhovian protagonist of Chekhov's "The House with the Mezzanine."

But then, this was 1890s Russia—far away and a really long time ago. Here and now, to be sure, everything is drastically different, to the point of being diametrically opposite.

November 18, 2016

Trump's America has voted for him not *in spite* of his outrageous antics, his buffoonish behavior, his ugly rhetoric and utter vulgar shamelessness, his cruel propensity for mocking people with disabilities and the weak of the society, his gleeful constant incitement of violence and his unadorned racism, xenophobia and nativism, his heedless self-proud know-nothingness, his predatory misogyny—but *because* of all of the above. He is the first presidential contender in decades to articulate, loud and clear, just what they were thinking themselves but were afraid to say publicly. He has legitimized their darker selves, has let them know in no uncertain terms that it is OK now not to be "politically correct" and to say exactly what they feel and think of all those *other* Americans, the *not-real* ones, the arrogant ones, who have been looking down on them, the real

Americans, for too long and somehow have managed to take over their country, the America that used to belong to them, the *real* Americans, Trump voters—to show all those snooty intellectuals, foreigners, Muslims, Jews, Hispanics, blacks, gays, feminists, you name it, just who exactly is back in charge in America. Enough is enough! Make America great again, the way it used to be before all those others had taken it into their heads that they also . . . Well, one gets the point.

That's why it is more likely than not that even if–or when, rather—Trump and his happily unscrupulous aiders and abettors in Congress do manage to wreck the economy, plunge the country and the world into deep recession, start dismantling Medicare and doing away with Social Security, the angry America of Trump voters still would continue to support him, stand firmly behind him, even in the face of its own mounting economic misery, because . . . well, make America great again! Because being able to express freely their unabated rage at and contempt for that collective *Other*, to let all those others know in no uncertain terms who's the new old sheriff in town again and where to go, is beyond any tangible monetary value to them, more important than their own and their families' well-being, let alone those of the world at large and the planet on the whole. It's about no longer having to feel ashamed of who they are.

November 19, 2016

> With Trump as president, the only
> thing we have to fear is everything.

November 19, 2016
P & T

Putin is the president of the country where I was born and spent the first thirty years of my life, and of which I used to be a citizen, back when it was called the Soviet Union and had no real presidents.

Trump is the president-elect of the country I have been a citizen of for the past twenty years.

Putin reminds me of a lot of guys I grew up with, or alongside of, or else unhappily crossed paths with as an adult, back in Leningrad.

Trump reminds me of a number of arrogant bloviating asshats met at different points of my life both in the former USSR and in the US.

Putin likes Trump.

Trump likes Putin very much.

Putin does not want to be like Trump.

Trump does want to be like Putin.

Putin is Putin.

Trump is Trump.

Putin is.

Trump is.

Putin is short and trim.

Trump is tall and overweight.

Putin is smart and and cynical and deeply corrupt and well-organized.

Trump is smart and stupid and deeply corrupt and chaotic.

Putin has a small crew of personal food-tasters traveling with him everywhere.

Trump eats overcooked steaks and bucketfuls of KFC.

Putin does not drink alcohol.

Trump does not drink alcohol.

Putin is colorless and soft-spoken.

Trump is cartoonishly flamboyant and has a voice sounding like a chorus of bullfrog mating calls.

Putin's skin has a natural pasty pallor.

Trump's artificial tan makes him look like an orange alien with morbidly ashen eye sockets.

Putin's hair is nothing to write home about, and not even worth mentioning in the first place.

Trump's hair is the Shakespearean mare of the night.

Putin is the banality of banality.

Trump is the pointlessness of pointlessness.

Putin, although his naked torso is nothing to write home about either, frequently takes his shirt off for the photographers, because his electorate, especially its larger female contingent, likes the idea of Russia's de facto tsar being a macho man.

Trump, mercifully, prefers to keep his clothes on in public, perhaps because of that botched Donald Duck tattoo he is rumored to have on his lower back since the dark days of his rebellious youth, or just because he is a billionaire and the suits he wears always are very expensive and pleasant to look at.

Putin exercises with obsessive dedication, doing endless laps in his Olympic-size pool at his Novo-Ogarevo estate every morning.

Trump has no time for any such foolishness.

Putin is secretive.

Trump is childishly boastful.

Putin is much richer than Trump.

Trump is much poorer than Putin.

Putin knows you and thinks you are a loser.

Trump does not know you but also thinks you are a loser.

Putin speaks fairly fluent German and a tiny bit of English; at the very least, he was able to memorize and subsequently to croon out the lyrics of "Blueberry Hill" a few years ago, much to the delight of the always well-informed and principled American movie stars in attendance that night at his

Novo-Ogarevo residence outside Moscow: Sharon Stone, Kurt Russell, Mickey Rourke, and Goldie Hawn.

Trump apparently is a monoglot and has never attempted to sing any Russian songs (which is a good thing), although two of his three wives, past and present, speak with a distinct Slavic accent (which, admittedly, is a non sequitur).

Putin was born in a lower-than-lower-middle class family and raised in a rambling communal apartment in the anguished roiling heart of the so-called "Dostoyevsky Petersburg" area of central Leningrad.

Trump was a child of wealth and privilege born in staid Queens, New York.

Putin, growing up, had never heard of Queens, New York.

Trump, growing up, had never heard of Leningrad, USSR—or even if he had, he still hadn't.

Putin was a subpar student with behavioral problems at school.

Trump was a subpar student with behavioral problems at school.

Putin, as a child, was an insecure little jerk, by some scattered anonymous accounts . . . and to that, without ever meeting him back then, I can attest.

Trump, growing up, was an overly confident little jerk, according to most everyone who knew him then.

Putin is.

Trump is.

Putin, both as an adolescent and later on in life, was able to forge some strong friendships with a variety of like-minded peers, ones he would continue to rely on and further cultivate mafia boss–style, eventually bringing that motley and distinctly delinquent posse of his lifelong friends and low-level KGB agents into the higher echelons of Russian power and bestowing upon those most devoted to him personally many billions of dollars' worth of untold riches appropriated at the expense of ordinary Russians by the criminal oil-and-gas corporation called Russia, of which he is a CEO.

Trump has never been good at making or keeping friends, relying instead first upon his father's political connections, then on shady networks of pointedly unscrupulous business and lawyerly characters (you get mentored by Roy Cohn, you end up forever striking bargains with the devil), and eventually upon his own children—and, in particular, his son-in-law, scion of New York's real-estate royalty.

Putin, in his early youth, studied judo, so as to become strong and invulnerable and a good future KGB agent; and some of his closest friends, such as his former coach and now one of Russia's richest men, subsequently emerged from that tight-knit circle of Leningrad judokas.

Trump claims he used to be the best at every sport he ever played in high school and then in college, especially at baseball, where he simply was the best of the best, better than any professional baseball player of the time.

Putin, as the man he is today, was formed by the rough milieu of the gloomy interior courtyard of his childhood and adolescence, where he would be spending most of his out-of-school time in the company of other underage *shpana*, or minor hoodlums.

Trump, as a child, already was the man he is today: a madly driven striver, a heedless bully in whom his stern, penny-pinching father had instilled, as an unshakable cornerstone existential principle, the notion that all that matters in life is always winning, at all costs.

Putin, for whose star-crossed impoverished and crushingly unremarkable ilk being possessed of an impossible Olympic-level athletic prowess or becoming part of the state's repressive machine were the only two conceivable venues for getting ahead in life, had dreamed of joining the KGB ever since watching (and then endlessly rewatching) the immensely popular 1968 Soviet film *The Shield and the Sword*, an epitome of sentimental hackery depicting the superhuman exploits of the mythological Soviet secret agent among the top tier of Wehrmacht command in Berlin during World War II; and while still in the eighth grade of middle school, he came to the Leningrad KGB headquarters (the so-called "Big House," over on Kalyayeva Street, at the corner of the stately Liteyny Prospect, down by the river: easily the ugliest, most sinister-looking building in the city) to offer "the organs" his services as their eyes and ears among his unsuspecting, barely pubescent classmates (he was listened out and then smiled at gently, encouragingly there, in the Big House reception area, and was told to return in a few years, when he grew up; and that he sure did, upon high-school graduation; the rest is history).

Trump, a man of simple and straightforward ambitions, had always only wanted to be incredibly rich and just as unimaginably famous: just that, nothing more; is that too much to ask?

November 22, 2016

I was born and lived for thirty years in a country ruled by the worst of people, in a boundless secluded territory occupied by unassailable evil—although, in fairness, it was not until I was at least sixteen that I finally started arriving at the latter realization in earnest—and I can tell you that, in my experience, it is fully possible to go through any darkness that surrounds you, no matter how long it may last, without too much damage to the core of who you are, but only provided you keep resisting it, even if only passively and not making too big a deal out of it, by refusing to surrender to its vastness and accept it as your preordained destiny.

November 24, 2016

"A fire broke out backstage in a theatre. The clown came out to warn the public; they thought it was a joke and applauded. He repeated it; the acclaim was even greater. I think that's just how the world will come to an end: to general applause from wits who believe it's a joke."
—Søren Kierkegaard, *Either/Or,* Part I

November 24, 2016

Russia was a major factor in Trump's electoral victory. Putin has every reason to be congratulating himself now.

Reagan used to call the old Soviet Union "the evil empire," but Putin's Russia fits that designation to a much greater degree—for indeed, evil, the opposite of good, happens to be its primary nonmineral export now. Unlike the senescent Politburo members of several decades ago, Putin is under no illusion with regard to his ability to compete with the West economically or militarily. Instead, his overriding project generally is to prove to the West, as well as the rest of the world, that it is no better than Russia, in that the people of the West, en masse, are just as ignorant, gullible, apathetic, easily deceived, and manipulated as the great majority of his, Putin's, supporters. Boundless cynicism, rather than obsolete crude military might, is his primary weapon, and the progressively more efficient new Western digital technologies serve as the instantaneous error-proof means of its delivery to a multitude of the Western world's weakest points. His main ontological thesis, and the sole apparent self-justification of his ridiculously protracted rule, is based on his firm conviction that democracy is a sham and merely the thin veneer of hypocritical subterfuge covering the unvarnished surface of ordinary, unadorned, par-for-the course corrupt authoritarianism.

This time around, he's been proven right in that contention of his. His strenuous efforts to influence the US presidential election have paid off. In Trump, he now has a US president who, in effect, is a typical Russian oligarch—or else, no better, the new, American edition of Italy's Silvio Berlusconi.

Widespread ignorance is incompatible with democracy.

November 24, 2016

TOP 5 DISTINCTIONS BETWEEN DONALD TRUMP AND THE AVERAGE RUSSIAN OLIGARCH

1. Trump doesn't speak Russian.
2. Trump is poorer than the average Russian oligarch.
3. Trump's admiration for Putin is sincere.
4. Trump is like an attention-starved child constantly in need of praise.
5. Trump can destroy the world with one push of a button.

November 25, 2016

The story of the 2016 presidential election in a nutshell:

A shameless person ran a shameful campaign and won an ugly victory, by losing the popular vote by an unprecedented margin but garnering the fervent support of the morally or educationally challenged 25% of the American electorate.

In Russia, people of Trump's ilk are called colloquially *bespredel'shchiki*—literally, those with absolutely no limits to how low they would be willing to go, with regard to their words or deeds, in pursuit of their personal objectives.

"O God, I could be bounded in a nutshell, and count myself a king of infinite space. . . ."

November 26, 2016

As a little boy, I saw Fidel Castro once from a stone's throw away, while sitting on my grandfather's shoulders. This was in Leningrad, in front of the then-new Frunzensky Department Store on the Moskovsky Prospect, the city's main transportation artery. Castro, flanked by some uninteresting people, was standing in the slow-moving "Chaika" cabriolet, waving benevolently at the ecstatic multitudes with little Soviet and Cuban flags in their hands on both sides of the Prospect, which in this particular spot, bucking up over the foul-smelling Obvodny Canal, is quite narrow. Fidel was bearded and young. I too was waving and hollering something, perched on my old-Bolshevik grandfather's shoulders.

Back then, they were playing on a loop two Cuba-related songs on the flat felt black disc of the kitchen radio: "Cuba, My Love" and "The Barbudos March." Both I knew by heart, sang all the time; and I could punch out the tune of each with one finger on the "Red October" piano in our room in the mid-sized communal apartment on Egorova Street, in the roiling Dostoevskean heart of midtown Leningrad.

"Red" as in "Red Army." "October" as in, October 25 (old style)—or November 7 (Gregorian Calendar)—the glorious day of Lenin-led Bolshevik revolution in 1917.

My grandfather and grandmother lived on the outskirts of Moscow and visited Leningrad once a year.

In our rather small, oval-shaped room in that communal apartment of my childhood, around the time of Fidel's visit to the Soviet Union, there were one large bed, one old fold-out cot our live-in nanny slept on, two small children's beds, a dining table, my father's desk, and a small nightstand for the tiny KVN TV-set with a palm-size screen and a set of two connected thick glass lenses one put over the screen, having filled the space between the two with water beforehand, to magnify the on-screen images. One wall was fully occupied by a floor-to-ceiling wood-burning stove, and on each of the countless pale-blue ceramic tiles lining it Tzar Peter purposefully striding along with a pipe in his mouth was depicted.

It was a bright, sun-filled day. The moment, beautifully protracted, lasted but a few seconds, and then he was gone for good.

November 27, 2016

The great Russian writer Andrey Sinyavsky (literary pseudonym: Abram Tertz)—whose political show trial in February 1966, along with that of his fellow writer Yuli Daniel, marked the birth of the modern dissident movement in the USSR—famously said to the court in his last word that he and the Soviet regime were incompatible "on stylistic grounds."

That's how, along with the majority of other American citizens, I feel about Donald Trump: we are totally and completely incompatible on stylistic, aesthetic grounds. After the dizzying array of remarkably ugly things he said during the campaign, and considering the shamefully dishonest kind of self-centered life he has lived to date, accepting him as the leader of the American people—and indeed, the de facto leader of the free world—would be an act of extreme tastelessness; and an act of self-betrayal. It just cannot be done. He is entirely contemptible and unacceptable.

Plus, of course, climate change and the Supreme Court.

It is not much more complicated than that.

November 27, 2016

Look, I hate to break it to you, but if you have spent decades reading the greatest authors in the history of literature— from Homer to Garcia Márquez, from Sappho to Vonnegut, from Euripides to Eugenides, from Georges Sand to George Saunders, from Faulkner to Franzen, from Tolstoy to Pynchon, from James Joyce to Joyce Carol Oates, from Camus to Roth, from Flaubert to Flannery O'Connor, from Gogol to Gaiman, from Chekhov to Atwood, from Milton to Grossman, from Woolf to Wolfe, from Bocaccio to Bolano, from Brodsky to Dostoyevsky, from Wallace Stevens to David Foster Wallace, from Borges to Nabokov, from Dante to Conan Doyle, from John Donne to Donna Tartt, from Goethe to Hemingway, from Poe to Kafka, from Proust to Agatha Christie, and so on, infinitum; this is just scratching the surface—but then one day you went and did something as unalterably outlandish as voting for the spiritually illiterate and altogether entirely immoral Donald Trump . . . well, I fear you may have wasted all that lifetime of bettering your soul.

November 28, 2016

He is the first president of the United States who lies constantly, daily, routinely, unabashedly, like a spoiled eight-year-old boy unafraid to be caught. In that sense, he is the first postmodern American president—and God help us, we have not the foggiest where that murky postmodernist curve of his insanity is going to take us in the end. And half the population of the United States has been conditioned to believe anything coming from the mouth of this ur-fascist demagogue, by decades of getting its free-floating anger and racial resentments stoked and brought to boil on vile half-truths by the increasingly more reactionary and ignorance-bound Republican Party. I cannot possibly tell you just how dangerous I believe this moment in history is, for all of us, for the entire world.

November 29, 2016

 Donald J. Trump
@realDonaldTrump

@HighonHillcrest: @jeffzeleny what PROOF do u have DonaldTrump did not suffer from millions of FRAUD votes? Journalist? Do your job! @CNN

9:14 PM – 28 Nov 2016

What PROOF does any Trump supporter have Donald Trump is not a complete IDIOT?

November 29, 2016
What it would have to take at this point, I would suspect, to puncture through the iridescent gaseous swirl of steadily expanding toxic Trumpean chaos, would be for someone with a remaining national reputation for integrity—John McCain, for instance—to come out and say, looking straight into a battery of cameras: "Enough is enough. There are times when one can no longer stay silent, party loyalty notwithstanding. My fellow Americans, it pains me to say this, but at this point, it is my firm belief that our president-elect is a deeply disturbed man, and as such cannot fulfill the obligations of the office of the president. There, I have said it. Now let's think of how to start extricating ourselves from this godawful mess of our own creation."

Admittedly, this is unlikely to happen, until and unless he does something so egregious that, even the most hidebound of those wonderful public servants would recoil from him in disgust.

November 30, 2016

"America will never be the same again," many say sorrowfully. "Not after Trump. America will never fully recover from this moral collapse."

That is true. But so what? Nothing ever gets to be the same as before. We are never given the opportunity to be the same as we used to be, hard as we may try to fool ourselves and Mother Nature. We just keep on living, steadily getting older, and then (spoiler alert) we die. And so it is with everything, states and societies included.

And what does recovery mean, in this context, anyway? Do countries ever recover from anything to their own and history's satisfaction? The question is also the answer. Germany had Hitler, and now it's a different Germany; an infinitely better and massively remorseful one. The Soviet Union had Lenin and Stalin and millions of innocent people killed or otherwise destroyed for nothing, and now there is no Soviet Union—and present-day Russia, though by no means a democracy, but rather a fairly putrid autocratic kleptocracy run by morally reprehensible people, still is a very far cry from the Soviet Union circa the Stalinist purges. Will Russia recover from its current illness of toxic Putinism? Maybe; maybe not. Has Argentina ever recovered from Peron's dictatorial rule? Spain—post-Franco? Perhaps; perhaps not. Again, what is recovery? Once broken inside, people and countries stay broken until the end, although on the surface they look quite whole, with all their faculties seemingly intact. But there remains inside an undiminished area of permanent displacement. One never fully recovers from having been broken once. It's like losing one's innocence: you can't unlose it. Or it's like being accosted for the first time, as a child, with the sudden shattering realization of your mortality. You cannot erase the damage caused by being alive. Nothing worth recovering is ever fully recoverable. Yet still, that inner brokenness also is what gives a person or a country a greater, more reliable strength, in a long-term perspective, than one they otherwise might possess, if either had never known the devastating impact of a barely survived existential crack-up. And what, really, is "never"? The same as "always": a nanosecond amid the timelessness of the boundless universe.

Trump, Putin, sundry other ur-fascists, demagogues, and authoritarians. . . . America will, of course, recover from the bad shock and subsequent heavy hangover of Trumpism, but it also will—at least for a while—be a different, less self-congratulatory and more chastened America. Russia, eventually, will get rid of the noxious fog of Putinism—hopefully (and if not, too bad, but maybe not, if such would happen to be the verdict of history, the mother of truth, as per Cervantes), but it certainly will be a different Russia, perhaps a smaller one, and one less burdened with a host of dangerous aggressive impulses borne out of an explosive admixture of wrongfully understood, wounded national pride and the fantastical notions of a global historic mission.

And so will we all. We will always. We will never.

Mikhail Iossel
December 2016

December 1, 2016

At his "thank you" rally in Cincinnati, Ohio, right now, Trump almost immediately launches into a rant about an extremely dishonest press, turns it into a thirty-minutes of hate, mugging, gloating, yelling, and whipping up murky waves of malevolence; promising to build the most beautiful wall in the world, repeal Obamacare, stop immigration from Muslim countries "dead-cold-flat;" vowing to "drain the swamp," shouting at a protesters, telling her to "go back to mommy," while lying repeatedly, just lying away, about too many things at once to mention, floating through his own eerie barren, fact-free reality, claiming a landslide victory and, surprisingly, neglecting to bring up the fact of having lost popular vote by an unprecedented margin, then reluctantly going back to the teleprompter and with a disinterested air calling for national unity and exhorting his fellow citizens to "dream big," then commencing to holler about himself again, bragging about his "landslide" again and fulminating against the many thousands of mythological Muslim immigrants supposedly streaming across the country's borders, then switching back to settling old scores with the media, airing his innumerable little grievances, waging his little vendettas, going on and on about the extremely dishonest media and other losers who hadn't expected him to win: an unsettlingly Mussolini-Berlusconiesque, heavily jingoistic, altogether extremely bizarre kind of spectacle. The crowd is chanting "Lock her up!" He is smiling benevolently. What the hell is this? This is banana republic-grade stuff. He clearly does not want to be president—he wants to keep on campaigning: a mentally unbalanced seventy-year-old man clowning away in front of a raucous crowd of ignorant, misguided, angry people . . . an extremely dangerous man, the minority president epitomizing the worst of America.

December 3, 2016

I don't believe that just because Donald Trump is ignorant, arrogant, reckless, rash, greedy, corrupt as hell, vindictive, cowardly, paranoid, self-centered, mendacious, insecure, intolerant, hypocritical, bigoted, misogynistic, has the attention span of a luna moth, and has not read a single work of literature in his adult life—that just because of all that, he couldn't still be a great president, as many of those who voted for him were convinced he would be.

December 7, 2016

Rulers I've Survived

Khrushchev was a genial, mercurial half-literate folksy boob with a blood-drenched past and a bitter resentment in his heart against Stalin, who had humiliated him for years, by making him play a clown in front of other glorified flunkies in Stalin's inner circle.

Brezhnev, a unibrowed bubblehead, was a once-handsome hedonist, genial womanizer, good-natured lover of good food with good drinks in good company, childishly vain and boastful—a nonreflexive, instinctual, middle-brow Party conformist who in different historic or geographic circumstances almost certainly would have spent his time on Earth as a perfectly ordinary person with an entirely and harmlessly conventional life, rather than being forced to play the improbable role thrust upon him by malevolent iron-fingered fate: that of the increasingly more dim-witted and incoherent, thoughtlessly cruel, poor stroked-out fool, obscenely bemedaled pagan idol perched, heavy and immobile, on top of an ugly power pyramid in one of the most repugnant dictatorships ever known to history.

Andropov, a sort of an epicurean Savonarola, possessed of Machiavellian wit, cold seething ambition, a strong vengeful streak, and boundless cynicism, the much-dreaded former longtime head of the omnipotent KGB, a terrible amateur poet and a connoisseur of fine whiskeys, was far and away the most dangerous among post-Stalin Soviet rulers, who in his mercifully short tenure in the above-said capacity of the world's second most powerful man had succeeded quite remarkably in reimmersing the Soviet Union in the viscid atmosphere of pervasive Stalin-era fear and pushing the planet ever closer toward the very edge of a nuclear catastrophe.

Chernenko, Brezhnev's lifelong shadow and drinking buddy, a thoroughly nondescript Party apparatchik from Siberia prior to meeting his benefactor, was effectively dead, and definitely and characteristically brain-dead, even at the moment of his nominal assumption of General Secretary's office—a transparently desperate time-buying move on the part of the Politburo old guard—so there is no point, really, in discussing him at any great length here.

Gorbachev was a frenetic, chaotic busybody, gurgling of rain in a rusty drain pipe, a faithful Party man who ended up killing the Party, full of sound and fury, smiles and belly laughs, wonderful intentions and quixotic ideas invariably falling victim to a myriad of bureaucratic snafus; a Southern-accented clown in statesman's attire, a statesman in a clown's costume, a tyrant-cum-liberator, an exhaustively garrulous, starry-eyed dreamer with no follow-through, of the kind people love to despise at the time but tend to feel fond about in wistful hindsight.

***

(As for Donald Trump, in a parenthetical aside, he would have been a godsend to the old Soviet ideological-brainwashing machine, of course, complying to a T with with every single stereotype of its unremitting and relentless anti-American propaganda.)

December 8, 2016
A seventy-year-old child with a host of rotten habits and severe psychological problems, lashing out viciously and indiscriminately at any slight real or perceived—a dystopian minority president, immensely ignorant and vengeful, the absolute worst type of person ever to be put in any position of power, thoroughly averse to the actual work of the presidency, interested only in continuing to hold his Nazi-style rallies and surrounded by an unholy coterie of incompetents, racists, conspiracy buffs, bullies, and hateful ideologues: history has decided it's time to punish America for its relentless glorification of ignorance with its first openly and unmistakably fascist president.

December 11, 2016
It is brave of the US president-elect to side with the Russian secret services in a matter of grave national security for his

country, lashing out at the CIA in order to defend the honor of his role model and apparent puppet-master, Vladimir Putin.

December 11, 2016

It is, of course, an interesting question to ponder, from a purely academic perspective: is Trump a straight-up Benedict Arnold, doing Putin's bidding for some heretofore unknown nefarious reasons of financial or, possibly, blackmail-related nature—or merely Putin's honest "useful idiot"? If someone were to ask him that question, couching it in as mild a phrasing as possible, I don't think he would even understand it, because . . . well, how can something—anything—that's good for Trump be bad for America? He only knows one form of patriotism: self-love.

December 11, 2016

"So then. Washington is ours."

Aleksandr Dugin—Russia's leading fascist "philosopher," a prominent public "intellectual" with unfettered access to the highest echelons of Kremlin power and a frequent propensity for articulating the latter's unspoken mind—reacts to Trump's electoral victory.

December 12, 2016

Laugh at him, as a means of "de-trumpifying" your brain, I would suggest. There is nothing he deserves more than being mocked and ridiculed, constantly, mercilessly. Having him on your mind for hours on end every single day can drive one insane, quite literally so, because unlike him, we have the essential capacity for reflection and need to keep re-examining our lives in order to reassure ourselves we are not wasting our lives in a barren ocean of chaos the way he has wasted his own existence. What you can laugh at, you cannot be afraid of—and we are not afraid of him or the kind of America he stands for: we despise him, and to some extent we pity him, too, because— God, what a waste of humanness.

For eighteen viscous years, along with the rest of Soviet people, I lived under Brezhnev's progressively more ridiculous, stagnant, and pointless rule, in a similar barren ocean of chaotic entropy Trump is currently attempting to impose on the US— and with every year, especially beginning in the mid-seventies, there was a massive increase in the number of political jokes (*anekdoty*) about Brezhnev circulating around the country in millions of daily iterations. We all were dissidents, back then, when we were telling or listening to those *anekdoty*. Like most of my friends, I myself could tell a good couple dozen of variably funny Brezhnev jokes in one sitting. And we all knew then, beyond a shadow of a doubt, that while Brezhnev, strictly speaking, was still alive, the chaotic anti-ideology of Brezhnevism we all were supposed to believe in was as dead as a doornail.

By contrast, in Stalin's times, there were not, and could not be, any dissidents, and hardly anyone was foolish enough to tell any irreverent jokes about Stalin or the Soviet life in general: too great was the sheer weight of fear saturating the country's atmosphere, too real and indeed imminent the prospect of any such suicidal daredevil's being overheard and reported on to the omnipresent NKVD by a situationally disloyal friend or questionable relative or shifty communal-apartment neighbor in need of improving his living conditions.

One could not laugh at Stalin, except in the privacy of one's own troubled mind only (not even in a whispered nighttime pillow conversation with one's spouse, because . . . well, are you really sure you know him, her all that well?)— Death alone, unimpressed with all the mountains of money he had been throwing at his pseudo-scientists in search of eternal life for himself, was able in the end to take care of him—but Brezhnevism, to a considerable extent, I am convinced, eventually fell victim to its own patent and ultimately unsustainable ridiculousness.

Laugh at DT, I would suggest. To him, this would be like dying inside a thousand times per day.

Whatever is laughable is defeatable.

December 15, 2016

A racist, a birther, a bigot, a xenophobe, a sexual predator, a consummate con artist, a shameless yahoo, an ignorant buffoon, a stubborn nonreader of the US Constitution, a human embodiment of flagrant antispirituality, an admirer of the most egregiously thuggish dictatorial strongmen on the international arena, and, quite possibly, a traitor knowingly accepting in the course of the campaign massive amounts of disinformational help from his unholy patron and America's sworn enemy, Vladimir Putin; and finally, the reality-denying loser of the popular vote by an unprecedented margin—how, with all that in mind, can any self-respecting person recognize a man like that as his or her rightful president?

December 16, 2016

Let me suggest why the Russians' strenuous concerted effort to subvert US election and hand the presidency to a highly manipulable fool might be a bigger deal than if the US were to attempt similarly interfering with the upcoming (in 2018) presidential election in Russia:

1. What presidential election? "Don't make my slippers laugh," as per the popular idiomatic Russian expression. Putin will just reappoint himself president, and that

will be the end of the whole show; and everyone in Russia knows so, and will vote (or not vote) for him in full apathetic awareness of that ironclad eventuality.

2. What, you say, if some unsavory, highly damaging information about Putin and his inner circle, with regard to their mind-boggling financial machinations and/or their Kaligula-esque personal lifestyle were to become public, as a result of the US secret services managing to hack into the closed-circuit Kremlin electronic communication channels? Still absolutely nothing would happen. Still "don't make my slippers laugh." Of course, people in Russia know full well that Putin and his unholy coterie of merry megathieves are as corrupt as hell, just breathtakingly and wantonly dishonest and unimaginably wealthy—but so what of it? He is the tsar, if a quasi-democratically elected one—and all of the country's immense riches (and Russia, just to remind you, is the richest country in the world, in terms of its mineral resources), belong to him, by an inherent right, by the natural order of things—to him and, by extension, to his favorite boyars. Good for him, Putin, with his KGB wiles, to have been able to be made the tsar of Russia by fickle-fingered destiny. If you or I or any other person in the country were to find ourselves in his gigantic shoes, many a Russian would tell you, we'd all be behaving in the exact same manner, enriching ourselves through the wazoo and getting rid of those foolish pesky opponents standing in the way of our doing so, because—well, sure, why not and how could that even be any different? If you're the tsar, you can do whatever you want. That's the way it goes in life. . . . You can't stain Putin's reputation in

Russians' eyes, in other words: it's made of nothing but a steely blob of stain.

3. But the still-remaining free media? The newspapers? Television? The Internet? The independent investigations? The . . . Haha. "Independent," you said? "Free"? That's a good one. "Don't make my slippers laugh." Hack away, Americans, hack away.

December 17, 2016

 Donald J. Trump
@realDonaldTrump
China steals United States Navy research drone in international waters - rips it out of water and takes it to China in unpresidented act.

7:30 AM – 17 Dec 2016

Donny, you orange-haired, short-fingered drowning research drone, China is trying to tell you something, but you, sadly, are too stupid, too childish in the brain, to get the message.

Unpresidented, huh? What an excellent adjective! Describes you to a T. You're a regular wordsmith, aren't you?

Congratulations to everyone who voted for this moron.

December 22, 2016

What happened in the US on November 8?

Too many Americans have come to take democracy for granted.

Ignorance is incompatible with democracy. Ignorant people tend to have difficulty telling the difference between freedom and its absence.

December 22, 2016

 Donald J. Trump
@realDonaldTrump

The United States must greatly strengthen and expand its nuclear capability until such time as the world comes to its senses regarding nukes.

8:50 AM – 22 Dec 2016

He is a heedless bratty teenager, full of complexes, whom some staggeringly reckless, stupidly childish adults for some wholly irrational reason have decided to entrust with the world's largest and most potent nuclear arsenal. The rest of the world must now deal with the distinct possibility of having, at some point in foreseeable future, to reap what those strongman-craving Einsteins have sown. I would challenge any one of them to read this horrifying tweet aloud and then try to explain just how exactly "greatly strengthening and expanding nuclear capabilities" by the US would cause the rest of the world, including such nuclear states as China or Russia, to "come to its senses regarding nukes."

Good Lord.

December 22, 2016

There are more of us out there—those who see that uncommonly reprehensible and dangerous man, Trump, as an unmitigated disaster on every human and political level, and who oppose him vehemently, loathing and despising him in equal measure—than there are those supporting him blindly and cheering him on. Simply put, we are more numerous than them. We are better educated than them, across the board, too, and possess more knowledge about the world outside North America. There are no KKK members, white nationalists, bigots, and antisemites among us: they all, en masse, belong to Trump, body and . . . what in other, less drastically damaged people, is usually thought of as that ephemeral substance, soul.

Why then are they on the attack at this time, aggressively attempting to remake the country into a bona fide ur-fascist state and threatening to upend the world with the sheer cumulative force of their heedlessness and parochial narrow-mindedness? Why is the evil of Trumpism currently advancing and why we are retreating?

Because evil always is more unified than the good. It knows no doubts and feels no pangs of conscience.

We must organize and resist.

December 23, 2016
The words "President Trump" make as much sense to me as, say, "Archbishop Scooby Doo."

And will be uttered by me just as frequently.

December 24, 2016
The presidential election of 2016, unlike any other in modern American history, was less of a political than an existential affair, what with the stark choice faced by the country being one between the Democratic nominee and The Unthinkable. The Unthinkable ended up winning, if by way of losing the popular vote to the tune of three million and with the vital help from the FBI Director and the kleptocratic authoritarian leader of the pan-European and indeed worldwide anti-democratic

alliance—and now what do we do, the large majority of Americans for whom the now-thinkable unthinkable can never become remotely acceptable? How does one adjust to living in a dystopian, ur-fascist world?

Think. Organize. Resist.

December 26, 2016

"We will remember not the words of our enemies but the silence of our friends."—Martin Luther King

December 30, 2016

 Donald J. Trump
@realDonaldTrump

Great move on delay (by V. Putin) - I always knew he was very smart!

2:41 PM – 30 Dec 2016

Let us understand what a strange and dangerous moment in American history this is: for the first time ever, and with a minority vote, America has elected a president clearly indebted to and in thrall with a criminal totalitarian ruler of its main ideological and geopolitical foe—with someone whose visceral hatred of America represents the cornerstone of his worldview.

December 30, 2016

If you support Trump, you support Putin. Because Trump admires and genuflects before Putin, and Putin has Trump in his pocket.

If you support Putin, you support unbridled corruption permeating all layers of society, widespread miserable poverty of the population, a lack of freedom of speech, an absence of democratic elections, the regular jailing and assassination of opposition politicians and independent journalists, all-out cynicism and deep envious loathing of America—among many other such fine things.

If you are a supporter of Trump, you are a Putin supporter. You may want to learn some low-level Russian, to be able to listen to Putin's droning drivel in the original.

If you are a Putin supporter, you are a supporter of Trump, and may consider learning some elementary, schoolyard bully–grade English, to become fully appreciative of Trump's moronic verbal ejaculations.

Learning foreign languages is a good thing.

December 31, 2016

Think a few short decades back. Think of what the public's reaction in the US would have been if some Republican (or even more so, Democratic) politician had stated that he favored Leonid Brezhnev over Ronald Reagan and the KGB over the CIA.

Imaginable? Not really.

But that's exactly what's happening now in the Republican Party.

December 31, 2016

Happy New Year, everyone! С Новым Годом!

For many of us—and for the US and the world at large—the mercifully departing 2016 was, in many ways, a harshly difficult year. It should not be all that hard for the nascent 2017 to make us feel grateful merely by turning out to be just a little bit better, kinder than its predecessor.

May our loved ones still be with us this time next year. May our friends still be there for us, and may we still be there for them at all times.

May we always have the wisdom to know the right thing to do in the year to come—and do it without regrets. May we be serene of mind and noble of spirit even through the darkest of times that may lie ahead of us.

May we be good to ourselves and each other. May there be peace in the world.

December 31, 2016

Donald J. Trump
@realDonaldTrump

Happy New Year to all, including to my many enemies and those who have fought me and lost so badly they just don't know what to do. Love!

5:17 AM – 31 Dec 2017

Lotsa love from the vile moron in chief.

The guy is just incredible. A true nutcase.

Mikhail Iossel
January 2017

January 1, 2017
Well, here we are now, on the other side, having survived 2017. We are stronger than we know. Things will be different now, even if they won't—and even if they won't, they still will. In the end, it's all up to us.

Happy trails through the year ahead, one and all!

January 2, 2017
None of this is too complicated: improving relations with Putin's Russia is impossible for America at this time in principle, because Putin needs America as an enemy, a foil in order to maintain the "besieged fortress" mindset among the increasingly more impoverished and embittered Russian populace; Putin's ultimate strategic objective with regard to America (and by extension, all the rest of the Western world) is not to destroy it or, conversely and hopelessly, attempt to catch up with it in terms of per capita wealth or military capabilities but, rather, to bring it down to Russia's own moral level, by means of corrupting and destabilizing its democratic institutions and generally demoralizing it, and thus to prove democracy to be worthless, useless, fatally flawed as a form of government. His overriding, if unarticulated, existential

ambition—to put in in grand literary terms—is to convince as many tens and hundreds of millions of people as possible out there, in Russia and throughout the Western world, that they are worse than they think they are, and that it's OK, for being bad is good, because it is the only natural way for human beings to be. In other words, he is your good old tired devil in the flesh, who at this point in his life would love nothing more than to be able to spend most of his days with his dogs and grandchildren, and to die knowing that, since evil trumps good in the universe, his life has not been a complete waste of time.

January 2, 2017

In his review of *Citizen Kane*, Borges cites a line from a G. K. Chesterton story: "There is nothing more frightening than a labyrinth without a center."

America, however, has become something even more frightening now, I'm afraid: a labyrinth without a center, filled with people unaware that they are in a labyrinth, and that the labyrinth they aren't aware they're in has no center.

January 3, 2017

We the humans will see great, wondrous, breathtaking things in our future: flying cars, space elevators, teleportation, people traveling beyond our solar system, finding cures for all diseases (including aging), communicating with extraterrestrials, forming underwater civilizations, etc., etc.—but we will never, never, never-ever, never-ever see Donald Trump's tax returns.

January 4, 2017

Hillary Clinton has decided to attend Trump's inauguration, according to her statement, so as "to be able to witness the peaceful transfer of power" (a hallmark of American democracy) to someone who, in the course of his campaign, routinely called her "Crooked Hillary," led thousand-voiced chants of "Lock her up!," promised to put her in jail, publicly mocked a disabled person, advocated for torture and other war crimes, spewed unabashed racism on a daily basis, had no idea who David Duke was, publicly mocked a woman's bout with pneumonia, labeled Mexicans criminals and Muslims terrorists, attacked a US-born judge and impugned his integrity on the grounds of his ethnicity, bragged on tape about grabbing women's genitals with impunity, rated women on a scale of one to ten based solely on their looks, expressed admiration for a foreign dictator and referred to the latter as a stronger leader than the sitting US president, spread paranoid conspiratorial theories, and, in a sheer demonstration of his contempt for the tenets of American democracy, time after time suggested that if he lost the general election, it would mean that the political system was "rigged."

January 6, 2017
Imagine a yearning for validation so enormous, it can be slaked not even by the glory of the presidency. He is just one gigantic black hole of howling need, and he is about to become the most powerful man in the world.

January 6, 2017
Back in late Soviet Union, there was no more despised category of individuals—not only among the intelligentsia, but generally across the spectrum of the society—than the KGB: deeply amoral, inherently cruel, coldly manipulative people with no heart and no conscience, no sense of decency, and a starkly negative capacity for compassion with others. After the USSR fell apart, amid the widespread panic and round-the-clock

burning of incriminating paperwork inside the Lubyanka, Yeltsin had whimsically decided to pass up on the seemingly natural opportunity to declare the KGB a criminal organization. The rest is history. The "organs" managed to survive, by repairing and regenerating themselves—and in 1999, in due course of perverse historical developments, an unrepentant, committed lifelong "kagebeshnik" became the ruler of Russia—and some seventeen more years later, in a recruiting triumph of unprecedented proportions, the latter was able to succeed, quite beyond his own most halcyon expectations, in helping the more retrograde segment of the US electorate to make his virtual transatlantic kindred spirit a president of America.

January 7, 2017
In response to Trump saying that only "stupid" people would not want good US-Russian relations:

Look, Trump, you, at least nominally, are the new president-elect of the United States, and Russia has just committed a bona fide act of war against the country you, as of two weeks from today, will be duty-bound to defend against any and all of its enemies. There is a reason why the dictator of Russia wanted quite so badly to see you as the new American president, rather than Hillary Clinton: precisely because, right after Russia has committed an act of war against your country, you think it is appropriate to be calling for improved relations with Russia, while simultaneously having the breathtaking gall to label everyone who does not agree with your adoration of Putin "fools," or stupid people. You are unbelievable, Trump: an unprincipled, ignorant, mentally sick buffoon constantly balancing on the precipitous edge of treason and willing to sell your country down the river for a pat on the back from Putin.

January 9, 2017
If I were looking for one adjective to describe Trump and his world adequately, it would be "tasteful." He is the real "people's billionaire." Everything about him fairly screams of good taste, heightened spirituality, and philosophical devotion to simple living. He is a true Spartan, or perhaps an adherent of Diogenes, in league with Liberace or Leona Helmsley. One shudders at the thought of how garish, gaudy, and tawdry by comparison with his modest gold-plated abode, straight from the cover of a Harlequin Romance whose main protagonist is Fabio's hair, must be the tacky, shamelessly opulent McMansions of such spoiled members of pampered Hollywood elites as Tom Hanks, say, or, indeed, very prominently, Meryl Streep. That is why ordinary Americans love Donald Trump: they know he understands them and their problems, because he is, in effect, one of them.

January 10, 2017
As a schoolboy in summer camp once, according to his teacher's recollections, young Vova Putin, alone among his peers, volunteered to chop off the head of a duck to be boiled for the communal supper that evening. He wrapped his frail frame in a length of red cloth for the occasion, proclaimed himself an executioner, and wielded with visible satisfaction the large, fearsome-looking rusted axe provided by a drunk local woodsman.

January 10, 2017
As the president of the United States in Chicago is extolling the virtues of democracy and appealing to the better angels of human nature, in New York the president-elect is defending himself on Twitter against the allegations that Putin has him on tape either urinating on people or being urinated on.

January 12, 2017

After the smartest, most decent, eloquent, and inspirational of American presidents in modern history, there comes the vilest, tawdriest, shallowest, meanest, most vulgar, demagogic, and dishonest one, all aglow with manifest derangement. The gods of history, known for their warped sense of humor, have decided once more to remind America, lest it keep its complacent ways, that there still dwells at least just as much gloomy darkness as there is light in its collective soul. Well, what's to be done about it? Light every candle in the house. No night lasts forever.

January 12, 2017

The enemies of America throughout the world are rejoicing these days: the new American president is at war with his own intelligence community, possesses no concrete knowledge about anything, admires the dictator of Russia, reviles and suppresses the nation's press, hates democracy, and is loathed and despised by the majority of Americans.

January 13, 2017

 Donald J. Trump
@realDonaldTrump

Totally made up facts by sleazebag political operatives, both Democrats and Republicans - FAKE NEWS! Russia says nothing exists. Probably . . .

6:11 AM – 13 Jan 2017

Trust Russia! I do! With every fiber (if I know that word) of my, um, being! I trust Russia implicitly, more than any intelligence, way more than the CIA or MI6 or whatever, because . . . who wouldn't? When was the last time Putin ever lied, especially about having *kompromat* on someone? I don't really trust myself, so I don't know for sure if those tapes of me in Moscow exist, or even whether I exist myself, but if Putin says there's nothing there, then there is nothing.

January 13, 2017
The secret of Trump's success in dealing with the press, and in life in general: extreme, total, and absolute shamelessness.

January 14, 2017
On the news of the "Steele dossier":

This is chilling.
What we have here, apparently, is the worst case of treason in American history.
In five days, the country will be inaugurating a traitor.

January 15, 2017
After the most intelligent and dignified of presidents in modern American history comes a stunning clinical narcissist, ignorant buffoon, and likely traitor. The pendulum of history is swinging too wildly for its own good, running the risk of getting a whiplash.

January 15, 2017
Time, which is but our shared perception of history, has a way of teaching lessons in shame even to the most obtuse among people. Consider that a mere half century ago, it was deemed

perfectly acceptable for many millions of Americans to declare themselves in public unabashed racists—and who in his or her right, unimpaired mind, without grading into downright derangement, would openly admit to being one now?

Generations of Germans, to cite the most glaring of recent historic examples, have learned, with time's insistent assistance, to be ashamed of and for their Hitler-loving forbears, who were just like them, by and large, in every single respect, save for an accidental yet crucial factor of an earlier birth decade. The same, in application to their countries' own history, could be said of the modern-day generations of Italians or Japanese.

The time will come, and perhaps sooner than we know, that the Americans of the near future will similarly be ashamed of this, current moment in their history, and of those among their predecessors who, due to excessive recklessness or bitterness of spirit and mind, had voted in as US president someone with the likes of whom no decent or self-respecting person should ever feel any trace of affinity.

January 15, 2017

A conservative pundit on TV just said, while admitting that P-E Trump's behavior may be somewhat, um, abnormal: "But sixty-three million Americans cannot be wrong."

That is a well-thought-out statement, and it deserves an equally considerate response.

Here is my response: "Hahahahahahahaha!"

January 15, 2017

One hundred years after the Russian Bolshevik revolution of 1917—the Great October Socialist Revolution, in ironclad official Soviet parlance—America is about to inaugurate its first openly antidemocratic, pro-KGB president.

January 16, 2017

Brief Character Sketch

Vladimir Putin, former low-level KGB functionary, Leningrad-born, sixty-four, is immensely and unimaginably wealthy, loves dogs and is suspicious of people, swims multiple laps in Olympic-size pool every morning, has twenty-six known luxury residencies within his boundless domain, resolutely suppresses freedom in all its manifestations at home, jails or kills his political opponents, richly rewards his cronies and friends of long standing, presides over a vast star-crossed country with a rapidly contracting and disintegrating and heavily militarized economy and an angry and embittered population beset with dire and deepening poverty and a massive host of social ills, does not drink or smoke, waxes nostalgic over the great Soviet Union of yore, despises America, loathes democracy, used to be duck-faced in his salad days and now looks like a bored rat overdosed on Botox, fears death, and secretly sends his trusted moneyed emissaries to different remote corners of the world to ferret out the putative recipes for immortality, has just had his vapid and clinically vainglorious de facto puppet elected as the new US president, and knows full well that he could no more afford ever to step down from power than the supreme mafia boss to make a public announcement of his impending retirement.

January 16, 2017
Reflections on a photo of Soviet Premier Nikita Khrushchev doing the "Pepsi Challenge" with then US Vice-President Richard Nixon, Moscow, 1959:

Visualize now Putin instead of Khrushchev, and Trump in Nixon's stead. Substitute the look of anxious anticipation in

Nixon's eyes with that of boundless, obsequious adoration in Donald Trump's fishlike peepers. Instead of the fake hero of the Russian Civil War, Kliment Voroshilov—the one on the right, he of the pointlessly nonplussed, moronically furrow-browed aspect and fashionable "I'm just a suburban Soviet pensioner" straw hat—picture, say, Igor Sechin, the ugly-as-hell head of Russia's largest state-owned oil corporation, Rosneft, and his bosom buddy, the sonorous leonine Texan Rex Tillerson, the ExxonMobil CEO and, at present, PEOTUS Trump's pick to run the State Department: Rosneft and ExxonMobil have a signed agreement, worth $500 billion (with a "b"), to develop a vast swath of Russian oilfields, but they cannot consummate their beautiful financial relationship because of those darned sanctions imposed by Obama on Putin for the latter's annexation of Crimea (VERY UNFAIR! SAD! PUTIN GOOD, OBAMA BAD!); and so, as soon as Trump becomes president (Putin, with a slight incline of his ovoid bald cranium, raises the little plastic cup of lovely refreshing Pepsi to his bloodless thin lips, in an understatedly congratulatory gesture) and Tillerson, his Secretary of State, the sanctions will be lifted, and then. . . .

"*Vashe zdorov'ye, gospoda! Za mudryj vybor amerikanskogo naroda! Za nashu nerushimuyu druzhbu!*"

January 18, 2017

Putin's dedicating the majority of his press conference in Moscow yesterday to the discussion of prostitutes in general (people who believe in collusion between Russia and the Trump campaign are "worse than prostitutes"; etc.) and Moscow prostitutes ("best in the world") in particular is a classic case of an expert spymaster handling his asset, in effect sending Trump a none-too-subtle reminder: "Oh yes, I do have those tapes, pal."

January 18, 2017

In two days, the world will become an immeasurably more dangerous place.

Thanks, Trump voters.

January 18, 2017

Loathe him, despise him, mock and ridicule him—but don't hate him, because then you would become like him.

January 18, 2017

It is going to be refreshing, palate-cleansing, after eight years of Barack Obama, finally to have as president someone with no dignity, no class, no capacity for intellectual curiosity, no hobbies, no pets, no ability to express himself in complete sentences, no desire to read books or learn anything new about the world, no facility for sympathizing with other people, and absolutely no interest in anything except sex, money, and, above and beyond all else, talking about himself.

January 18, 2017

"... *a route obscure and lonely, Haunted by ill angels only.*"

—Trump's life, as per Edgar Allan Poe's "Dreamland"

Which last, incidentally, happens to be the land we are about to enter now: one of difficult, troubled, ominous, viscous dreams, haunted by ill angels only, from which one finds it impossible to awaken.

January 18, 2017

Trumpism is moral entropy. Putinism is moral atrophy. The former is an inchoate, chaotic stage of the latter. Both seek to delegitimize the essential goodness of human nature and bring everyone down to the same baseline level of all-out cynicism, by ceaselessly stressing the ultimate primacy of material self-interest over the much-ridiculed selfless nobility of spirit in people's lives. But while Putinism already is a fait accompli in Russia, Trumpism still is an American project in progress. A large majority of Russians either tepidly support or apathetically accept Putin as their country's totalitarian ruler. A large majority of Americans, at this point, hold an unfavorable view of Trump and his toxic notion of America. If and when—hopefully and almost certainly, never; but then, one never knows—most Americans, somehow, inexplicably, following foolishly in Russia's somnambulistic footsteps, either will become Trump supporters or the fatalistic pessimists willing to acquiesce to the seemingly inevitable evil of his permanent vulgar dominance over the American society, Trumpism, instantly transformed into an anglophone version of Putinism, will triumph for decades to come in the land of Lincoln.

January 19, 2017

Obama, as president, called upon the best in human character. Trump, a grotesquely flawed man, will be constantly appealing to the absolute worst in people. We can only survive his ill-gotten rule with our dignity intact by steadfastly refusing to accept the absurd notion of his normalcy. There is nothing normal about him. He does not represent us. His ugly, dystopian vision of America is not ours. He must not be allowed to gain any purchase on our minds. We are the only ones who can and will defeat him.

January 19, 2017

Don't be downhearted. Feel energized instead. Evil is taking over in America. We have a clear enemy now. Everything is out in the open. The air is filled with ozone. It's time to resist.

January 19, 2017
On television: New Yorkers lining 5th Avenue and watching Trump's LaGuardia-bound motorcade in silence, with gloomy and disdainful expressions, the way citizens of a vanquished nation watch the entrance of an occupying army into their capital, in old documentary footage. Which is what, in essence, Trump and his retinue are to the great majority of New Yorkers: an occupying force.

January 19, 2017
As is well-known, in many hotels around the world—including, for instance, the one I was just staying at in Tampa, Florida, the other week—there is no 13th floor: the 12th is followed directly by the 14th. (Superstitions better not be taken lightly by those whose livelihood depends on the psychological comfort of large masses of people.) I would suggest, in a similar vein, that the 44th US president (Barack Obama) will, in the collective mind of the future generations of Americans, end up being succeeded directly by the 46th (whoever she or he may turn out to be), with the nominally 45th being strictly a temporary presidential placeholder, called Trump (just Trump, and nothing more), not worthy of his own number for reasons of his burgeoning illegitimacy and dizzyingly spectacular inadequacy to the office. And so, I would imagine, it may eventually be reflected in future history textbooks: "The 44th US president was followed by Trump, followed in turn by the 46th US president. There was no 45th president in US history. Instead, there was Trump."

January 20, 2017
The day Donald Trump was inaugurated 45th president of the United States

We exist at this moment.
That will have to suffice for now.

January 20, 2017

 President Obama
@POTUS44

It's been the honor of my life to serve you. You made me a better leader and a better man.

6:09 AM – 20 Jan 2017

January 20, 2017
This is not a hallucination. This is reality. Welcome to the dark times, the age of dishonesty and mendacity, unbridled avarice and ignorance, bigotry and traitorousness—and, above all, the age of the dumb in America.

January 20, 2017
. . . but then again, the worst human being ever to occupy the White House has already been, um, president for forty minutes now, and so far, the world is still here. And we are still here with all our faculties intact. Small steps, tiny increments of time. Only 1,461 days left to live through. (2020 will be a leap year, hence the unfortunate extra day.)

January 20, 2017
In response to a WashingtonPost.com opinion piece, "A Most Dreadful Inaugural Address":

A hateful, vengeful, dishonorable, ignorant, worthless man.

January 21, 2017
The day of the Women's Marches across America and the world

January 21, 2017
On the day of likely the largest peaceful global protest in history, the primary cause and main target, the maniacally self-obsessed and uniquely unqualified, newly elected minority president of the United States—blithely unburdened by his record-low approval numbers and the sheer volume and intensity of the pure loathing and indignation he has managed to generate all across the country and throughout the world—traveled to CIA headquarters, largely empty on a weekend afternoon, to offer reassurance and encouragement to the small segment of the agency's workforce in attendance, after spending weeks by turns mocking and vilifying American intelligence; and there he stood in front of CIA's Memorial Wall of agency heroes, more than one hundred nameless stars carved into white marble, and proceeded to warble disjointedly about the number of times he had appeared on the cover of *Time* magazine, to lie stupidly about the size of his inauguration crowd, to vituperate against the dishonest media, to suggest with chilling light-heartedness that perhaps the US would get "another chance" to appropriate Iraqi oil, to crow about his own, like, intelligence, and so forth—a hollow, morally bankrupt, entirely shameless, and altogether unworthy and unfortunate man, certain to be judged with utmost severity by history.

January 22, 2017
In response to news reports that on Trump's visit to the CIA, those cheering and clapping when Mr Trump spoke were not CIA staffers but people who accompanied Mr Trump to the briefing:

This is going to be a permanent feature of Trump presidency, borrowed directly from an authoritarian playbook: his personal traveling "applause brigade." Can you see any other American president, from Lincoln to Obama, doing that: paying his personal applauders? Not really. But obviously, any modern-day illegitimate ruler's power, from Lenin and Stalin to Brezhnev and Andropov to Putin and the latest of North-Korean Kim's, invariably has rested on and was measured by the length and intensity of sustained applause greeting his public pronouncements.

"Long live our dear leader, the supremely wise and eternally young Comrade Donald Johnovich Trump!"

January 23, 2017
Wouldn't it have been nice if, standing up to the microphone to deliver his inaugural address at the National Mall three days ago, Donald Trump had suddenly smiled beatifically down at the expectant crowd in front of him and said, "My fellow Americans, instead of giving a divisive speech, I would like to share with you today one of my favorite quotes, which comes from Hermann Hesse's *Siddhartha*: 'My real self wanders elsewhere, far away, wanders on and on invisibly and has nothing to do with my life.' Think about it, my fellow Americans." And then just sat down quietly.

January 24, 2017
There are the unwelcome times when, through no free choice of your own, everything suddenly becomes political in your life. Sometimes these periods of heightened civic turmoil pass by relatively quickly, and sometimes they last one's entire lifetime, since history operates on a whole different scale of chronology than its human subjects. It always, I would suggest, starts when

a sharp needle of profound disillusionment in your country enters your heart—and once that's happened, the needle stays in there. Then the heretofore primary components of your life start falling by the wayside, your very life as you used to know it gets put on hold—a massive waste of time. But them's the breaks. You may wish you were more like some among your circle of friends, capable of remaining serene of spirit and existentially untroubled in the face of the rapid gathering of nonfreedom, the coagulation of darkness in the air all around you—but, alas, you do indeed not have a say in the matter. You are who you are and no one else. Everything becomes political in your life, and all other aspects of your daily being suffer from neglect as a result. But, well, life knows each of us better than we know ourselves, and is solely in charge of deciding what we should be doing at any given point in time, despite our sincere interior protestations to the opposite. There is no arguing with it. We are who we are. Things are the way they are.

January 25, 2017
Trump effectively designates FOX News as State TV.

One of the first things Putin did upon coming to power seventeen years ago was to start steadily, piece by piece, dismantling Russia's independent television.

 Donald J. Trump
@realDonaldTrump

Congratulations to @FoxNews for being number one in inauguration ratings. They were many times higher than FAKE NEWS @CNN - public is smart!

6:16 PM – 24 Jan 2017

January 25, 2017

It feels as though a wicked enemy of America, a vengeful fascist ignoramus, has managed to seize power in the land, doesn't it? But he did not have to invade America from the outer space or the boundless snowbound expanses of eastern Siberia. He was, of course, democratically elected, if, admittedly, with considerable assistance from Russia and the wily FBI Director—by the decisive minority of angry and predominantly under-educated American voters who freely chose nonfreedom for themselves and, unfortunately, their country writ large.

January 27, 2017

In response to Trump's failure to mention Jews in his statement on Holocaust Remembrance Day:

In his Friday statement commemorating the victims of the Holocaust—a statement most likely written by his senior advisor and chief ideological guru, the prominent white nationalist and known anti-Semite Steve Bannon—Trump neglects to mention Jews once.

Oops.

Oh well, no big deal. Trump may not even have heard about the Holocaust before, so that's kind of excusable.

No, he is not an anti-Semite himself: he is just a deranged narcissist, an airheaded situational bigot, a rabid, vile demagogue and xenophobe. But yes, indeed, his daughter has converted to Judaism and his toxic son-in-law is Jewish. And he definitely won't be going that route, taking the anti-Semitic path, until and unless it becomes absolutely necessary, essential from the standpoint of his popularity with his core base.

January 27, 2017

All it would take—or, at least, what would be a strong first step in the right direction—would be for whoever happens to be interviewing him for television in any given instance, just to interrupt him in the middle of his repeating a bald-faced lie, and to say, politely yet firmly, "That is a lie, Mr. President. It has been thoroughly debunked, and you know it. With all due respect, you are lying now."

January 28, 2017

DONALD CALLS VLADIMIR

—Hello, Donalld.

—Mr. Vlad, so fantastic to hear your lovely voice, sir! I been missing it terribly this whole past week!

—Donalld, how many a times I must to tell you to not call me Mr. Vlad? It is not a my name. I am not a Vlad the Impaler.

—Impala, sir? Like, Chevy Impala? GM is a disaster, let me tell you. Total failure. I told them, "After Ford, you're next. If you want to shut down your factories here in the US and relocate to . . ."

—Donalld, shut up.

—I'm sorry, sir. You're right. Won't happen again. I just get passionate, you see, big leagues, when it comes to saving American jobs and . . .

—Donalld, shut up. Listen me carefully. We here in Russia are not too much happy of you, at this far. You not been doing that we told to you to be a doing. You go to a head with what we told you to do in America too quickly, too. Much too. It will to lead to crash and to burn. You impatient and like child. Americans will to become suspenisve. Already they is. It's too unpresidented. Too fast. Our for you agenda must to be interduced in America more peacemeally. Hurriedness only appropriate when you try to catch lice. Listen me. I am going to quote for you the words of song of your past American group, name TLC: "Do not go chasing waterfalls. Please stick to the rivers and the lakes that you are used to. I know that you are going to have it your way or nothing at all, but I personally think you are moving too fast." You understand what I say, Donalld?

—Yes, sir, I do I understand. I am sorry. 100%. I know what you mean. But I just get so damn passionate, you know, big leagues, and in a hurry to carry out your beautiful agenda for America. You, sir, are a great man. Permission to speak freely? I admire you, sir. You are my number-uno hero. 100%. I . . .

—Donalld? Donalld. Shut up. You not is getting that *kompromat* tape to back. No way, Jose. Ah, and to speak incedentally about Mexico and of what impatient fool you are.

—But sir? Look, I am not doing all this to get that tape! Which doesn't even exist . . . does it? How could you even . . . I honestly think you are an incredible, fantastic, amazing human being. I . . .

—Donalld, shut up and listen me. We are not go to excuse your debt you owe us that we own you. Okay? It is not to go to happen. So stop be babbling like a waterfall and listen me good: you must to immediately start critiquing me, strongly, to calling me dictator, despot, violator of human rights and annexer of Crimeas, and hacker of your DNC . . . Run-DMC, heh heh. You roger me? You must to go medieval rhetorically on my so-called ass, as said your Tarantino. Credibility, Donalld! You not have it, and you still is losing it. What was that which you did on Mexican front? Chto eto bylo? That was stoopid. Why build idiotic wall when you cannot to keep your promise to make Mexicans must pay for it? Not wall, Donalld, but instead, if serious, if you man, you must to start a hybrid war in Mexico, with the hands of their own Mexican polite green men, and to annex large part of it. No minced steps! That will be more manly thing doing. Just I am saying. You roger me?

—Yes, but . . . But, Mr. Vl . . . but sir! How can I in all honesty insult you? My tongue won't turn in my mouth to do that! I can't speak badly of you. I cannot tell a lie! I truly admire you, big leagues. You are a fantastic person. But maybe, if I could have that tape. . . .

—Donalld, you are not get that *kompromat* from us. It is too good for us to be apart from. We, with colleagues, we watch it on every night almost, and we all laugh our asses on the floor and admiring your devil-like fantasy. You are an amazing . . . what is the American word, vers libre? . . . Ah, no: pervert. Yes, you are perv, as my assistants say you people say in America. Perv. I found my thrill on Blueberry Hill, in the presidential suite in Ritz-Carlton Hotel in Moscow. Hehe. Ah, Donalld, Donalld. You are such touching and moving child! I almost love you! Almost. . . . OK, Donalld, now speak it: Vladimir Putin is a tyrant and aggressor. But we must be looking for ways to a better mutual cooperation with Russia, because what the hell other choice do we have? Right? Kapish? Say it!

—But sir. . . . OK, Vladimir Putin, is a . . . I don't know the man, but if he thinks highly of me, I'll take the compliment, OK? Totally. Big leagues. He's a strong leader, and I will be a strong leader like him, only for America. Sir, I just can't do it. . . . I . . . I can't! Maybe if you could forgive most of that debt, then. . . .

—Donalld, do you know that popular old song by former popular England rocker and guitar player Eric Clapton—"I shot the sheriff, but I did not shoot the deputy"? It is of your choice, Donalld, who is to be you, the sheriff or his deputy. I also must to reminder you, because I is on the roll now, your popular rapping singer, Mr. LL Cool J, who rapped, long time ago, "Mama said knock you out!" Consider me is that mama in this specific case. I'm gonna knock you out, Donalld! See, I been here for years, rocking my peers, putting suckers in fear, making the tears rain down like a monsoon! . . . And etcetera. Do you kapish me now? Or do you to want for me quote another words to some another American song for you, which you will not certainly like, big ligz?

—I understand you, sir. Totally. I hear you. You are an incredible person. But a tyrant. But a fantastic person still. But a dictator. But an extremely strong leader. But a . . .

—That's better, Donalld. But not perfect. But better. Practice, practice! . . . OK, you can go now. I'm to leave you with this quote from words to lyrics of a song by Mr. Jay-Z: "You are a child of destiny, you are the child of my destiny, you are my child with the child from Destiny's Child."

January 30, 2017

All this pre-election talk about Pence's potentially becoming the most powerful VP in history, in light of Trump's unique unfitness for office, has now been proven moot, since the de facto position of the most powerful person in Trump's administration by this point has been firmly occupied by the Rasputinesque Steve Bannon: the most powerful white supremacist, Leninite, and anti-Semite in modern American history.

January 30, 2017

This, in a nutshell, is the situation: we have a maniac—malignant narcissist, bereft of compassion and empathy, infinitely vacuous and ignorant—occupying the most powerful office in the world and being manipulated every step of the way by a devious white supremacist and anti-Semite bent on Leninist-style destruction of the existing world order. This, to put it mildly, is a bad spot for America and the rest of the world to be in—the worst, perhaps, in the ultimate perspective, since the rise of Nazism in Germany. Yesterday they came for the Muslims—the most vulnerable and easily vilified group of people in the eyes of the million-strong army of bigots and xenophobes constituting the new regime's core base of support. Jews tend to know intuitively what is likely to follow . . .

A specter is haunting the Western world, and America in particular—the specter of fascism.

January 30, 2017

Obama has only been gone for ten days, but these last were filled to the brim with unspeakable ugliness, and it feels as though he's been away from the White House for a decade. From Obama to Trump. . . . It's as if, the day following Einstein's death, an angry drunk clown with orange hair and eyelash-less bloodshot eyes walked unsteadily into a Princeton auditorium, hiccupping and belching, and announced in a hoarse voice to horrified students, "OK, losers, now I'll be your new quan . . . quant-whatever physics and stuff, like, professor. That Einstein guy was a disaster, total failure."

January 30, 2017

Trump, in one fell swoop, has fulfilled Osama bin Laden's innermost, utmost dream—the one he lived and died for: to get the Muslim world to view America as the enemy of Islam, a crusader nation.

Good job, Trump voters!

Mikhail Iossel
February 2017

February 1, 2017

If you have a Trump voter/supporter in what Nabokov called "the basic text" of your life, have her/him, circumstances permitting, read aloud—aloud—the remarks made by Trump this morning at the White House, in honor of the Black History Month.

If they agree and proceed to do so with an air of confidence, in a clear voice, sans visible embarrassment, without turning red once, or shaking their head or rolling their eyes, without stammering or sighing or finally interrupting themselves and muttering "good lord" and refusing to keep on enunciating this murky juvenile stream of jejune conscience, please know they probably are beyond hope of salvation and . . . well, if they are your friends, they may no longer be, sadly, because their noggins have been captured and colonized from within by invisible alien brain-eaters.

February 2, 2017

In response to a Politico.com article, "White House nixed Holocaust statement naming Jews":

Wink, wink, nudge, nudge—hey, anti-Semites, Holocaust-deniers, I'm on your side, know what I mean?

February 2, 2017

This is a highly dangerous time for the open critics of Putin's regime in Russia. The new US president is a Putin admirer at best, and Putin's puppet at worst; and the new US secretary of state, until last month and for a number of decades the head of the world's largest oil corporation, is Putin's personal friend and de facto business partner, standing to gain hundreds of millions and perhaps billions of dollars in oil revenue from the lifting of Obama administration's sanctions on Russia. The new US president's national security advisor, a conspiracy theorist with a mean authoritarian streak, is an unabashed Putinophile. How likely, realistically speaking, would those excellent dudes be to raise their voices in defense of largely nonexistent democratic freedoms in Russia, if and when doing so becomes a matter of life and death?

Not. Very. Likely. At. All.

Putin knows he's got a free hand to do whatever he goddamn well pleases with his opponents now. And it already, as ever, is a matter of life and death.

Today, for the second time in two years, one such brave man, Vladimir Kara-Murza, is fighting for his life in Moscow, in a critical care unit, having apparently been poisoned again by FSB agents.

Dark is the road ahead. But there is no choice in the matter, no chance of a change of heart for those already braving it.

February 3, 2017

 Donald J. Trump
@realDonaldTrump

Professional anarchists, thugs and paid protesters are proving the point of the millions of people who voted to MAKE AMERICA GREAT AGAIN!

6:48 AM – 3 Feb 2017

"Paid protesters." This, from the very outset of his rule, has been the repeatedly stated and reinforced centerpiece of Putin's system of values: all protesters against his regime in Russia— or in Ukraine, for that matter, prior to the overthrow of his puppet Yanukovich there—must be paid by the enemies of Russia and by his personal enemies: most notably, the US State Department and the nefarious cabal of unimaginably rich international cosmopolites and enemies of traditional orthodox values in Russia, bankers and financiers, such as George Soros. No one can be protesting against him of his or her own free will, people can only be motivated by material self-interest, financial incentives, in order to go out into the streets and protest. People aren't that stupid—to protest against nonfreedom for free.

Trump is borrowing language directly from Putin here, in this and other instances. Trump is Putin's representative in America. Trump is America's leading Putinist.

February 3, 2017
Trump has let it be known that he wants women who work for him to dress "like a woman."

I would really like for Trump to start dressing like a chihuahua in winter, or else like a constipated wolverine, or else like Louis XIV of France, the Sun King.

February 4, 2017
Back in the Soviet Union, at different times throughout late seventies to mid-eighties, I used to know several smart, talented, educated, self-aware, and generally well-meaning young people who, seemingly out of the blue, would join the Party (CPSU), under one version or another of the standard rationalization of such a manifestly unseemly, downright repugnant (in every

"normal" person's eyes) decision that in order to fight evil, one had to gain access to its source first, its inner mechanism, because one could not realistically hope to improve the admittedly disastrous situation in the country without becoming, willy-nilly, part of the only force (an unequivocally evil one, granted, but . . . where were the alternatives?) with the practical power to do so, in the end—that in effect, according to every one of them, those lovely and ambitious but perhaps slightly disingenuous young people, they were going into the heart of darkness without any consideration of the benefits the Party membership would bestow on them but, rather, with nothing but their brightly burning hearts they were prepared to pluck out of their chests to light the path for the rest of us, the huddled masses, and, for good measure, with boxes of matches in their pockets, in order, yes, to dispel from within the impenetrable darkness engulfing the country.

Well, guess what. There were no happy endings there. The darkness had swallowed them all.

Don't play games with evil.

February 4, 2017

Trump's principal project: delegitimizing truth itself

February 4, 2017

One crucial difference between America and Russia: America has always been stronger than any one person, in the end; Russia, unfortunately, never has.

February 5, 2017

My quick, brief take—on living in alternative reality:

The author provided a link to his NewYorker.com article published this day titled "Life Under Alternative Facts." The full text appears below.

There was no real cognitive dissonance existing in the minds of most people in the Soviet Union of the nineteen-seventies and eighties. Everyone knew that everything said on the radio or on television, everything (with the exception of weather reports or sports results) was a blatant lie, spoken pro forma, just because that's the way things were and had to be: outside, it was dark or light or drizzly or sunny or cold and snowy or pleasantly warm or too hot for comfort—and on the radio and on TV and in newspapers and magazines the untold legions of official-propaganda folks talked about the kind of reality which did not remotely exist in the reality of Soviet people's lives.

Just because from dawn to dusk everyone was forced to hear on the radio and read in newspapers that everyone's life in the Soviet land was wonderful and was going to be infinitely better still, and that everyone else out in the capitalist world envied the happiness of Soviet people's lives, no one was duped into thinking this was actually how things were, neither in their own lives or in the lives of people all around them, in their cities and villages. Everyone knew the truth, even in the absence of any alternative, more reality-bound source of information.

Everyone knew how things were in reality. How could one not? One had one's eyes and ears and one's own life to live.

Everyone knew that the country was mired in poverty and decay and stagnation and degradation, drowning in lies and cynicism and all-out drunkenness. Everyone knew that they, the Soviet people, lived in a veritable funhouse of a giant isolated world unto itself, in the parallel reality of that endless hall of crazily distorted mirrors. People were not fooled, to put it mildly. Still, there was nothing they, including myself and everyone I knew, could do with or about that understanding. There was no place for them to take it, to pour it out on. Being exposed to constant, relentless irradiation by that funhouse reality, forever a swim in a sea of lies, had made people lethargic and apathetic, cynical and fatalistic, dumbfounded into mute infantilism, drunkenness, and helpless rage in the meagerness of their tiny private, personal worlds. Their worlds were small and filled with sameness. People lived their lives in a state of permanent shell shock, like dynamite-blasted fish still somehow capable of swimming.

This is what constant, permanent exposure to alternative reality does: it deafens and deadens you.

February 7, 2017

Kellyanne Conway told CNN this afternoon that the numerous untruthful remarks made by so-called president Trump are no more important that the truthful ones he also makes from time to time.

That is a beautiful, ironclad logic. Let's see . . . It is true that Stalin killed millions of Soviet people, but is that fact more important than the one that he also did NOT kill millions more of them? Because he could have killed everyone in the country, including himself, but decided that wouldn't be the right thing to do. Good on him. That's what historians should concentrate on.

February 8, 2017

. . . en route to DC, ready to help Trump swamp the drain in the rain, circumstances permitting. It would be fascinating, I think, to be able to see the world through his eyes for one split second: the view must be radically new and drastically unimaginable, like that possibly reflected in the unblinking retina of a rainbow frog falling topsy-turvy from the overcast sky over Manhattan.

February 9, 2017

Writing from the Association of Writers & Writing Programs conference in Washington, DC:

There are no clear parallels between Russia and America, let alone between the old Soviet Union and the US. The two countries' histories have next to nothing in common: one, in the main, is the narrative of freedom, the other—that of a sad lack thereof. Americans are not Russians: they are not inured to being subjugated by the powers that be and are instinctively unwilling to accept the pitiable roles of the meek hostages of malevolent fate. It is exciting and instructive, at this particular moment in time, to be in DC and surrounded by thousands of writers, people of the word, all united by the determination to take their country back from the minority forces of vile small-mindedness, self-proud ignorance, intolerance, xenophobia, and basic indecency.

February 10, 2017

Insanity is not a passing illness, akin to common cold. Power is its ultimate ferment and catalyst. Encountering no resistance on account of its carrier's growing degree of authority, it blooms and blossoms and mushrooms with madly accelerated fervency amid the lunar landscapes of the afflicted mind.

America, your president is a deeply deranged man.

February 11, 2017

One of the—admittedly, alas, rather minor—corollaries of the unmitigated tragedy of Trumps's election: it no longer appears to be a fad, among a certain segment of liberal intellectuals, to dig Putin as the only world leader out there, presumably, with the chops and the moxie and all that to stand up to, you know, America's global expansionism, etc. The bloom is off the stinking rose. Putin, via his outrageous meddling with the US elections, has been revealed for all to see for what he really is: a kleptocratic murderous thug with a messianic complex, and the archenemy of democracy.

February 11, 2017

America, by and large, has always been the rambling home of free-spirited troublemakers. The old Soviet Union, by contrast, could be viewed as a combination of a kindergarten for grown-ups and a bootcamp.

Just one more reason why it would be impossible for Trump to pull off a Putin in the White House.

February 11, 2017

One of the primary reasons Putin, between 1999 and the mid-2000s, was able to transition the inchoately democratic post-Soviet Russia to full-fledged autocracy: the fundamental absence of an independent judiciary.

Therein lies the essential difference between Russia and America: right now, with Republicans controlling both houses of Congress, it is the judiciary—people in black robes—serving as the only real obstacle in Trump's path to autocratic, fascist rule . . . when people in black robes would have to start taking orders from people in brown shirts—and then, in the spirit of making America great again, would be replaced altogether by people in white robes with pointy hats.

February 12, 2017

Every would-be authoritarian, wittingly or not, aims to crush people's will and capacity for mental resistance, by the sheer ubiquitousness of his nauseating presence in their lives; to subjugate them intellectually with blatant lies, maddeningly contradictory statements, and manifestly outlandish assertions. In order to be made safely governable and easily manipulable, people must be driven insane with the disorienting uncertainty of their, suddenly defamiliarized, reality. It is, for most people, truly a terrifying recognition—that the theretofore reliable center of stability in their lives suddenly has been replaced with the heart of darkness, the howling whirlwind of chaos. The primary purpose of chaos is chaos itself, but the practical result of it is the exhaustion on the part of everyone except its, a priori indefatigable and infinitely needy creator. Mental tiredness leads to cynicism, and cynicism is the essential prerequisite for giving up the resistance and giving in to the chaos of mind-bending alternative reality. That's the core of an authoritarian's unarticulated game plan: to force people to accept as something natural, par for the course the status quo of deepening unfreedom. It is therefore crucially important for people to stay awake and alert and not to lose their capacity for indignation . . . as indeed happened in Russia just a few short years after the nondescript soft-voiced, diffident apparatchik Vladimir Putin's timid and near-accidental assumption of power. At first, there seemed to be nothing to worry about: he was just a harmless protector of the preexistent status quo, a bland protector of Western-oriented oligarchs' sudden fortunes. Before too long, however, the promise of Russian democracy was dead and, much to everyone's confused dismay, it already was too late to force Putin to reverse the course he was on and go back to the point of no return. All bad things happen when people stop paying attention, draw back into themselves, turn their gaze inward for the seeming sake of saving their sanity.

There are times when the path of least resistance necessarily runs through the greatest expenditure of energy.

February 12, 2017
America is no late Soviet Union, and Trump, admittedly, is no Khrushchev/Brezhnev/Andropov/Chernenko, but oddly (and almost nostalgically, although . . . not really) recognizable to a former Soviet citizen is the regenerated permanent sense of existential uncertainty stemming from the realization that your life, along with the lives of everyone you care about and indeed the fate of every other person in the country, is in the hands of someone with an alien and obviously hostile and chaotic mindset and warped mentality, someone inherently cruel and unpredictable even to himself, driven by a limited sense of vile impulses: a deranged man surrounded by a clique of cynical opportunists and amoral sycophants. Life, for unknown reasons of its own, has a circular pattern. It is imperative for America to resist this man's hold on power.

February 13, 2017
It's only been three weeks, but already it feels like he's been so-called "president" for at least three years, you say? Patience, patience. Give it a little more time—and in a few months, the very mention of his name, let alone the sound of his voice or the sight of his mug on television, will be causing 75% of the country's population to experience an instantaneous involuntary vomiting reflex. And then, somehow, one way or another, by hook or by crook, just like that, he will be gone, because no nation can possibly survive a situation when three-quarters of its citizens are constantly throwing up, jointly and separately. . . .

February 14, 2017

A quick reminder: the US is currently being governed by a bunch of confused evil clowns because to a whole lot of perfectly sane people the supremely qualified woman was just, you know, not likeable enough.

February 14, 2017

At this very moment, one could imagine, Trump is sitting on the gilded padishah-sized bed in his White House office, snugly bathrobed and barefoot, in front of a muted TV screen, his orange head cradled in his delicate little hands, and wondering in helpless agony, as is his wont in times of trouble, "What would Putin do in this situation?"

He knows the answer to that hypothetical, of course: it ain't no electromagnetic engineering. Putin, quite simply and naturally, would have a couple of opposition leaders and several particularly eager investigative reporters liquidated, a dozen or two more arrested and thrown in the clinker to cool off; and he also would have the owners of such disgustingly irreverent and despicably dishonest, fake-news publications as the *New York Times* and the *Washington Post*, forced, on pain of finding themselves in a world of eternal pain, to sell the above-said dirty assets to a couple of Putin's pocket multibillionaires—and presto! Problems solved! Everyone immediately falls silent and gets moist-eyed in an excess of happiness.

Oh, but alas . . . "Oh, to be like Vladimir!" Trump's full, finely curved, sensuous lips are whispering inaudibly. . . .

And indeed, why can't life be as kind and benevolent to him as it always seems to be to Putin? Why can't he, King Trump, be like Putin? Why? Why?? Why must life—his life!—constantly be so relentlessly UNFAIR and SAD?!!

February 18, 2017

> **Donald J. Trump**
> @realDonaldTrump
>
> The FAKE NEWS media (failing @nytimes, @NBCNews, @ABC, @CBS, @CNN) is not my enemy, it is the enemy of the American People!
>
> 1:48 PM – 17 Feb 2017

"Enemy of the people," huh? Someone's been reading up on the Stalinist era of Soviet history—right, Donald? Well, good for you! Better late than whatever. But do you know what Stalin, with the help of his trusted NKVD, did to enemies of the people? Of course you do. That's right: he had them exterminated "like rabid dogs," by the hundreds of thousands. If the media is the enemy of the American people—in particular, the willfully ignorant and morally flawed, less-than-decent people, ones constituting the great bulk of your electorate—well, what are you waiting for? Those purveyors of fake news over at CNN, CBS, ABC, NBC, the *New York Times,* and the *Washington Post*—they need to be dealt with immediately. Don't lock them up— shut them up for good! That would do wonders for the atmosphere of unity in the country. Make America Great Again, baby, like Stalin's Soviet Union or Putin's Russia! The next exciting step on your agenda, also rich with the possibility of mass purges: the collectivization of America's agricultural sector.

February 20, 2017

I can only imagine just how stunned into momentary disbelief millions of people in Russia felt when they heard the American president, of all the people in the world, use the innately, congenitally terrifying, onetime and still-recent death sentence of a phrase, "enemy of the people"—and especially in reference to the free press.

February 22, 2017

You wake up in the dark, groggily turn on the TV, hear the words "Today President Trump . . ."—and then, a few last semiconscious moments later, "The weather in hell today is going to be lovely, with scorching rains, clear crimson skies, and torrential sandstorms. . . ."

February 22, 2017

. . . my quick take—on dictators and whiners.

The author provided a link to his article published at NewYorker.com on this day titled "Five Rulers and One Presidential Press Conference." The full text appears below.

I lived under five rulers in my "first" motherland. With the possible exception of one—the only one still among the living—all were what most normal citizens of the free world would be justified in calling moral invalids, in terms of their essential worldview.

The First was a hot-tempered vulgarian, buffoonish utopian, and deliberately clownish boor with a characteristically cruel, blood-drenched past, but, in stark contrast to his monstrous immediate predecessor and that leader's hideous heritage of infinite terror, he was possessed of no predilection for ceaseless mass murder nor for continuing to keep the vast, and vastly insecure, country (a veritable self-contained parallel universe unto itself) in a miserable state of complete isolation from the rest of the world. Too whimsically unpredictable for his inner circle's liking, too overtly populist and rashly impulsive in his determination to "thaw out" the permanently petrified country, he ended up being overthrown (but not killed: a first), in a peaceful palace coup.

The Second, a childish, vainglorious bumblehead and uncomplicated connoisseur of life's simpler pleasures, an immensely proud wearer of every medal or any other shiny sign of distinction ever issued anywhere in the world, took his sweet time—eighteen long years' worth of growing mental and physical decrepitude, as he withered on the vine of swelling irrelevance, amid the country's inexorable descent into the torpid swamp of economic stagnation and psychological depravity—to relieve his bitterly apathetic subjects from his unremitting daily presence in their lives. There was not a moist eye in the land when his metal-plated coffin, while in the televised process of being lowered into the grave, in the very heart of the heart of the country, suddenly proved to be too heavy for the funeral servants' hands and tumbled into the hole with a loud crashing sound.

The Third—ruthless and vengeful, elephantine of memory, exceedingly smart and coldly calculating, heavily Machiavellian (as befit a longtime head of the country's omnipresent and lethal secret police), outwardly Westernized to the teeth, herringboned and bespectacled, Scotch-sipping and tennis-loving, given endearingly to bouts of hack versification, superficially sophisticated, suave and polished, prim and proper, fanatically dogmatic, and, in all, dangerous in the extreme—mercifully shuffled off this mortal coil after less than fourteen months on the throne. He was felled by a chronic kidney ailment, having succeeded quite nicely nevertheless, even over such a minute stretch of history, at restoring the never-dormant atmosphere of Big Fear throughout the land, as well as at inching the world ever so much closer to the brink of nuclear annihilation. Had *he* been allotted even a third of the Second's tenure . . . well, I, for one, most likely, would not be writing this now, and you, I am afraid, might not be reading anything, either.

The Fourth, a clear placeholder and time-saver of a ruler, was at least half dead, both metaphorically and literally, even at the moment of his nominal elevation to the pinnacle of power. And, because hardly anyone among the general public had ever heard the otherworldly sound of his halting voice, let alone been able to register a single instance of him saying anything remotely consequential—and seeing that, as per the common knowledge, the only reason anyone was even aware of who he was to begin with was the random circumstance of his having been the Second's faithful lifelong sidekick, drinking buddy, and card partner—no one really cared when he quietly gave up the ghost in a snow-white hospital bed. There was no perceivable difference between his existence and nonexistence, as far as any of us were concerned.

The Fifth was a bouncy, altogether unserious, overly accessible, ever-smiling and glad-handing, motormouthed, hyperkinetic lightweight of a ruler, in the contemptuous view of the majority of my former fellow-citizens. He was a totally un-tsar-like windbag with an ominously shaped (mark of the Devil?) birthmark on his forehead, completely incapable of instilling fear in (ergo, of commanding the respect of) the increasingly restive populace (which, by and large, over the many centuries of the country's existence, has always tended to have difficulty with the fanciful, abstract notion of itself as an agglomeration of people of free will, partial masters of their own destiny, rather than just scattered handfuls of the dust of history). Well, he, The Fifth, as stated earlier, was the only reasonably *normal*, comparatively relatable, recognizable human being in the bunch. Nowadays, at eighty-six, the man who, wittingly or not, gave the people of his and other countries freedom is the most broadly and intensely hated political figure in the country's recorded history. And the monstrous ruler who died two years before I was born, the one personally responsible for the wholesale extermination and the ruined lives of many millions of his innocent subjects, happens to be one of the most universally admired.

Khrushchev, Brezhnev, Andropov, Chernenko, Gorbachev—why did I recall them just now? Because, I suppose, it has just occurred to me that not one of them—not even the voiceless and half-dead Chernenko or the incoherent and ultimately loony Brezhnev—would have humiliated himself quite as deeply and comprehensively, to the same degree of perfectly unbidden self-revelation, as the new US president did with utmost naturalness during the afternoon of February 16, in full view of tens of millions of people across the globe, in the course of a seventy-seven-minute emotional striptease performed under the thin disguise of an impromptu White House press conference. Not one of them, those five, would have given as much as a second's thought to the possibility of permitting himself to be perceived by others as so desperately, nakedly needy, so irrevocably overcome with self-pity. Cultural difference? Go figure. They were dictators, but they were not whiners. Make of it what you will.

February 24, 2017
Trump just now at the Conservative Political Action Conference (CPAC): "A few days ago, I called the fake news the enemy of

the people, and they are. They are the enemy of the people because they have no sources. They just make them up when there are none."

I wish this pathetic, dim-witted excuse for a human being had lived in the Soviet Union under Stalin. Then, in a momentary, final glimmer of helpless illumination, he would know the meaning of that phrase, "enemy of the people," as he would be led, sobbing and slobbering, on gelatinous legs, to his execution, having been unloaded from the back of a covered truck at the edge of the city, along with thousands of others slotted to be shot in the back of their heads on a daily basis. He would know then, with utmost clarity, what it felt like, to have been branded an enemy of the people.

February 24, 2017

They were waving little Russian flags with Trump's name on them during the latter's speech at the Conservative Political Action Conference (CPAC) earlier today. They almost certainly, bless their hearts, had no inkling those were indeed Russian flags they'd been handed out of the blue by mischievously smiling strangers outside the CPAC convention hall. They saw Trump's name and thought—well, this must be the brand-new flag of the wonderful new country called Trumputinlandia. But those, of course, were Russian flags. Well, stuff happens. . . .

Still and all, this might be an interesting question to consider: would they actually prefer to live in Russia, those innocent flag-waving CPACers, given the opportunity? Most likely, not, of course—not in any literal, physical sense: they don't know any Russian, for one thing; and they also would be unpleasantly surprised, one would surmise, to discover just what a poor country Russia is, in terms of per capita consumption. Well, OK. One wouldn't want to trade down one's consumption—that would be un-American. But . . . would they like for America, under Trump, to be a bit more like Russia maybe, only one with a greater variety of yoghurts and potato chips?

They probably would.

Because they do want a strongman in their lives. A forbidding father figure. Someone to promise to take care of them when the going gets tough—and it only keeps getting tougher all the time. Someone to tell them what to think, and when to think nothing. Someone to assure them that being their worst selves is OK.

Simply put, they want a dictator.

They want someone to make all the important life's decisions for them. Someone to tell them he'll protect them from anyone who is not like them. Someone with enough ironclad determination to close down the newspapers and TV channels that confuse them with contradictory information— and ones that have the temerity to criticize their leader, their father-figure, their dictator, too. Someone capable of jailing and killing those he would call the enemies of the people.

They want to live in an authoritarian society. They don't want to be free if that means they would have to be the ones solely in charge of their own lives. Freedom is onerous and complicated, and involves too many other people, most of whom look and think differently from them. They are un-American Americans, they don't want other Americans to be unlike them. They are the anti– Statue of Liberty Americans. They are the pro-Putin, pro-Trump Americans.

Those little Russian flags they'd been waving, ever so gullibly, were quickly confiscated from them by the vigilant CPAC overseers. But one can continue waving the flag of any figurative Trumputinlandia even in its literal absence from your hand. Un-Americanness is a state of mind. Once having been seduced by the siren call of nonfreedom, one will not give it up again for anything.

February 25, 2017
I, Donald J. Trump, will not be attending the White House Correspondents' Association Dinner this year, because I know all those enemies of the people there will be making fun of me, mocking me mercilessly, which I totally cannot take, because I am a humorless loser, an apoplectic barrel of useless protoplasm, and also because I know I am an impostor, an illegitimate president. I hate you all, normal people. I have never felt happy once in my entire, unbelievably shallow, pointless life. Please wish everyone well and have a great evening!

February 28, 2017
The constant, relentless, and ultimately pointless drive for continuous material self-enrichment at all costs, defining the existence of the likes of Trump and Putin with his pocket oligarchs, is the clearest indication and most immediate consequence of one's extreme spiritual impoverishment. A waste of a life—that's what happens to those who don't read books.

February 28, 2017
The father of Ryan Owens, the SEAL killed during the failed raid in Yemen, is refusing to meet with Trump and is demanding an investigation into the circumstances of his son's death, for which he blames Trump personally. The hastily approved raid (Trump was enjoying dinner while greenlighting it) was a fiasco that has yielded, so far, no intelligence. Tonight, just now, in front of the cameras and the entire nation, Trump has exploited

that tragedy—for which indeed he bears sole responsibility—and turned it into a sickeningly elaborate sequence, cynically taking advantage of the fallen man's widow's grief. Smiling upon her benevolently, he ad-libbed, referring to the length of the standing ovation, during which Carryn Owens also stood to applaud, "Ryan is looking down right now, and he's very happy because I think he just broke a record."

The young man who lost his life because of Trump's incompetence and vainglorious stupidity "just broke a record." In Trump's warped worldview, even the dead care most of all about record-breaking applause.

Mikhail Iossel
March 2017

March 1, 2017

My quick take—a few thoughts in connection with the second anniversary of Boris Nemtsov's assassination:

Iossel provided a link to his article in ScoundrelTime.com, "Because They Could: How We Are Not Russia." The full text appears below. On February 24, 2017, he had posted an abbreviated version on his timeline.

On February 27, 2015, a stone's throw away from the ominous fishbone of the Kremlin's Spasskaya Tower, they killed the charismatic and universally beloved leader of the Russian political opposition, the former Russian First Deputy Prime Minister, Boris Nemtsov, with four bullets to the back. Effortlessly friendly and quick with a smile, altogether brilliant (one of the country's most talented young physicists, in another lifetime), Nemtsov was the very soul of the country's opposition movement. They killed him because they hated and feared and envied him, to be sure, but mainly they did it just because they could.

Who were they? We know who carried out the assassination: people who had arrived to Moscow from the autonomous republic of Chechnya, with indirect connections to the ruler of Chechnya, Ramzan Kadyrov. We do not know for certain who ordered it. It did not have to be Vladimir Putin. It did not have to be Ramzan Kadyrov. We do not know if it was them, directly. But it was, nonetheless, the universal, eternal, timeless Russian *them*.

They could, and they did.

"We have a lot of killers, got a lot of killers. You think our country's so innocent?" Donald Trump shot back at Bill O'Reilly in a FOX News interview that aired before the Super Bowl. O'Reilly, at a loss for words, spread his arms in a helpless gesture.

Before they killed Nemtsov, they—the same faceless *them*—killed, in a similar matter-of-fact fashion, in an equally quiet and cowardly manner, a large number of other disagreeable individuals of public renown: independent journalists, human rights activists, members of the political opposition, and other such excessively eager truth-seekers. Anna Politkovskaya, Sergey Magnitsky, Aleksandr Litvinenko, Sergey Yushenkov, Yuri Shchekochikhin, Paul Klebnikov, Natalya Estemirova, Mikhail Beketov, Nikolai Girenko, Valentin Tsvetkov, Stanislav Markelov, and Anastasiya Baburova—those would only be the most notable names of those they killed. They killed them because they were angry with them, of course—but, again, first and foremost, they killed them because they could. They could, and so they did. They could—and they still can, and even more so than before.

Is this the Russia Trump loves?

"You think our country's so innocent?"

Them. The names are not important. They are *them*: those in or close to power, convinced beyond a shadow of a doubt that their lives are infinitely more important than ours or anyone else's; those willing to do anything to anyone standing in the way, however obliquely, of their constant self-enrichment. They are *them*, and they are there. Our country—the one led (if not quite represented) by Donald Trump at this point in history—certainly is not "so innocent," but *they*, those *them*, cannot do anything they want to whomever they want *here*. That is still the crucial difference between here and there.

Memory takes me a good thirty-plus years back, to the old USSR. In addition to being an unsuccessful applicant for an exit visa to the US and a former engineer-cum-security guard at the Leningrad Central Park of Culture and Leisure (charged with guarding the city's only roller-coaster, or "American Hills," in Russian), I was then a member of the Leningrad underground *samizdat* literary community. They—essentially the same timeless *them*—were in the full bloom of their supreme power in the country. *They* were personified on two particular separate (and equally insignificant) occasions by two identical sets of faceless hulking hoodlums freelancing for the Leningrad KGB, who quickly and expertly and dispassionately beat the old crap out of immaterial little me in front of my apartment building late at night, aiming half-heartedly for my vital internal organs so as not to leave visible marks on my face or on my body, apparently, for being disrespectful and irreverent and too cute by half, when I politely (I'd thought) turned down their routine "offer" to cooperate with them by informing on my fellow *samizdat* writers. They had me pummeled for the same simple reason: because they could.

They wanted to punish me for my reckless insolence, and so they did. "Next time we're gonna fucking kill you," one of those massive faceless gentlemen with broken noses, former boxers gone to seed, said nonchalantly in a flat nasal voice over his shoulder after the second of those beatings, as the two of them walked away unhurriedly from my crumpled little form, prone on the ground. They laughed good-naturedly, understandably pleased with themselves, because their effortless, quick work on me was done, and they had more cases just like mine waiting for them on a constant basis. Life was smiling on them.

But I didn't get killed next time. Much to my surprise and understandable relief, there was no next time. They didn't kill me: I just wasn't worth it, in their estimation—a lightweight, a total nobody. Had I, on the other hand, been somebody perceived by them as someone even a little peskier, more bothersome and somehow, tangentially, threatening to their clear designs on life—well . . . Mind you, they didn't decide not to have me killed because, all of a sudden, they took pity on me. That would indeed be a laughable assumption. They could have me killed with the batting of an eyelash, but to them I wasn't worth the effort of batting an eyelash.

Boris Nemtsov, however, was an entirely different matter, thirty-plus years later, two years ago. He did represent an existential threat to the eternal, timeless *them*. He made them feel bad about themselves, and he significantly complicated the process of their constant self-enrichment. So they had him killed. They could always do anything to anyone there. They still can. And everyone there has always known as much: that one is always living on borrowed time and in occupied territory. "They can do anything to anyone there." I keep repeating this so as not to forget that simple mind-boggling truth. There is no hiding from them anywhere, while one is still within their reach.

Two years ago, they killed one of Russia's best and brightest, noblest, and most fearless people. They did it because they could. They could—and they did.

March 2, 2017

The thing to understand about Trump is that he essentially is a typical mid-list Russian oligarch, wholly amoral and entirely dependent on Putin's benevolence. The only difference between him and all the rest of them is that he doesn't know any Russian—that, plus the quaint little fact of his being president of the United States.

March 3, 2017

This is not about fomenting anti-Russian hysteria. This is not about Russia, as such—it is about Putin's Russia. There is a world of difference between the two. This is about Putinism: a perniciously criminal ideology of aggressive state-sanctioned cynicism and amorality, premised on extreme corruption and legalized lawlessness. Trump, wittingly or not, owing to his general mindset and psychological makeup, has become the leading representative of Putinism in the US. This is not the new "Red Scare": this, rather, is "Rot Scare"—or "Rat Scare," if you will.

March 4, 2017

Leave Putin alone! Let Putin be! America has been so grossly unfair to him! It's all our own fault, just as everything that soon is about to come to light concerning Trump's being on the take with Russians for years will turn out to be Obama's and Hillary's fault! Indeed, what could he, poor besieged Putin, possibly have done but lash out at us, think about it objectively, after we heartlessly surrounded him with NATO bases, "poking the old shirtless bear," so to speak, making him feel extremely threatened and vulnerable and betrayed and heartbroken and all but openly provoking him to try and reestablish the pre-post-Soviet geopolitical order within his immediate, you know, domain; yes, and also after we, and Hillary in particular, chided him, repeatedly, ever so humiliatingly, as if he were a guilty child, for his human rights violations (as if we were not gross violators of human rights ourselves!), for imprisoning and assassinating Russian independent journalists and his political opponents (as if we were so innocent ourselves, as if Obama has never jailed or ordered the assassination of a single American journalist or his own political opponent!); yes, and after we imposed sanctions on him, Putin, once again, after he (yes, bo-ring!) annexed chunk of his neighboring state's territory (yes, that Crimea thing, Ukraine, blah blah blah) and unleashed a so-called "hybrid" war in southeastern Ukraine (yes, that old Donbas thing, killed lots of people there, yada yada, but what choice did he have?), in understandable hopes of virtually destroying Ukraine in order to teach them naive West-worshipping Ukrainians a valuable lesson in the true meaning and limits and overall negligible usefulness of that thoroughly fake Western democracy (as if we ourselves never invaded other countries, never annexed chunks of their territory, us, the blameless US; and as if Ukraine was even some sort of independent state, when Putin clearly doesn't believe so himself, Ukraine-wise, because in his view, and in the enlightened opinion of most Russians, Ukraine is not even a separate country, and never has been, but just happens to be a smaller version of Russia: Little Russia, as it has been called historically; and as if Ukraine and all those tiny Baltic states, all that post-Soviet territory, was not his, Putin's, rightful area of control, sovereign zone of influence, since it was our, US fault to a large degree that the Soviet Union fell apart in the first place; we're such hypocrites!); and finally, and especially, after we placed more sanctions on him, for his supposedly . . . ok, definitely, but so what, hacking into our elections and trying to influence their results, possibly in cahoots with the Trump campaign, yeah, OK—now, that really beats the band and what have you, as if we ourselves never tried to influence elections in Russia, like in 1996, the last time they hand real elections there, when that drunk Yeltsin ran against that old-style communist, Zyuganov, and we put our thumb on the scales there, trying not to let Zyuganov win, even though he was a favorite from the start; and as if we never tried to influence the Israeli elections, either; and as if we never . . . Oh, where does one even begin, going back all the way to the nineteenth century—our whole history is one unending succession of the kinds of things next to which Putin's possible minor and excusable transgressions would seem like the folly of a priest smoking a guilty cigarette on the sly in back of the church on a Sunday morning!)—OK look: leave Putin alone! Leave him out of it! That's new McCarthyism, blaming Putin for anything that's our own fault! The new Red Scare! Trump is Putin's puppet, you say? Yes, that, too, is our own fault! Hillary should've run a stronger campaign, should've visited Wisconsin or Michigan even once in October-November! We shouldn't have ignored the legitimate, economically-racial grievances of white working-class people! Trump is on us, totally! Putin only did what any strong national leader would do seeing an opportunity to take advantage of the woeful state of affairs in his main geopolitical rival's camp! That's why Russians love Putin so much, because he's a strong and tough leader, and why they loathe us Americans! Stop blaming Russia! Blame Obama! Blame Hillary! Blame, uh, blame Gary Johnson, blame Bernie, blame millennials, blame UFOs, blame yourself, even blame Bannon, if you must! Blame whoever and whatever, just leave Putin be! We are just as bad as or worse than Russia or the old Soviet Union has ever been! We are the worst, the source of most evil in the world! Leave Putin alone!

March 5, 2017
Sixty-four years ago today, on March 5, 1953, one of the most prodigious mass-murderers in human history, Iosif (Joseph) Stalin, bit the dust in a pool of his own urine on the floor of his Kuntsevo residence.

March 6, 2017
Life goes on—just not in the same way as before. A different kind of life. A life of uncertainty engendered by the constant gnawing realization that your country, and indeed your very existence, are in the hands of the sort of people any normal person would readily identify as moral degenerates. It's been lived before, that kind of life—in another place, another time.

March 9, 2017
No, getting Trump elected president was not Putin's primary objective. It just turned out to be, in the end, a nice corollary result of his efforts; a pleasant surprise. His overriding goal, in working assiduously to make hash of the 2016 presidential elections, was to compromise the American electoral system as a whole, to demonstrate for everyone to see the intrinsic weakness of the American political process, to sow further doubts about the essential nature of democracy as a system of government and a way of life, both in the minds of his apathetic majority in Russia and people all across the Western world; to undermine the strength of the Western alliance by tarnishing and diminishing the image of America as the world's sole superpower, and, perhaps on a more local scale, to throw into a tailspin from the very start the broadly anticipated Clinton presidency.

Trump was just, very conveniently, there: a permanent fixture on the radars of Russian intelligence, presenting of himself a temptingly useful vehicle for the realization of the aforesaid multipronged plot against America: a suitably amoral, shallow, childishly vainglorious and boastful rich guy, famous for being famous and beset with a host of prepubescently perverse, insecurity begotten sexual fantasies. For years he'd been coming to Moscow, looking for the elusive white whale of a megalucrative deal, and the Russians kept stringing him along, while at the same time dutifully registering and documenting his nocturnal escapades in front of dozens of hidden cameras in penthouse suites of five-star Moscow hotels. For years he was being kept afloat with Russian oligarchs' cash, while serving effectively as an American laundromat for their untold sums of shady money. Now he is Putin's man in the White House.

This is both dauntingly complicated—and not quite complicated at all.

This is not a conspiracy theory, either—one could come up with a much more elaborately provocative one, after all, if that's what one had in mind—but just a perfectly plausible version of the present state of the US-Russian relations. Relentlessly exposing the perfidious nature of Putin's regime, and the perniciousness of Putinism as its governing ideology, has nothing to do with bashing Russia or fomenting xenophobic sentiment among the nonxenophobic majority of the American electorate. There is nothing wrong with shedding light on Putin's Russia as the world's current ground zero of corrosive cynicism and wholesale denial of the importance of human freedom.

March 10, 2017
Kindred spirits:

The essence of Putinism: "Everyone has a price."
The essence of Trumpism: "Morality is for losers."

March 10, 2017

Many people wonder why Donald Trump never seems to smile.

In order to answer that question we must turn to science. Science tells us that the only animals that bare their teeth as a sign of friendliness and/or when they experience happiness are humans and chimpanzees. Thus, the mystery is solved: Donald Trump never smiles because he is neither a human nor a chimpanzee.

March 11, 2017

Some Americans—Glenn Greenwald, for example—seem to believe that the US is the primary source of all evil in the world, and that, consequently, everyone who is openly anti-American (such as, prominently, Vladimir Putin, his regrettable flaws as a person and an authoritarian ruler notwithstanding) happens to be a global force for good. That is a bitter, dyspeptic, and generally rather repugnant stance, on basic moral grounds, but Glenn Greenwald and people like him are entitled to it, as American citizens, and are free to express it as frequently and vociferously as they would like, exercising the essential human right they effectively would be denied or find it much too dangerous to put to practical use had they been Russian citizens, for instance, intent on publicly espousing the view that Russia (rather than the US) is the source of most evil in the world.

March 12, 2017

I don't get this whole "Leave Russia alone! This is not about Russia! Russia had nothing to do with Trump's victory! This is McCarthyism! Red Scare! John Birch society! Witch hunt!" movement. Oh, poor, innocent, unjustly maligned Putin! So unfair! He is so misunderstood! Sure, he did interfere in the 2016 US presidential election, and he did so with the express purpose of inflicting as much damage as possible on the Clinton campaign, and he did use WikiLeaks to deliver the "hacked" information to the American public/American media/Trump campaign, and a number of Trump campaign aides did meet with Russian officials/Russian intelligence during (and following) the campaign (and forgot to mention it to anyone, until the information of those meetings was unearthed by journalists, at which point they did remember: "Oh yeah . . .") , and Trump's close old friend and confidant and onetime advisor Roger Stone did communicate with WikiLeaks regularly and, by his own admission, had been in touch via email with the infamous Guccifer 2.0 (an aggregate name, apparently, for a number of Russian hackers that broke into the DNC computer network, etc.); and generally, more and more assertions contained in the Christopher Steele dossier on Trump are being confirmed (and all of them will be proven correct, before too long, I would dare to predict); and Trump's relationship with Putin/Putin oligarchs does seem exceedingly suspicious (he effectively served as a laundromat for some of the oligarchs' money in the US, as in the case of one Mr. Dmitry Rybolovlev, proud owner of Trump's former property in Florida, who paid for the latter 2.5 times more than Trump had two years prior, and whose private plane always and mysteriously found its way from Moscow to the very same locations Trump was holding his rallies at in the final days of the campaign; what was that all about, considering Rybolovlev is reported to be one of the oligarchs most dependent on Putin personally and financially and therefore most suitable for the role of Putin's personal emissary?); and in all, the possibility of collusion between Trump campaign and the Russian intelligence appears to be increasingly high and should be investigated in full exhaustive detail, because . . . because—are you kidding me? How could it not be investigated as thoroughly as possible? Why wouldn't it be? What could be the possible reasons for NOT investigating it to the hilt?

Seriously, I cannot think of one such valid reason. Can anyone? What's the deal with that "Russia had nothing to do with it!" hue and cry? Russia didn't, but Putin did. The Russia of Tolstoy and Mandelstam didn't, but the Russia of Stalin and Putin surely did.

I just don't get it.

March 17, 2017

Not even the most wild-eyed official Soviet propaganda of 40-50 years ago, in the zenith of its righteous class fury, ever conceived of a character of an American president quite as shallow, ignorant, narcissistic, stupid, pettily vindictive, and altogether pitiful and pathetic as the current occupant of the White House. And that's saying something, believe me.

March 23, 2017

Has there been another time in US history when the president and his staff were under investigation for treason?

March 23, 2017

The old Soviet Union, for better or worse, did have an ideology to challenge that of the Western world—a poorly synthesized mélange of Marxist-Leninist posits premised on the theory of permanent class struggle and the wholesale denunciation of capitalism and bourgeois democracy. Many Western intellectuals, over the decades, had found themselves seduced by that illusory, utopian alternative to the society of harsh inequality in which they lived, becoming in effect the archetypal useful idiots for successive Soviet rulers.

Putin's Russia does not have a self-sustaining ideology of its own, unless one counts unbridled Darwinism and legitimized all-out mafia-style corruption as viable elements of one. But Putin's Russia does have a vast supply of criminal money, trillions of dollars, stolen from the people of Russia over the last decade and a half by the Putin-led private criminal oil-and-gas corporation "Russia." With that filthy lucre, in the absence of any uplifting spiritual incentive, Putin's regime is buying by the hundreds and thousands—no, not the intellectuals (it has no abiding need and feels strong instinctual contempt for those)—but the more easily corrupted and otherwise manipulable among various-sized Western politicians and plutocrats: from Schroeder to Berlusconi, from Le Pen to Orbán, from Manafort to Flynn to Trump. *Pecunia non olet*, you know.

March 28, 2017
Putin in Russia, Trump in America: in due time, each country's separate past, left undealt with, comes rushing back with a vengeance.

March 28, 2017
Boris Nemtsov, Anna Politkovskaya, Sergey Magnitski, Natalya Estemirova, Yuri Shchekochikhin, to name but a few: Putin, whose entire life has been one of the tireless and brutally efficient pursuit of wealth and power—the life, effectively, of a human rat (no knack on those innocent animals)—is not worth the pinkie nail of any one of the above brave and strong, brightly smart, deeply honest and altogether remarkable people. And yet, all of them are dead, having been killed for standing in the way of or shedding light on his and his cronies' continued unchecked criminal acquisition of wealth and usurpation of power, and he is still alive, pointlessly and, in a larger, karmic sense, offensively.

March 28, 2017

Today, Trump ordered an end to all federal action on climate change. Let that sink in. The future generations of the people of Earth, including your own children and grandchildren, oh the enlightened Trump voters, will think of you without kindness. Stupidity has consequences.

March 29, 2017

Russia has the infrastructure of a democratic state but no democracy. The great majority of participants in the nationwide anticorruption protest of March 26 were very young people, those born and raised within that ugly societal paradox, who have never known any other Russia or lived under the rule of anyone other than Vladimir Putin. Unlike the older generations of Russians, they are not inured and have not been conditioned by previous, "Soviet" experience to the rank cynicism that is the cornerstone of Putin's ideology; and unlike older Russians, they do not depend on television as their primary source of information about the world at large. Russian television has been under Putin's total control since shortly after he became president seventeen years ago, but the Internet is a whole different matter: it exists beyond Putin's will and outside his domain. Now yesterday's adolescents have reached the age of being able to take a clear-eyed look around them—and much to their revulsion and indignation, they are realizing that their country's political system is rotten to the core, rife with corruption and criminality; that everything they've been hearing all these years from Putin and his cronies has been one big fat shameless lie, and that, simply put, they are living in a country of triumphant fakery, ruled by thoroughly amoral people, mega-thieves and cold-blooded murderers.

And they have decided they are not going to stand for it.

Mikhail Iossel
April 2017

April 3, 2017

Reagan, Trump. . . . My quick trip down memory lane.

The author provided a link to his NewYorker.com article, "A Reagan—Trump USSR Winter Dream." The full text appears below.

In another lifetime, back when I was a very young man in Leningrad, USSR, my friends (my fellow *samizdatchiks*) and I would be stunned to hear the rare American visitors to our semiunderground literary club—experimental poets and avant-garde writers from California and New York—criticize Ronald Reagan, and in the most vehement terms, too! Despite our inadequate command of English, we understood the gist of their diatribes, and we just couldn't believe our ears: Reagan! Our Reagan! Our only hope! How dare they be against him, say such unjust and hurtful things about the great man who had vowed to destroy us, the evil Soviet Union, and consign us to the ash heap of history! We were counting fervently on his being able to do just that: to destroy, once and for all, the indestructible USSR, our hateful motherland, the only country in the world we'd ever known!

It was, as we tried to communicate to our uncomprehending visitors, none of our business, and didn't matter a whit to us, what exactly Reagan was doing to the American economy or those (what were they called, you just said?) air traffic controllers, or whatever. The American economy could withstand Reagan. All the problems could wait until after he had delivered on his solemn promise to us! Leave our Reagan alone, we tried to tell them! Let him be! Don't attempt to replace him, please! Let him destroy us first!

In the ensuing silence, filled with sadness, we gazed out the dark window of the mansard loft, located in a dilapidated and otherwise unpopulated, soon-to-be-demolished building that we had claimed for our impromptu gatherings—a stone's throw from the pointedly ugly edifice of the Leningrad KGB headquarters. There, in the eternal winter of our simmering discontent, loomed the frozen river, and the blurred outlines of one of the seven major bridges spanning it. Its opposite bank— an unbroken string of majestic architectural landmarks—could not be seen, only guessed at, in a gathering blizzard. Night, indifferent to everything, had spread its vast wings across all of the boundless country's eleven time zones. This was our world. The future was unknowable to us, just as our own past would become strangely unfamiliar to those of us still left around a lifetime later. We were burning with a yearning to be destroyed. Our visitors from another planet looked at us with gentle pity.

This was a long time ago. Trillions of cubic meters of water under all the bridges of our lives.

I remembered that distant episode the other night, seemingly out of nowhere, while perusing an independent Russian news site and half-listening to some agitated pro-Trump pundit on TV attempting to count the ways in which Donald Trump was similar to Reagan: both were Washington outsiders, straight-talkers and straight shooters, both were Democrats turned Republican, both had been TV stars before diving into politics, both were pro-life and strongly in favor of tax reductions, both initially had been dismissed as frivolous candidates by the arrogant political establishment, both were extraordinarily charismatic, both focused like a laser beam on enforcing border security, both aimed to make America great again. . . . Both were largely ignorant and incurious and believed in social Darwinism at its cruelest and did some serious damage to America's image in the world, I appended in my mind, yawning. Although, to be fair, one of them did play a major role in ridding the world of the Soviet scourge by successfully scaring the hell out of the Politburo oldsters with his dangerously reckless space-bound bluff, his illusory zero-sum game of geopolitical chicken, thus luring them into a final, and entirely unsustainable, military-spending surge.

At that moment, by an oblique association, I imagined what it might have been like if, through some insane fluke of history, Trump, instead of Reagan, had been the American president back when I was a very young man in Leningrad. That, of course, was wild conjecture—a dystopian-slapstick kind of tale. For one thing, Trump most certainly would not have vowed to destroy us, the Soviet Union. Rather, he would repeatedly be calling Brezhnev and Andropov strong leaders and praising their intelligence and their brutal decisiveness in confronting the slightest manifestations of ideological dissent. At infrequent White House press conferences, he would be citing Brezhnev and Andropov's ninety-nine-percent approval ratings among Soviet citizens. "You think we're so innocent?" he would be saying sardonically, in retort to Tom Brokaw or Dan Rather. "You think we never invaded and occupied other countries, even bigger ones than Afghanistan, or downed some random passenger planes? You think we don't have thousands of political prisoners in the . . . what's that word you just said, 'gulag'? Give me a break, will ya? And listen, I think when Andropov calls me brilliant, I'll take the compliment, O.K.?"

I laughed quietly, and my cat, sleeping on my desk next to my computer, opened one green eye and focused it on me briefly, nonplussed. She was right. It was too late for laughter. Let sleeping cats lie.

April 3, 2017
. . . first, unstructured thoughts:

Two tragedies occurred in Russia today.

One was a shrapnel-bomb blast on subway train in St. Petersburg: ten people killed, as of this writing; dozens severely injured. This happened in the very heart of the city's subway system: there hardly is a Petersburger who wouldn't have passed through one of the two stations in question, Sennaya Square and Technological Institute, once or more often in their lives. In my case, it would have been hundreds of times, since most of my trip downtown from my part of the city had taken me along that "blue line" subway route.

At this point, it still is hard to comprehend: my city, even after thirty years of my living far away from it—the most beautiful city in the world, the city of my childhood and youth, the city of my life, where I was born and spent my first thirty years, where the oldest of my friends live—was hit by a bomb, blown up. My heart is breaking, filled with a dull ache. It feels, clichéd as it may sound, as though part of my own being has been exploded and gone up in acrid smoke. It feels as though all of us—people for whom that city is the city of their lives—have been violated.

The second tragedy—admittedly, a less brutally corporeal and more cerebral one, yet still blood-curdling in its implications—is that just minutes after the news of the explosion had reached the electronic media outlets, the "Russian" Internet—the Russophone segments of Facebook and Twitter—fairly erupted with confident assertions that this was "the regime's" work, a "black-flag" operation undertaken in order to divert the public's attention from the country's growing protest movement, the sudden emergence as an active and potent political force of a whole new generation of Russians—the young people, eighteen- and twenty-year-olds, those born "under Putin," who never knew any other Russia but Putin's Russia and any national leader other than Putin, and therefore ones not injured by the experience of previous falsehood-based "Soviet" life to the blatant lies, hypocrisy, and overt cynicism that are the hallmark of Putin's rule.

Let that sink in: the very first thought to cross the minds of an untold number of people in Russia was that the bomb explosion in the St. Petersburg subway was the work of Putin's regime intent on changing the current antiregime course of political developments in the country, diverting the millions of increasingly discontent young Russian people from their concentration on the cosmic levels of corruption and inequality in the country, and using the subway attack as a pretext for cracking down on any and all forms of public dissent, precluding even the minute possibility of open discontent, and banning all future rallies and protest marches. The use of terrorist acts to tighten the screws is a national tradition in Russia.

It was regime's own work, the untold number of Facebook posts and tweets in Russian are asserting—and how could they not be? Who would be able to convince all those thousands upon thousands of posters of the opposite, given everything they and everyone else with a connection to Russia has come to know all too well about the nature and the general modus operandi of Putin and his regime: after the highly suspicious and likely "black-flag" explosions0 in apartment buildings in Moscow, Buinaksk, and Volgodonsk, and the discovery by vigilant tenants of an explosive device of a similar nature in the basement of an apartment building in Ryazan at the outset of Putin's rule, immediately prior to Putin's using the fact of those bombings as a pretext for starting the Second Chechen war; after the mysterious deaths of the prominent investigative reporter and the famously incorruptible politician involved in looking too closely into the details of the above tragedies; and after the terribly botched and still unexplained "Nord-Ost" hostage crisis in the Dubrovka Theater in Moscow, where more than 100 hostages were killed by the mysterious gas used by the FSB "rescuers"; and after the horror of Beslan, where hundreds of children were killed as a result of another rescue operation gone terribly wrong and lied about just as terribly in its wake; yes, after all those lies, after the veritable torrents of lies with regards to the annexation of Crimea, the "hybrid" war in Donbass, the shooting down of the Malaysian passenger plane over southeastern Ukraine, after the polonium poisoning of Alexander Litvinenko in London; after the murder of Sergei Magnitsky; after the as yet unresolved assassinations of the leading opposition figures and independent journalists—who would possibly believe the regime? It has long forfeited its right to be believed. It has covered itself in layers of illegitimacy.

The old Soviet Union, way back when, in another lifetime, had fallen, in large part, under the weight of its own lies, as a result of the great majority of its citizens' losing the last shreds of faith in it. It had delegitimized itself out of existence. Back then and there, we, Soviet citizens of old, used to read Soviet newspapers instantly and automatically converting all "pluses" into "minuses" in our heads as a habit of simultaneous mistranslation: whatever was stated there, we knew, was a lie—whatever or whoever was praised, was bad by default; and whatever and whoever was vilified, was just as unquestioningly good.

This is the predicament Putin's regime is finding itself in, at this point: it won't be believed, no matter what. No matter what it does now, what kinds of proof it is going to present, what presumed apprehended culprits it is going to parade in front of the TV cameras, it will not be believed. It will never be able to cleanse itself off of the layers upon layers of lies and illegitimacy it has covered itself with over the past decade and a half. This is a Russian tragedy, the tragedy of Putin's Russia, the second tragedy of April 3, 2017.

April 4, 2017
For today's barbaric chemical attack by Assad, Trump is blaming . . . Obama.

An American president blaming a war crime committed against children by a foreign dictator, on the previous American president. For crying out loud, does not this pathetic man have even a tiny shred of decency?

Nope. Not a shred.

April 4, 2017
Confucius said: "Life is really simple, but we insist on making it complicated."

Confucius, allow me respectfully to disagree: Life is really complicated, but we insist on making it simple.

April 10, 2017
In response to a NYTimes.com article, "How Soviet Dissidents Ended 70 Years of Fake News":

This is an interesting but, IMHO, a thoroughly confused piece by Gal Beckerman. The Soviet dissidents "ended" nothing. 99% of the Soviet population had never heard of those brave people, the Chronicle editors, much less seen the actual issues of the publication. 99% of the Soviet population at the time never got to hear the severely jammed short-wave Russian broadcasts of the Voice of America or the BBC, let alone Radio Liberty. 99% of the Soviet people at the time thought the high-profile Soviet dissidents (Bukovsky, Orlov, Shcharansky (now Sharansky), even Sakharov, and others) to be some sort of cantankerous crazies just looking for trouble and hoping to convert their ill-gotten fame later on into financial backing from their imperialist sponsors at the Pentagon and the CIA (TsRU), et al. 99% of the Soviet people in the 1970s–80s knew without the Chronicle that the regime and its political system were rotten to the core and were going to fall apart sooner or later; but unlike the Chronicle editors and other dissidents, they saw no reason or possibility for themselves to attempt hastening that end, no more than one would attempt to hasten the arrival of warm weather or the end of the interminable rain falling from the gray sky for days on end.

A well-meaning piece, perhaps, but one informed by wishful thinking or an excessively streamlined interpretation of Soviet history.

April 10, 2017
Happy Passover, everyone!
We are stronger than our enemies.

April 11, 2017
Barack Obama, who, according to Trump, was not a real American, hosted a Seder at the White House eight times during his presidency.

Donald Trump, who is more American than a carrot pie, has just skipped his first one. That makes a lot of sense, from his political perspective: he has hurt his core base of anti-Semites and white nationalists quite enough already, by giving increasingly more visibility to that Jewish-globalist son-in-law of his and slighting the true-blue, Jew-loathing Americans like Steve Bannon in his administration. David Duke is feeling heartbroken, and that's just needlessly cruel—breaking David Duke's heart. Cruel—and unwise. Without the enthusiasm of anti-Semites and racists, could Trump be reelected? Unlikely. His finely tuned political intuition has never let him down, and he knows he needs to cool it with all that Jewiness, at this point.

So then, goodbye for now, weird Jewish suppers. Hello again, all-American double cheeseburger.

April 11, 2017

In response to a Bloomberg.com article about remarks made by US Secretary of State Rex Tillerson to European diplomats in Italy, "Tillerson asks why US Taxpayers Should Care About Ukraine":

Oh, indeed. What an excellent question, Rex. Why should US taxpayers care about anything at all? Why should they care about Syria, for instance? Why should they care about Europe? Why should they care about art or literature? Why should they care about the fact that your boss's incessant golf outings to his Florida dacha cost them, US taxpayers, millions of dollars per week—or that his administration is comprised of plutocrats and multibillionaires, or that you and your oil company stand to gain hundreds of billions of dollars should the European and US sanctions on Russia be lifted? Why indeed should US taxpayers care about the lawyer Sergei Magnitsky murdered by your personal close friend Vladimir Putin's regime? What's

Hecuba to them? Why should US taxpayers care about anything that does not directly influence their own bank accounts, or anything that concerns anything happening more than ten miles away from their own homes?

US taxpayers, in your judgment, are a bunch of egotistical, unsympathetic yahoos, right, Rex? Your probably think every US taxpayer is like you or your boss or your boss's core electorate. You are wrong, Rex. Wrong. You're a fool, Rex. US taxpayers are ashamed of you.

April 11, 2017
Not-Evens:

Not even Hitler gassed his own people. Not even Stalin threatened the world with nuclear weapons. Not even Lenin ordered summary executions of orthodox priests. Not even Vlad the Impaler impaled people at random. Not even General Westmoreland sanctioned the use of napalm in Vietnam.

All true, of course. But by the same token . . .

Not even Genghis Khan mocked disabled reporters. Not even Ivan the Terrible played so much golf at taxpayers' expense. Not even Caligula tweeted such adolescent nonsense first thing in the morning. Not even Ayatollah Khomeini boasted publicly about grabbing women's genitals. Not even Pol Pot hung out with so many Russian mobsters. Not even Idi Amin refused to release his tax returns. Not even Mussolini gave such stupid nicknames to his political opponents. Not even Saddam Hussein lived in a more tastelessly decorated penthouse. Not even Grand Inquisitor Torquemada slapped his name on so many tacky skyscrapers. Not even Jeffrey Dahmer managed to lose one billion dollars in one year while running a casino. Not even Robespierre called Mexicans rapists. Not even

Emperor Hirohito had less of a sense of humor. Not even Mao Zedong lied about the size of his inauguration crowds. Not even Attila the Hun had as little understanding of the US Constitution. Not even Vladimir Putin has a more charming smile. Not even the rain has such small hands.

April 12, 2017

Today is April 12, Cosmonautics Day—an official Soviet holiday. On April 12, 1961, Colonel Yuri Gagarin, twenty-seven, was launched into space and spent 108 minutes up there, having orbited the Earth once and, in a parallel development, having observed no traces of God's existence above us.

I was very small at the time, but still remember the sheer vertiginous, otherworldly happiness breaking out and engulfing everyone all around me right after the momentous news had poured forth from the flat black felt dish of the communal kitchen radio, in legendary announcer Yuri Levitan's preternaturally sonorous and solemn voice. "Attention! Moscow is speaking! All the radio stations of the Soviet Union are reporting! We are broadcasting a TASS (Telegraph Agency of the Soviet Union) report!" The entire vast Soviet country went mad with exhilaration, as if God himself had come down from the firmament and promised immortality to each and every one of us. I remember feeling befuddled.

For most of my childhood, between my ages of eight and seventeen, our family lived on Cosmonauts Avenue, in a large "micro-district" on Leningrad's southwestern edge. The elementary-through–high school I went to, School #511 of the Moskovsky District of Leningrad, was located on Yuri Gagarin Avenue, a ten-minute walk away.

Another lifetime.

April 13, 2017

Assad is denying the use of chemical weapons on innocent civilians. Putin is denying Assad's use of chemical weapons on innocent civilians. A grizzly bear interviewed by a local radio station has strenuously denied ever defecating in the woods.

There is a Russian saying to describe people like those two: "You can pee in his eyes, and to him it'll just be God's morning dew."

April 16, 2017

The old Soviet Union had an official ideology, if a thoroughly demented one, called communism. The Soviet state motto was "Workers of the world, unite!"

Putin's Russia does not have any clear governing ideology, except for that of cynicism and greed and an obsessive determination to bring the rest of the world down to its level of moral turpitude, in order to feel better about itself. Its unarticulated motto is, "Bad people of the world, unite!"

Putin's Russia is considerably more dangerous than the former Soviet Union, because it is infinitely flexible ideologically and has absolutely no limits to how low it would be willing to go in pursuit of the above objective.

April 17, 2017

Longish text out for a spin:

Putin, Russia, Trump, Assad. "Some viewers may find these images disturbing." Death abounds everywhere.

As I am writing this, on a rainy April afternoon, multiple people in different parts of the world are killing scores of other people. Assad uses poison gas on children. Trump reciprocates with a missile strike intended to send a clear message to Assad that this level of barbarity will not be tolerated. What will Putin, Assad's benefactor, do now? He'll think of something, no doubt—and all of us will be the first to find out, if and when he does. Is Trump about to send a similar message to other countries, such as North Korea, for instance? That could start a nuclear war, which is a worrisome perspective. Enquiring minds want to know.

Bannon calls Kushner a "cuck" (note to self to look it up in Urban Dictionary) and a "globalist" (that is to say, the sort of person Comrade Stalin was wont to call a "rootless cosmopolitan"). Stupid and ridiculous stuff. I didn't need to know this.

Bomb blast in St. Petersburg metro. The very first thought to cross the minds of millions of people in Russia: could Putin have been behind this, in some way? Sad, but true. Eleven killed, dozens wounded. Some viewers may find these images disturbing.

Decades ago, in another life, there was a rather lengthy stretch of months when I would be passing through those two "blue line" stations, "Technological Institute" and "Sennaya Square," almost on a daily basis.

The sheer fragility of human existence. Sometimes, and often, it feels like a miracle to me, that I've been able to make it this far in life—well past the middle of my life's journey, in point of fact—with most of my basic faculties relatively intact.

Truck attack in Stockholm. Such ugly, cowardly brutality: ploughing a heavy vehicle into a crowd of unsuspecting bystanders. One must be a rabid dog of a human being to do such a heinous thing. A dim-witted, angry loser brainwashed to the point of total inhumanity.

Relentless is the drumbeat of predominantly bad news from all across the world. Facebook, Twitter, and other social networks are keeping one updated on a microlevel, with print and electronic media providing the chaotically instantaneous "big picture."

An uncommonly good man, kind and decent and loved by everyone—a talented and popular forty-two year old Russian novelist, father of two—has died in a Tel Aviv clinic of stomach cancer. A venerable Russian poet, fellow Leningrader, one of the originators of the literary samizdat movement, has died in Germany at the respectable age of eighty-one. Easily the most likeable of the entire cohort of still-living ex-Soviet cosmonauts, veteran of a record number of space missions, Georgy Grechko, has died in Moscow. He had the kind of face that looked as though he was constantly smiling—and perhaps he was . . . constantly smiling, the lucky guy. He was eight-six, which is the age my father would have been now.

We, the news consumers, are getting what we—most of us—always thought we have wanted all along: being fully immersed in the unstoppable flow of world's micro- and macrodevelopments, even at the cost of constantly taking on an infinity of nonhealable little wounds. But this, for many, is proving to be too much. The world, engulfed in turmoil and steeped in violence, keeps coming at us all at once and from every conceivable angle, in ceaseless waves of simultaneous dispatches—and one's brain, unable to cope, is fairly drowning in this permanent deluge of hyperawareness. There is no hiding—not for any meaningful length of time—from all that excessive and irreversible knowing. No matter how disturbing the images, they cannot be un-seen. Every new random bit of heartbreak is undeniable. Everything is unfolding in the real time of our lives. We no longer have the luxury of *not-knowing* anything.

Everything is right at our fingertips and directly before our eyes. There is a severe shortage—the old Soviet-style *defitsit*—of *not-knowing* in our lives.

Twenty-five centuries ago, Plato wrote in *Phaedrus*: "The only problem with seeing too much is that it makes you insane." Insane, huh. What would he have said after watching cable news for an evening and then spending a few hours on Facebook and Twitter? Oh, probably nothing. Insane is insane.

Or take Proust. In *In Search of Lost Time*, we read, "That abominable and sensual act called 'reading the newspaper,' thanks to which all the misfortunes and cataclysms in the universe over the last twenty-four hours, the battles which cost the lives of fifty-thousand men, the murders, the strikes, the bankruptcies, the fires, the poisonings, the suicides, the divorces, the cruel emotions of statesmen and actors, are transformed for us, who don't even care, into a morning treat, blending in wonderfully, in a particularly exciting and tonic way, with the recommended ingestion of a few sips of café au lait." In other words, according to Proust, we don't need to know anything happening in the immediacy of our lives that we cannot see with our own eyes or hear from someone we trust (presumably, not the powers-that-be, because in a society with no independent sources of information, the rulers always are liars).

It feels almost strange, quaintly poignant to recall now that back in another lifetime, some three-plus decades ago, in a whole other world that is no more, many young people of a certain restless disposition, myself included, feeling lost and isolated in their hostile and self-enclosed habitat, were experiencing an entirely different predicament: an acute dearth of information about the world writ large and even about their own country; a massive surfeit of *not-knowing*.

***

Back then and there, people like us lived much the same lives, shared the same endless low-slung sky, went to the same food stores with hardly any edible food in them, saw no point in complaining about things entirely beyond their control, were paid next to nothing for doing an equivalent amount of work and were quite OK with that, knew how to exist just fine without money, were not allowed to travel abroad or say publicly anything demeaning about their demented rulers and so forth, and considered all that to be not much stranger than the fact of their having been born in the first place or human beings' inability to inhabit the Moon, tried repeatedly and in vain to make out more than just a few shredded sentences at a time in the invariably jammed-by-the-regime short-wave radio broadcasts in their language by so-called "enemy voices" from the unimaginable outside world, drank copious amounts of noxious red rot-gut and DDT-infused ersatz-port, had virtually no hangovers and felt no particular dread at the thought of dying young, read on public transportation secretly obtained banned books concealed daringly inside the tattered covers of some harmless classical novel or a collection of children's poems, tended to wear exaggeratedly bored facial expressions in the presence of any figures of political authority, despised their demented rulers to the point of almost pitying them and never bothering to speak about them with each other, trusted no sober stranger, knew better than to get enmeshed in dangerously slippery conversations or tell politically dubious jokes in mixed company, considered themselves to be consummate gimlet-eyed cynics, were childishly naïve and unspoiled for ordinary people their age, put together underground literary magazines, often thought of themselves in the third person, kept in mind at all times that their lives were fully at the mercy of their demented rulers, sometimes were fun to be around, liked getting together in dank basements or echoing mansard lofts of uninhabited or soon-to-be-demolished buildings for drinking that poisonous stuff they drank and talking about everything and nothing and reading aloud their own and others' writing and so forth into the wee hours of the morning, sandpapered the inner lining of their throats with the acrid gray smoke of the country's most popular *papirosy* bearing the name of the inoperative and ipso facto redundant giant northern waterway built by the free labor of hundreds of thousands of emaciated political prisoners, said lots of pretentious stuff with self-conscious smiles and fell silent all at once at uneven intervals of time in order to focus their diffuse stares on some invisible point in far-off darkness, equally loved and feared solitude and its absence, felt sad and a bit scared visualizing the immense gray space of empty nothingness un-punctured by words and sentences all around them, did not believe in God and didn't believe God believed in them, had no idea what to do with their hardened immortal souls or their permanently confused and officially nonexistent collective subconscious, felt nostalgic for the sharp smell of chlorine mixed with the reek of fried cabbage in the endless dark halls of the communal apartments of their childhoods, pictured themselves as human bats speaking mainly in order to echolocate themselves in time and space by the refraction of their voices off the walls of rooms and buildings or any other hard surfaces, took on faith nothing written in newspapers about the historically doomed Western world of rotten capitalism or even about their own country, were not sure about the exact meaning of the adjective *Orwellian*, hardly ever watched TV news, had their teeth on occasion drilled and extracted without anaesthesia, loved America for the obvious reason that they were supposed to hate it and so on and also because it was feared and reviled and envied by their demented rulers, hoped against hope America would liberate them some day by destroying their country's ruling regime, realized with a touch of sorrow that they probably were never going to see with their own eyes either America or the rest of that unimaginable vast world beyond their malevolent motherland's monstrous boundaries, stole on a drunken whim aluminum forks from greasy spoons and other public eateries and were unable to explain to themselves or to each other what they had done this for, pondered briefly the self-erasing nature of memory once it was committed to paper, viewed the sphere of sexual relationships as just about the only one where the thought of the ruling regime rightfully never once entered their minds, fell in love easily, said things like "love is a self-inflicted wound," awoke before dawn in a state of unaccountable happiness and with their hearts hammering away in their chests, were startled momentarily by their own reflection in the mirror, wished they could see themselves the way other people saw them, saved up for weeks and months by recycling their own empty wine bottles in order to buy Western rock records or a pair of verifiably genuine American jeans from wily and elusive black-marketeers, were waiting secretly and with a serious measure of protective self-irony for something unimaginably good to happen to them, had all kinds of mutually exclusive thoughts about themselves, fancied themselves to be the kind of people who owned nothing of material value and owed everything to the wonderfully malleable language into which they did actually feel lucky to have been born, had dreams more beautiful and colorful than anything they had ever witnessed in their reality, had lingering existential doubts concerning the reality of their own existence, said things like "life is but a brief interval between two eternal silences," looked straight ahead or under their feet while walking in the city and paid zero attention to the ubiquitous and totally meaningless visual propaganda aggressively saturating most of the available empty space overhead on every street corner, ignored altogether or laughed contemptuously at the unremitting ecstatic proclamations on the radio and on television as to how their country was the most glorious one in all of human history and the envy of the entire progressive mankind and how its matchless chess players and ballet dancers and cosmonauts left their Western counterparts far behind in the dust of history, gazed out the streetcar window into the meager gray afternoon light and wondered without really wondering why good and talented people tended to die young while the openly bad and evil ones seemed to keep on living forever, thought of how strange it was to have been born at all and at that specific point in time and geographic locale, failed to fail better repeatedly, knew that the rest of the world feared and despised their country, wondered how it had to feel being a foreigner and not one of them and to have to think and express oneself not in their native language, paused to consider whether people ever thought in words at all or in thought clouds only, felt ashamed to be treated like kindergarteners in a boot camp by their demented rulers, imagined with a twinge of embarrassment that the entire civilized world was laughing at them and their country with its constant *defitsit* of everything and even such frivolous and ridiculous items as goddamn toilet paper, felt both amused and offended by the general bourgeois triviality of the Western world's thinking, wished those arrogant foreigners could also experience even once the bitter satisfaction of using as toilet paper the upper half of the front page of the country's most sacrosanct newspaper with the stupidly dignified jowly face of the country's supreme demented ruler on it, called themselves in jest (among themselves) the enemies of the people, joked that everyone in the land of enemies had to be an enemy of the people, lay fully clothed on their beds in their rooms on their sides with their faces to the wall and their eyes open and unseeing and tried to visualize the unimaginably vast and foreign world writ large out there, yearned to be part of the infinite outside world, wished they could know the truth of everything happening in the world every second of every hour, longed to become immersed in the sheer ceaseless tidal flow of the unimaginable foreign world's happy and tragic developments, knew they were not allowed to know about anything permanently good happening in the historically doomed world of rotten capitalism or anything seriously bad occurring in their own country, felt fed up with their forced all-out not-knowing, hated the empty gray vacuum of their no-lives, wished they could die and be reborn and start living anew in the unimaginable outside world and be everyone and everywhere at once there, said things like "living is finite but dying is not," believed on some inchoate level of childish naivety that people in America or anyplace else in the free world a priori had no valid reason to complain in earnest about anything in their lives because of their having already been lucky enough to avoid the fate of having been born in the land of ultimate nonfreedom, mused aloud if becoming different killed one's memory or whether the only way one could really see anything was on condition of being blind, said things like "my true home is my language" and "every sentence we ever write down is a proof but not a justification of our existence," felt angry about being angry and miserable about being miserable so damn often and had no inkling at all that misery was their peculiar little kind of happiness and that their all-encompassing forced not-knowing was in effect a safeguard of sorts for their unrecognized and misinterpreted inner peace, said things like "life is life and who cares how it passes so long as pass it does," were uncertain of everything except the lifelong steadfastness of their unquenchable thirst for as much information as possible about the world and almost certainly would have laughed derisively and said that was just insane talk if someone had suggested to them in passing just then that decades later and long past the middle of their life's journey there would come a time when they would surprise themselves by beginning to half-miss the simple not-knowing of their distant youth in that unimaginable another lifetime of their then-present and would indeed almost wish to return to that whole bizarre and shortage-ridden bygone world of *not-knowing*.

April 17, 2017

Today the President of the United States phoned the dictator of Turkey in order to congratulate the latter on becoming Turkey's dictator-for-life.

Nice.

From George Washington to Donald Trump—from the mountaintop to the bottom of the garbage dump.

April 19, 2017

St. Petersburg journalist Nikolay Andruschenko died today after a brutal beating last month. He had reported on the government's mob ties, corruption, and police brutality.

From Russia, with warm greetings from Trump's spiritual kin and benefactor, VVP.

April 21, 2017

In response to a TheGuardian.com article, "What do Donald Trump voters really crave? Respect":

This feels a bit frustrating, due partly to the word's endless mantic repetition. Respect? Based on what? The mere fact of one's being a sentient consumer of oxygen does not merit automatic respect. People—separately, not jointly—are owed only a presupposition of their general innate humanness and goodness, until and unless they prove one wrong on that count, and the basic measure of a priori civility. Respect, on the other hand, is not unconditional. It is earned, not granted automatically. Automatic respect toward an unknown individual is but a form of camouflaged condescension. Automatic respect can be accorded an office or an institution, but not necessarily the person associated with the latter. One respects the office of the US presidency—and rightfully, by extension, respects Barack Obama, as well, but despises the hell out of Donald Trump. One respects the hallow symbolism of the Oval Office—and is repulsed by the racist, anti-Semitic pig Ted Nugent, besmirching it with his presence last night, upon Trump's invitation. One respects another person's right to hold an opinion different from his or hers, but not the person as such, sight unseen, word unheard. You want others' respect? Start with not voting for a narcissistic cryptofascist, racist, sexual pervert and abysmal ignoramus—because by voting for him you essentially show your total lack of respect for the very people whose respect you seem to seek, "crave," and even insist on.

April 21, 2017

In response to an OccupyDemocrats.com article, "Trump Just Tried to Show Off for Italy's Prime Minister and Humiliated Himself":

"From Verdi to Pava . . . rotti. Good friend of mine. A very good friend of mine. Verdi, also. Great guy. Great friend. Amazing person. And I am a moron and a keen . . . would I know the word 'keen,' though? nah—and a total embarrassment to the United States of America. Also, Robert De Niro. Great friend of mine, unbelievable actor, even though he promised to punch me in the face. Great friend. Can't recall any other Italian names right now, but lots of great friends in Italy. . . . Ah! John Gotti! Great friend, amazing person."

April 21, 2017

In all fairness, it's not as if Barack Obama never used also to tweet out some threats to Iran or North Korea or a few adolescent insults aimed at random individuals or groups of people at 6 in the morning; as if he didn't also spend six hours a day on average watching cable news channels and frequently tweeting out an emotionally charged response to some inanity just mentioned on *Hannity*; as if he himself never lied every time he opened his mouth, never claimed that George W. Bush had wiretapped him, never did not have the slightest idea or the tiniest bit of curiosity about the contents of the health bill he was trying to repeal and replace, never talked about an armada steaming toward the North Korean shore when in fact it was headed in exact opposite direction, never bragged constantly about something he had not done, never spent every weekend playing golf at his own estate in the company of fat cats paying him personally $200,000 each per year to play golf at his estate and in his company; it's not as if Obama, too, never . . .

April 22, 2017

April 22. The man who ought to never have been born—whose name was borne with revulsion by the city of my life, whom as a child I was told I was supposed to love more than my own parents, who was proclaimed by millions of visual propaganda items on every street corner to be more alive even in his death than all the rest of us the living, for whom thousands of hosannas were sung day and night on the radio, in whose honor on a certain number of Saturdays per year the whole vast country was engaged in some meaningless menial activity, and who lay immobile and sallow-faced with hollow eye sockets and all waxen in his black suit and extremely dead inside the eerily bright glass cube guarded by heavily armed soldiers with inscrutably cruel features in the dark while the horrified five year-old me with my hand in my old-Bolshevik grandfather's large palm was moving past that awful glass cube in otherworldly silence—that man would turn 147 today.

April 23, 2017
In response to news at WashingtonPost.com that Trump's base is still behind him:

"88% of Trump voters say he has accomplished 'a great deal' or 'a good amount' so far."

My guess would be, that's because they are, um, dumb.

April 23, 2017

Donald J. Trump
@realDonaldTrump

Eventually, but at a later date so we can get started early, Mexico will be paying, in some form, for the badly needed border wall.

10:44 AM – 23 Apr 2017

This sentence, effortlessly transcending all boundaries of time and space and generally messy and convoluted to the point of being almost entirely nonsensical, is a product of a hopelessly ignorant mind mired in mendacity.

Your president, Trump's America.

April 29, 2017

America and the world have survived the first 100 days of the previously unthinkable and unimaginable: the rule of a vile, vulgar, infinitely ignorant and amoral, insanely self-obsessed, petulant child from hell. It can be done. One step at a time.

April 29, 2017

My last 100 days were infinitely more successful for America and the rest of the world than the first 100 days of the Trump presidency. And so were my dog's last 100 days, despite the fact that both he and I live in Canada. And so were your last 100 days, and your cat's, if you have one, or your goldfish's.

April 30, 2017

The leading figure of the Russian opposition, the country's most popular and charismatic antiregime politician, internationally renowned anticorruption crusader and 2018 presidential candidate, Alexei Navalny, had an acidlike substance thrown in his eyes yesterday by an unknown young hoodlum clearly affiliated with government structures and the secret services. In recorded video shown on TV, the attacker's face is blurred as he runs off to a waiting car, and so is the face of his accomplice continuing to hang out at the scene after the attack. Why the blurring? Well, because. Take a wild guess.

Navalny may lose an eye. He maintains his characteristic upbeat tone in his first social-media post after the attack.

This is Russia today.

Mikhail Iossel
May 2017

May 1, 2017
Let's give Trump credit for keeping the flames of our indignation with him alive and burning bright, by reminding America and the entire world on a daily basis, through his outrageous words and deeds, that he is a vile, ignorant, thuggish, craven, infinitely amoral and corrupt, dictator-loving cryptofascist moron who belongs in jail and has no business being within one hundred miles of the White House.

May 1, 2017
Trump says it would be "an honor" to meet with Kim "The Smart Cookie" Jong-un. So? Why no one criticized Dennis Rodman when he said the exact same thing directly to insane Kim's face a couple of years ago in Pyongyang, being visibly drunk? Just because Dennis Rodman has many more piercings and tattoos and is taller, younger, more eloquent, a whole lot better as a basketball rebounder, and probably more qualified to be president? I don't think it's fair to discriminate against Trump solely on the basis of his total cluelessness.

May 2, 2017
An old blind man in a long wintry line to the beer kiosk told me once, decades ago, in another lifetime, in a world

no longer in existence, in a glorious and terrible city that has since been re-renamed, that when he was a young prisoner in an eastern Siberian Gulag camp, he wrote poems for an imaginary fiancée at night, in pitch darkness, on scraps of paper bags that had been filled with cement, with an illicit stub of a lead pencil, by the light of his own eyes. I told him that was a nice metaphor, and he said in response, a little huffily, that it was pure nonmetaphoric truth. "Why do you think I've been blind for so many years now?" he added in a wistful tone, turning to me his desiccated face with empty eye sockets. "I burnt them out then. Still, no regrets. Just imagine that blue light in the night!" I told him, feeling a shiver of strange unease scamper down my spine, that I sure hoped his imaginary fiancée had subsequently appreciated those, doubtless lovely, poems of his.

May 3, 2017

"Russia is 'the greatest threat of any nation on Earth'," FBI Director James Comey said today at the Senate hearings.

He is right. Putin's Russia is the epicenter of cynicism and amorality in today's world, the fulcrum of the world's antidemocratic forces.

And America's demented current president envies Putin and admires him.

May 5, 2017

Putin and Trump are going all out for the fascist Le Pen.

Obama and Merkel have expressed their strong support for Macron.

Here is hoping France delivers Putin and Trump a big, fat smack across their faces on Sunday.

May 5, 2017
Being over the age of fifty is a preexisting condition. Being a woman is a preexisting condition. Having a breakable heart is a preexisting condition. Having a conscience is a preexisting condition. Being you or me is a preexisting condition. Being mortal is a preexisting condition. Being nonexistent is a preexisting condition. Not even the postexisting condition of being dead can guarantee one a favorable insurance rate.

May 7, 2017
Macron wins, in a landslide.

This is a victory for France, victory for Europe, victory for democracy everywhere.

It is a massive loss for Putin and Trump and the global forces of reactionary nationalist populism.

May 9, 2017
In response to Donald Trump's firing of FBI Director James Comey:

This is something that happens in banana republics: when the supreme leader starts feeling uncomfortable about being investigated, he fires (or worse) people in charge of the investigation. . . . I suppose we should be grateful that in the US investigators merely get fired, rather then fired at from the window of a car speeding by.

May 9, 2017
Trump is meeting the Russian foreign minister, Sergey Lavrov, at the White House tomorrow, to report the intermediate results of his efforts.

"Look, Sergey, tell the boss I'm trying. I'm doing the best I can, OK? I'm trying! I understand his impatience, but please explain to him the tough circumstances I'm in. He's got to appreciate my limitations: I can't simply fire all these damn Democrats and close down them friggin' newspapers, it turns out. Not right away, at any rate. One step at a time. I need more time. There is a difference between our situations. I know I owe him, I know he's unhappy, and I'm sorry, but I just need a little more time."

May 13, 2017
Trump giving commencement address at Liberty University.

Can anyone think of a less religious person, and a more egregious and prodigious sinner, than Donald Trump? Of the Ten Commandments, how many has he not violated? Only the rarely mentioned Eleventh one: "Thou shalt not badmouth dictators who have thee by the balls financially and also possess tons of *kompromat* on thee."

May 13, 2017
I am about to release a certified letter from one tremendous law firm, one of the best law firms in Guatemala, stating that I have never lived in the Soviet Union, with a few exceptions.

May 13, 2017
A bunch of torch-wielding alt-right Nazis in Charlottesville, Virginia, chant "Russia is our friend!" at Robert E. Lee Park.

In front of the Robert E. Lee monument.

Sure, why not. Putin is your friend, trumped-up mouth-breathers.

May 14, 2017
I immigrated to the US in 1986, became a US citizen in 1996, and never could have imagined at the time that twenty years later, 40+ percent of American voters would decide they no

longer had much use for democracy and would be just fine living in an authoritarian society instead—and would, as a result, elect as their president, by minority vote, essentially an English-speaking version of a typical second-tier Putin's oligarch: tacky and tawdry, infinitely vulgar, vertiginously ignorant, and sleazy and amoral as all hell.

History has a peculiar sense of irony.

May 20, 2017

On the occasion of Donald Trump's first visit abroad as president, to Saudi Arabia:

The first image of this American president abroad: curtsying with an ugly gold chain around his neck, like a circus bear, before a bunch of smiling tyrants and kleptocrats, in a palace owned by the royal family that finances international terrorism, denies basic human rights to women, beheads and stones to death hapless violators of barbaric medieval laws among its subjects, and tortures and kills its political opponents.

To say that Trump is a searing embarrassment to America would be an understatement of the decade.

May 24, 2017

In response to a photo of a dour-faced Pope Francis (in white) standing beside (all three in black) Donald Trump, Melania, and Ivanka:

One could write a novel based on this photo.

THE POPE is thinking: "I've seen many millions of sinners in my life, but this one. . . . Lord help me. There is just no soul to save here."

TRUMP is thinking: "This dude likes me. He really, really likes me! Could he make me an honorary saint or something? And also, four words: Trump Tower Vati Can!"

MELANIA is thinking: "Oh my God, what have I done with my life!"

IVANKA is thinking: "This look really works for me. Innocence incarnate. Totally launching new clothing line: 'Santa Ivanka'."

May 25, 2017

In response to British Prime Minister Theresa May saying publicly that she would remind Trump that intelligence shared between their two countries had to remain secure:

In a related development, later today I am going to confront my dog and tell him not to pee in public.

May 25, 2017

In response to yet another awful photo of Trump baring his teeth, this time at a NATO meeting in Europe:

Look at that lovely face. Yes, a national embarrassment. Except that the 25–30 or whatever percent of the electorate constituting his core support group comprises people who derive pleasure from being embarrassed, like a number of memorable Dostoyevsky characters. (They don't know who Dostoyevsky was, and neither does Trump, but Trump likes Putin, so they like Putin also, and Putin knows who Dostoyevsky was, because he had to read Dostoyevsky in high school, the famous Dostoyevsky novel set in the same city and the very same city area where Putin was born and spent his childhood and youth, and Dostoyevsky would have a lot of fun dealing with a Putinlike character, he liked Putinlike characters, those madly ambitious and immensely amoral and deeply repressed featureless snitches, so that would be an OK reference for

Trumpsters.) Well, the world will understand. At some point, America was bound to have a yahoo president, representing the million-strong army of American yahoos, insecure bullies, proudly ignorant America-firsters.

But it's a sad story, nevertheless—profoundly humiliating for America and alarming for the rest of the world.

May 26, 2017

It's as though this were yesterday, as the saying has it—but it was, in fact, sixteen years ago, in July of 2001.

St. Petersburg, Russia. An uncharacteristically dark July night. A thunderstorm is advancing on the city. There is a premonition of ozone freshness in the sharp, tangy air.

A large, disorganized group of American literary people, writing program faculty and participants, most slightly drunk and laughing, is pouring out of a fashionable new restaurant on the right bank of the river, in the immediate vicinity of Vasilyevsky Island, and off onto the embankment.

The University Embankment is largely empty, and there are no cabs in sight, but private cars, "privateers," periodically emerge in the dark perspective, traversing the embankment's length in search of wayward fares—and the two or three program assistants present, along with Jeff Parker and me, start hailing rides for the group and haggling about the price with the drivers. (Kazan Cathedral, directly behind whose hulk the program's hotel is situated, is but ten-minute automotive dash away, but the drivers would, of course, charge foreigners an arm and a leg if left free to do so.) I'm motioning with my hand to Denis Johnson and his wife, Cindy, to step over and get in a car; and he turns to her and says, "The big boss himself has arranged for our ride. We must be getting up in the world."

Later on, after the group has been set on its way back, I am sitting just outside a tiny café—a hole in the wall under a leafy overhang of tree branches—right off the bridge still on the right bank, with Arkadii Dragomoshchenko and Zina, his wife; and we're drinking cognac and coffee and looking at the gloriously illumined dome of St. Isaac's Cathedral, golden in the gathering velveteen darkness. There is a yellow-lit round space at the top up there, just above the dome; a circular living space, bathed in intensely yellow light: someone must be living up there!

I tell Arkadii and Zina a thought that has always, ever since early childhood, fascinated me: that someone may actually be living up there, on top of St. Isaac's, in that old circular space overlooking the entire city; some very old, eighteenth-century man, unaware of the century he's in, with mad Tsar Peter's old city still opening itself to his quiet view. There are old astrolabes, sextants, old maps of the Neva, ancient folios, whatever else, whichever other words of this useless nature I can come up with, up there, in that space. They are listening, nodding.

"A storm is inevitable," Arkadii says. "But such beauty, such incredible beauty—nowhere else in the world is it just like this. This intensity of beauty. Not even in New York, you must agree."

I nod. "Of course not."

"It's moments like this one's real life is made up of. Short discrete stretches of happiness," he says. "To put it simply. You can't get used to it. It's easy to get sentimental when you live in a place like this."

We keep drinking cognac with bitter coffee. The rolls of thunder are getting louder, nearer, more urgent. Pale lightning strikes the golden dome, buzzing like a celestial bee, and disappears, as if having been burned off by that parabola of gold in the night. The thunderstorm is directly above our heads, and a downpour will start any second now.

May 27, 2017

Imagine how different our world would have been if we'd never heard the sound of Donald Trump's mooing, lowing voice. His every word is a clump of dirt thrown at silence.

May 27, 2017

Some are suggesting I tend to oversimplify Trump's character, his primary motivations, and his thought process.

I wish I could agree: multilayered bad people, obviously, are more interesting (if also more dangerous) to deal with, in writing, than one-dimensional ones.

But, alas, I see no depth whatsoever to his persona. His brain-to-tongue connection strikes me as no more complex than the digestive process of a newborn puppy. As the Russian saying has it, "What's on smart one's mind is what on drunkard's tongue." Trump doesn't drink, technically speaking, and never has, but he's never needed to, either: he's always been drunk stupid, high as a kite on himself.

He may well be the least complicated and most simple-minded public figure in America today. That's exactly why he got elected by those who elected him. Kim Kardashian or David Hasselhoff would be like Robert Musil and Walter Benjamin by comparison.

May 28, 2017

Trump will not mourn the stabbing death of the two brave Americans who tried to defend Muslim women from a racist maniac on a MAX train in Portland.

The murderer most likely was Trump supporter, after all. And those he stabbed to death, while attacking Muslim women, may not have been—especially not the twenty-three-year-old recent college graduate.

So, no—Trump doesn't mourn the death of people who didn't vote for him or who didn't die at the hands of Muslim terrorists. He is not the president of all Americans—certainly not the president of the people of liberal, "sanctuary cities." He only is the president of the fascist Trumpland.

May 28, 2017
Comparative analysis of two world leaders:

Angela Merkel has a PhD in quantum chemistry and speaks several foreign languages, including fluent Russian.

Donald Trump speaks a dialect of English, started his adult life with banning black people from his apartment buildings, and later went on to found a fake university praying on the naive hopes of desperate, down-on-their-luck seekers of a better life for themselves and their families. He launched his political career by maintaining for five years that President Obama was born in Africa and never went to Harvard or Columbia Universities.

May 28, 2017
True fifty years ago, still—and even more so—true now.

"There is a cult of ignorance in the United States, and there has always been. The strain of anti-intellectualism has been a constant thread winding its way through our political and cultural life, nurtured by the false notion that democracy means that 'my ignorance is just as good as your knowledge.'"

—Isaac Asimov

May 28, 2017

Germany now is the leader of the free world.

America is voluntarily ceding to China the status of world's leading superpower.

Trump is a laughingstock throughout the world. Americans are thought of with pity and befuddlement.

Is this what Trump voters wanted, what with the majority of them having nothing to be proud of in their lives other than the yahooistically patriotic notion that "America is Number One, man!"?

Well, you'll have to give that up now, Trumpland, won't you—and all in exchange for feeling legitimized, reassured in your racism, bigotry, xenophobia, your pining for the past that never was. Well, OK. Was it worth it for you?

Oh, totally. No doubt about it. America first! If you look different from us or speak with an accent—get the hell out of our country! Feels great to be free to be vile.

May 30, 2017

The next American president—and I mean the real president, rather than any one individual in the contemptible succession of current constitutionally prescribed substitutes, such as Pence, Ryan, or, um, Hatch—will indeed have some serious explaining and apologizing to do before the rest of the world, starting with the Western leaders and telling them that, well, America had a temporary eclipse of her mind, an occlusion on her brain, a mental and psychological breakdown, a traumatic Trumpian episode, and was as a result taken over, for a relatively brief period in the historical perspective, by the unlovely minority combination of the most ignorant, most emotionally vulnerable, darkness-prone, vilest, and pathetically greediest segments of its electorate.

Some basic elements of the electoral framework would need to be seriously rethought, post-Trump, as well. The starkly antiquated Electoral College probably would need to go. A national soul-searching will be in order— a wide-ranging conversation about why it is better to be a decent and educated person rather than an ignorant and indecent one.

That broad national conversation would indeed need to include discussions about income inequality in America, gun sickness, kindness-deficit, and the unhealthy American habit of equating ignorance with spiritual authenticity and patriotism.

May 31, 2017

Yes, Syria, Nicaragua, and the US: the only three nonsignatories to the Paris climate accord. Three excellent world leaders. Assad is the smart one. Ortega, the best-looking. Trump is the one who tweets at midnight while falling asleep in the bathroom.

May 31, 2017

Does anyone seriously believe Trump actually knows what the Paris Agreement is? Of course not. He just knows that the rest of the world wants it, and wants the US to be among its signatories, so his natural first inclination is to punish those smartass European leaders who laughed at him back in Brussels a week ago, to show them who's boss—plus he senses the possibility of a nice deal materializing out of thin air. He's not used to giving away something for nothing, even if that something is an unequivocally good thing for everyone, himself included. "OK, I might consider not withdrawing from that thing you all like, but it'll cost you. Let's start with this modest proposal: two Trump Towers in the capital of every country that wants my kingdom to stay in the agreement. Plus one Trump golf course. Plus a few sweatshops for Ivanka's business. We could take it from there."

Mikhail Iossel
June 2017

June 1, 2017

Mike Pence is now talking about Trump, in his introduction in the Rose Garden, before the latter's announcement of yet another "America First" step back into knuckle-dragging medieval darkness, in exactly the same ridiculously overblown, panegyric way Politburo members in the old USSR spoke about Brezhnev, marmalade-faced and laughing inwardly, before bringing him out on stage and up to the podium at a Party congress—the stupid, disoriented, barely cognizant, pitiful, vaingloriously demented, mumbling old man. And then Brezhnev, hemming and hawing in a lowing, belly-deep voice and mispronouncing and mangling every other word on bold-typed pages in front of him, would start lying endlessly, hopelessly, pitiably, about how we were the greatest country and the luckiest people in the world. The only difference: back then, it was all in Russian.

June 1, 2017

Americans, Dear Leader Trump is offering you a simple choice: do you want to be citizens of America or citizens of the world? Do you want to be American patriots or rootless cosmopolitans? Do you trust them four-eyed educated types or are you with our proudly ignorant Dear Leader Donald Trump and other real Americans?

Do you want to be enemies of the people or enemies of the enemies of the people? He who is not with us is against us! If the enemy does not surrender, he is to be destroyed! We've always been at war with Eastasia!

June 1, 2017

I am a US citizen, and I am certain the great majority of other Americans, regardless of where they may live, feel the exact same way I am feeling right now: we want to say to the rest of the world we are sorry. Trump represents the minority of Americans, and he represents the worst there is in America. The large majority of Americans did not vote for him. Most Americans are dreaming passionately of the day when he is gone from the White House—and we all, to the best of our ability, resist his shameful presidency and do all we can to speed up the time of his departure. And when he is gone, America will be back in the world.

June 1, 2017

Following months of categorical denials, Putin admitted today for the first time that the hacking of the US elections may indeed have been done by some "patriotically minded" Russians.

May have been. He's not certain. He leans toward that conclusion, but he has no firm evidence to support it just yet.

The same patriotically minded individuals, no doubt, that invaded and annexed the Crimean peninsula in 2014, and then promptly unleashed the still ongoing "hybrid" war in South-Eastern Ukraine.

Note to Trump: no need to hem and haw and humiliate yourself any further on the subject. Your master has just admitted it: yes, he did it.

June 2, 2017

The US had its spot in the sun for a good long while, serving as a beacon of hope for the rest of the world for well over a century, but then the sheer accumulation of ignorance and bitter backwardness among its populace had exceeded some critical limit history was still willing to tolerate, and now, inevitably, other, more forward-bound and less victimhood-prone countries, most notably China and the strongest democracies of Europe, will step to the fore of human progress, because history refuses to stand still for any self-appointed losers.

June 2, 2017

When Putin gets cornered in an interview he realized too late he shouldn't have agreed to, he starts speaking rapidly, with great agitation, leaning forward, his voice rising, his face reddening, and he starts lying brazenly and stupidly and making crude and unfunny jokes and rude personal references. It is in those moments that one can see why Trump likes him so much: the two are cut from the same psychological cloth.

June 3, 2017

Trump's core supporters are deeply suspicious or downright afraid of the larger, outside world. They are not ashamed of Trump as the ultimate embodiment of the worst of stereotypes the rest of the world associates with the term "ugly American"—on the contrary, they thrive on Trump's boorishness, ignorance, bigotry, crudeness, cruelty, extreme yahooism, amorality, cynicism, organic inability to love anyone or anything, and general total lack of any spiritual foundation to his being; they feel legitimized in their own inner darkness by his open, self-proud hatefulness. What they perceive as a manifestation of their utmost patriotic "Americanness" is in actuality an expression of everything the Founding Fathers considered to be inimical to their idea of America.

The significant majority of Americans are capable of living at once in America and in the world writ large—and for them, Trump's grotesque persona is, of course, a source of keen embarrassment. The trauma caused to the collective American psyche by the vile charade of Trump's traitorous presidency will be long-lasting, because it will be impossible for anyone to forget, going forward, the previously unimaginable fact that 63 million American citizens willingly, and in many cases happily, had voted for someone whose character represents the full spectrum of the absolute worst features of human nature.

June 4, 2017

. . . reading a story, coming upon the sentence: "As everyone knows, smart is the new sexy."

As everyone knows. Well, OK.

But what happened to the old sexy? Where did it go?

The old sexy must be the new stupid. I feel sorry for it. The old sexy is not all that sexy anymore.

Here is another posit: "As everyone knows, stupid is the new stupid."

Trump is the new what the hell. Life is the new give me a break.

June 4, 2017

Putin, a former low-level KGB functionary and professional liar and snitch, catcher of damaged human souls, is an ignorant, none-too-sophisticated, remarkably vengeful and cruel, amoral and corrupt man, a murderer and a megathief, a thoroughly Dostoyevskean character and, in all, the sheer colorless embodiment of Hannah Arendt's "banality of evil." What could be the possible useful purpose for asking him any consequential questions when one knows with 100% certainty that he is going to lie in response? Why treat him with any measure of deference, as if he were a legitimate democratic leader, rather than a cynical usurper of power? Only, conceivably, in order to expose him for what he is as an interviewee: a thin-skinned, rude and crude and generally repulsive authoritarian ruler unaccustomed to being challenged or criticized by journalists. There could be no other reason.

June 5, 2017
One of the highlights of Megyn Kelly's interview with Putin in St. Petersburg: he still believes the CIA was responsible for the Kennedy assassination.

In the Soviet Union of his youth, and mine, this was considered an all but established fact, of course, and was invariably presented as such in untold multitudes of books and magazine articles. That's where Putin's head still is: stuck in the 60–70s Soviet Union. Once a *kagebeshnik* (derisive term for a KGB functionary), always a *kagebeshnik*. He is an ignorant, incurious, thoroughly uninteresting man, wily but by no means intelligent or sophisticated. Asking him any serious, probing questions is, to my mind, a waste of time.

June 5, 2017
Anyone trying to defend Trump's behavior at this point is going straight to hell, when his or her time comes. I can't reveal my sources, but I have it on absolutely reliable authority.

June 5, 2017
Remember the 1980s movies about the Russians invading America, such as, most prominently, *Red Dawn*?

Well, it has turned out, them resourceful Russians didn't need to bother actually invading America in order to take over the American presidency. All it took was a sufficiently large number of ordinary, non–Russian-speaking Americans with an authoritarian mindset, a massive reservoir of free-floating bitterness and resentment, an inherent fear of the outside world, and a deep-rooted distrust of the Other. The Russians invading America in order to dismantle its democracy have turned out to be Americans themselves, tacitly and tactfully guided in their anti-American endeavor by a handful of sympathetic Russians sitting comfortably in Moscow.

The next few posts are in response to news that Trump had called then–FBI Director James Comey to a private meeting in the White House, asked if he could "let go" of the investigation into Michael Flynn, asked for his loyalty, and asked if he is under investigation.

June 7, 2017

A plumber came to repair the kitchen sink faucet this afternoon, and I said unto him: "I need loyalty, I expect loyalty."

He didn't move, speak, or change his facial expression in any way during the awkward silence that followed. We simply looked at each other in silence.

Then I said: "Can you at least tell me whether I am under investigation?"

He looked me squarely in the eyes and said, "You are not under investigation."

June 7, 2017

At the coffee shop this afternoon, my barista, a tall guy named Jim, asked if I wanted extra pink sprinkles of my triple caramel frappuccino.

In response, I told him the Russia investigation was a cloud that was impairing my ability to act on behalf of the country, and that I had nothing to do with Russia, had not been involved with hookers in Russia, and had always assumed I was being recorded when in Russia. I then asked him what could be done to lift the cloud.

He responded that he was investigating the matter as quickly as he could.

June 7, 2017

When the door by the grandfather clock closed, and we were alone, my dentist began by saying, "I want to talk about that molar. It needs to be pulled. It was a good molar, but it no longer is, and it needs to go. I hope you can see your way clear to letting go of it, letting that molar go. It was a good molar, but it no longer is good. I hope you can let go of it."

I replied only that "it was a good molar."

I then got up and left out the door by the grandfather clock, making my way through the large group of people waiting there, including two cops and several plumbers and baristas.

I immediately prepared an unclassified memo of the conversation that just transpired and discussed the matter with my lawyers, also bringing to their attention the fact that I had no idea what the hell a grandfather clock was doing in a dentist's office.

June 9, 2017

I am going to leak some confidential information now:

In five minutes, I am going to have breakfast, and then I'll go for a walk with my dog.

The dog may not have wanted me to leak that information—he has a very different understanding of the concept of leaking to begin with—but I just went ahead and leaked it regardless, just now, without consulting him. If his lawyer (does he have a lawyer? Sure, why not; if Trump can have a lawyer, why not my dog?) may threaten to sue me for divulging confidential information about his client, I am ready. It will be my word against my dog's.

June 9, 2017
Like Trump, I spent some time in Russia/the Soviet Union (between the age of 0 and 30). Unlike Trump, I never lived anywhere outside Russia/Soviet Union between the age of 0 and 30. But, like Trump, I also always assumed I was being constantly recorded there, which is why, just like Trump, I had nothing to do with hookers in Russia/the Soviet Union.

June 9, 2017
This, in large part, is the source of my anger at Trump and those still backing him: prior to coming to the United States, I knew, based even on the general law of probabilities and despite my natural categorical disinclination to believe Soviet propaganda's constant assertions to the same effect, that people like many among Trump's core base of support did exist in America—racists, bigots, anti-Semites, xenophobes, shamelessly greedy persons, deeply and proudly ignorant ones—but I could never have expected they would be the ones, at some none-too-distant point down the road, to determine the outcome of the US presidential elections. In other words, to a significant extent, mine is the visceral anguish of a newcomer to the New World having his vestigial idealistic notions of America subverted, if not shattered altogether, by the growing coarseness of an increasingly incongruous American reality.

June 9, 2017

From time to time I am asked: what to do if one's friend is a Trump supporter? Nothing, in my opinion. There is nothing to be done at this time. Trying to appeal to the person's common sense or sense of decency, telling him or her that supporting Trump now is considered shameful and unacceptable anywhere outside those circles where it is also deemed par for the course to be an open racist, anti-Semite, or homophobe would be of no use. This is stronger than them. Watch—or rewatch—the classic late-70s film *Invasion of the Body Snatchers.*

Trump will have to go down first—as he will—for his supporters to start returning to sanity.

June 11, 2017

What's really insane about the current political moment in the US—and what drives the rest of the world crazy, I would wager a bet, is this question: how on earth do you go from Barack Obama and straight on to someone like Donald Trump as your president? What's wrong with your electoral process that it allows for such dizzying, manic oscillations between good and evil, extremely smart and downright moronic? It's just completely unnatural. Imagine if after this Pope, the college of cardinals had decided, entirely out of the blue, to make Ted Nugent the next one. "Yeah, totally, let's do it, let's get us Pope Ted XXII! That'd be so much fun! So freakin' cool! 'bout time we had a pope who hasn't even read the Bible once and basically spends all his time shooting at every animal he sees and posting anti-Semitic rants on social media. Enough of them professional believers in God! Fresh blood, that's what the Vatican needs right now! Time to shake the Vatican up! What kind of name is it, anyways: the Vatican? What does it even mean? Well, maybe Pope Ted XXII would know. maybe he would explain that to us."

June 11, 2017
What did Putin win?

OK, let's see. He did manage to install in the White House a weak-minded, comparably corrupt and amoral, uniquely unfit man, severely dependent on him financially and psychologically. Give him a round of applause. In that sense, he has been able to pull off the ultimate coup of infiltrating the White House and humiliating America in the way it has never been humiliated before, by any enemy, on its own territory.

What was he hoping to achieve? He was expecting, by controlling Trump, effectively to be able to control America's foreign and domestic policy also. He wanted, for starters, to have the crippling economic sanctions imposed on Russia by the Obama administration lifted. He wanted the FSB compounds in Maryland, also taken away by the Obama administration, returned to him. He wanted Trump, still just for starters, to recognize the legitimacy of the Russian annexation of Crimea. He wanted Trump to make Russia America's coequal partner in deciding the destinies of the world: the twinned, US-Russia super-superpower. He wanted Trump to close his eyes on any aggressive actions Putin potentially might undertake in the context of his pet project of restoring Russia within the old Soviet boundaries: invading one or all of the three former Soviet republics in the Baltics (Estonia, Latvia, Lithuania), for instance, or broadening the scope of his undeclared "hybrid" war in Ukraine.

In exchange—and in addition, obviously, to handing the election to Trump—Putin, of course, would have been willing to do deals with Trump and his associates. Putin and his oligarchs control trillions of dollars' worth of stolen oil-and-gas money, stashed away in a variety of murkily remote offshores and badly in need of washing. America under Trump was supposed to become a giant laundromat for those trillions of dirty cash. And also: how much is Mr. Trump worth—$3 billion? No offense, but that's a laughable sum, a pittance, by the yardstick of Russian oligarchs. Putin could make anyone Trump pointed a finger at a real, no-nonsense multibillionaire, on the scale of Deripaska, Abramovich, Usmanov, Rybolovlev, Vekselberg, Fridman, et al.

In short, Trump's election was supposed to be the beginning of a beautiful friendship between dirty Russian money and Trump andhis family and associates.

Sadly, that was not to be. Sanctions have not been lifted—and won't be lifted anytime soon. Those spy compounds in Maryland will not, most likely, be returned to the FSB, despite—or because of—all the talk to the contrary. America will not become a giant laundromat for criminal Russian money. Trump's associates will not become megabillionaires on the scale of Deripaska or Abramovich. So many lovely dreams along those lines have been shattered on both sides of the ocean.

What happened? What went wrong?

Well, for one thing, and most importantly, Putin, as is his wont, once again overestimated the real power of the American presidency. He thought an American president could subjugate the American political system to his will, strong-arm it it obedience. Putin does not believe in democracy as a form of government, convinced as he is that all the so-called "democratically elected" governments and their "democratically elected" leaders are corrupt by default, innately and inevitably, because in his model of the world, everyone is motivated solely by his or her self-interest, the "what's in it for me?" factor, and everything else—all this talk about democratic rule, systems of checks and balances, separate and coequal branches of government, honesty, decency, transparency, human rights—that's just something paid lip service to for purely cosmetic political reasons. There is little doubt Putin was and continues to be convinced that the American president, were he sufficiently smart, could indeed do all this by himself, through the sheer application of ironclad will and against the will of Congress: lift sanctions, recognize the annexation of Crimea, give America's tacit approval to the potential Russian invasion of other countries, and so on; and indeed: if he, Putin himself, was able to make everything work that way in Russia, why wouldn't an American president do something similar in America?

Trump could have admitted to Putin it would be beyond his or any American president's ability to fulfill any of the promises his presidential campaign had made to Putin, but he didn't do so at any point simply because he never had any idea himself as to how the American government works and what the basic difference is between a US president and a monarch an English-speaking "Sun King" Louis XIV. He was and continues to be naive that way.

What, then, has Putin accomplished, by this point, as a result of attack against America?

He's managed to sow further chaos and discord within American society and to distance and alienate America from its Western allies, as it has withdrawn into itself and effectively ceded the mantle of the free world's undisputed leader. That's a major accomplishment, in Putin's book. And the only one.

On the negative side of the ledger, Putin again, and even more vividly than before, has revealed himself as an international criminal and the world's most dangerous threat to democracy everywhere. He is even more of an international outcast now than he was back in 2014, in the wake of the

Crimea annexation. The large majority of Americans—those outside Trump's core base of support—view him as the main threat to the American democracy. The new French president, a quarter of a century his junior, repeatedly humiliated him at their joint press conference in Paris the other week, and Putin just stood there taking it meekly, because he can no longer afford being isolated from the leading economic powers of Europe, what with growing restlessness back in Russia and mounting dissatisfaction with his rule, especially among the younger generations of Russians. The chancellor of Germany, presiding over Europe's strongest economy, openly hates him.

Ultimately, the most important question: in what way has his successful effort to install Trump in the White House helped to improve the quality of Russian people's lives, so far?

It hasn't. Russia's economy is continuing to tank, and the country's prevailing mood is one of mounting resentment.

It was, in the end, a losing gamble for Putin: not the first one in his illustrious career of international mayhem, but hopefully, one of the very last ones.

June 12, 2017

The lasting damage of Trump's presidency: the world is never going to forget that the US is a country where something like a Trump presidency is possible.

June 12, 2017

In response to a WashingtonPost.com article, "Priebus, Cabinet members praise Trump in first White House meeting"

Thank you, Dear Leader, for bestowing upon the unworthy puny little us the celestial blessing of being able to serve you!

All these people would've made terrific low-level Party apparatchiks in old Soviet Union. They were born in a free country, raised in a democratic society—but what do you know: here they are, a bunch of perfect little totalitarians. Servitude, willful self-humiliating slavishness is an acquired skill.

I can just imagine the intensity of their hatred for the poor demented fool.

June 17, 2017

It is a sad, tragic even, tale: an idealistic seventy-year-old lifelong conman, starry-eyed and filthy rich and happily amoral, having been elected—by the less-well-informed minority of his subjects and with crucial assistance from the malevolent Eastern potentate named Pu "The Big Rat" Tin—to be the new king of America, comes to Washington, full of bluster and braying and demagogic fury and radiant and ambitious plans for his benevolent reign intended to enrich his family, his cronies, and his fellow plutocrats the world over . . . only to discover an inexplicable growing resistance on the part of his undervanquished and underjailed political enemies, who claim to represent the more-well-informed and therefore less patriotic majority of his kingdom's populace, through some nonsensical, meddlesome and totally ephemeral entity they call "the system of checks and balances." He attempts, in his noble barbaric ire, to fire them all, one by one, valiantly and with righteous crudeness, so as to clear the shining path for his beautiful monarchical agenda, but finds that the terrible nonmonarchical momentum of America's misguided history is too strong for one mortal conman to overcome, no matter how rich and quixotic or moronic he may be; and before too long, he is beset and all but rendered immobile, tied down by his delicate little hands and feet, by the foul multitude of those nasty, vicious, jealous, and envious ingrates, those piss-poor Lilliputians calling themselves "people's representatives," "independent judges," and "investigative journalists." Dancing madly and obscenely around his prostrate giant body, they squeal gleefully in tiny, gnatlike voices: "Impeachment! Impeachment!"

A truly heartbreaking story. A modern-day Shakespearean epic or maybe even a Hollywood drama.

June 21, 2017

"A nation can survive its fools, and even the ambitious. But it cannot survive treason from within," wrote Cicero two thousand years ago.

Can a nation, however, survive the rule of an ambitious fool who also happens to be a traitor but is too hollow and rotten inside to know the difference between treachery and common civic decency? Yes, it can, because a fool, no matter how powerful and ambitious, inevitably and before too long will reveal his true traitorous nature for everyone to see.

June 21, 2017

In response to a news photo of Trump and the Ukrainian president exchanging a dour stare in the White House:

Trump to Ukrainian President Poroshenko in the White House: "So, you the guy my master Vladimir Putin is pissed off at for your insolent unwillingness to subjugate to his will and turn your puny little country, which he doesn't even recognize as a separate country, over to him? That's not nice of you. My strong advice to you, from one billionaire to another, would be, go back and bend your knee before him, and kiss his ring—the one he stole from the Patriots' owner, Robert Kraft—and beg for his forgiveness.

June 24, 2017

What do a TV talk-show host in Russia and Donald Trump have in common?

Neither is allowed to criticize Putin, no matter how mildly.

June 26, 2017

Trump stated today that Obama is the person who really "colluded" with Russia.

Do you suppose he knows the meaning of the word "collusion"?

I would be inclined to say, "No, he does not," but I also remember that, according to Trump himself, he always has "the best words," while I never made any such claim about myself. In general, it cannot be denied that for an elementary-school first-grader, Trump is almost spookily precocious. So it is quite likely he knows something about the noun "collusion" and the verb "to collude" that neither I nor you, Reader, happen to know.

In light of that strong possibility, let me collude for you my day so far:

In the morning I colluded with a cup of tea and a plate of scrambled eggs.

Then I colluded with my dog and my cat, colluding both in the sense of feeding them, and then I colluded with my dog by taking him out for a walk.

Then I colluded, by e-mail, with the chair of my university department, to collude about some nonurgent matters of possible academic collusion with him.

Following that, I spent some time colluding with some TV news on my laptop, whose presenters were colluding, among other things, about Trump's collusion with the English language undertaken in order to accuse Obama of collusion, conclusion, collision, and contusion with Putin.

Later in the afternoon, having colluded with a stubborn little short story under revision, I met up at a downtown coffeeshop with the coordinators of the literary program I've been colluding with for many years, to collude with them over the upcoming collusion of said literary program with the Republic of Georgia, which is a small but exceptionally beautiful and altogether fascinating little country in Europe, where Trump owns no properties or golf courses and therefore has no idea and does not give a damn about where it is.

Having concluded that collusion, I colluded my way to my local supermarket, where I colluded to buy a bunch of various food products, with the colluded purpose of eating them eventually, although not all at once.

And now here I am, concluding this little collusion of a minitext and wondering (though not really), to quote the phrase colluded by Trump himself for the first time in all of human history, what the hell is going on.

June 27, 2017

In response to a news report that Russians rank Stalin as the "most outstanding person" in world history, with Putin second:

Stalin, Putin, Pushkin: three "most outstanding" persons in world history, as far as the citizens of Putin's Russia are concerned. Pushkin, I feel, was extremely lucky to have tied for second-third place with Putin. That's OK, though, he was a good guy, even though too much of a skirt-chaser, and a pretty good poet at that. But where is Ivan the Terrible? He also killed lots of Russians. No fair! It was not his fault he didn't have the technology of mass murder Stalin had at his disposal.

That's all you need to know about Russia, at this point in its history—or at any point in its history, for that matter—stuck forever, unchangeably, irredeemably, in its own medieval narrative.

June 27, 2017

If health care is not a universal human right, then being alive is not a universal human right, either.

Mikhail Iossel
July 2017

July 1, 2017
Whatever top-secret national-security information Trump will be able to retain inside his echoing head by the moment of his meeting with Putin next week, he will spill it all out the second Putin praises him as the smartest president America has ever had.

July 2, 2017
From time to time, I get messages—especially from my fellow former Soviet citizens—in which it is asserted that their authors have a number of smart, thoughtful, sophisticated, well-educated, culturally savvy, decent, intellectually and socially responsible friends of long standing who, counterintuitively enough, have voted for Trump and still continue to be Trump supporters.

Seriously? How very interesting! Good and smart people doing terrible and remarkably moronic things—that's so quaint, and so unusual! My inner Dostoyevsky is rubbing his figurative hands. Tell me more!

July 2, 2017
So yeah, well, there's this great old friend of mine, truly a wonderful person, smart, kind, and sensitive, with a terrific and offbeat sense of characteristically Jewish type of humor, immensely erudite

and wise, full of encyclopedic knowledge about the kinds of things I haven't even ever heard about (such as, for instance, the mating habits of the elusive poison dart frog), plus an excellent poet and professional-level amateur musician (author of the widely underknown "Symphony for the Theremin and Fifty-two Discordant Balalaikas"), generally a deep connoisseur of the arts and a master of far-flung international cuisine—but there's just one little problem: I don't know how and when it happened, but, you know, he of late has become, um, a bit of a Nazi, you know, and that, upsettingly, has begun to put some strain on our relationship. So now we mainly try to avoid any Nazi-related topics in our conversations when we meet, concentrating instead on poetry, music, exotic cuisines, and so on . . . although, admittedly, sometimes I find it hard to ignore that large black hole right in the middle of his chest—I just try not to stare—and occasionally, in his poems, he suddenly starts expounding on, you know, the need to kick all non-Aryan people (himself included, to be fair) the hell out of America, and all that kind of stuff. When he starts going into that mode, I just try to change the subject to, you know, the mating habits of the elusive poison dart frog.

July 4, 2017

Reflections on the upcoming meeting between Donald Trump and Vladimir Putin at the G20 summit in Hamburg, Germany:

They now will have a full-fledged "sit-down" meeting.

So they'll sit down. They'll sit down across the room from each other and will commence to gaze at each other in silence.

Thirty seconds. One minute. Two.

"Mr. Putin, it is an honor, believe me," Trump will say finally, earnestly, with an awkward smile of a hormonal hyena. "I've always been a big fan of yours, big fan. Matter of fact, just the other day, I was telling Melania I . . ."

"Where are my two spy compounds in Maryland?" Putin will cut him off brusquely. "When am I getting them back? And when are you going to lift those stupid sanctions on me already? My patience is wearing thin. My goddamn economy is falling apart. And where is my recognition by America of my annexation of Crimea? Where is my carte blanche from America to continue my undeclared 'hybrid' war against Ukraine? And that would be just for starters, Trump. I have other questions for you, too."

"I'm trying, I'm trying, Mr. Putin," Trump will say in a pleading tone, gesticulating wildly. "But it's not as easy as I thought it would be. Who could've known president is not the same as king in America? I know I owe you bigly, Mr. Putin, but. . . . You must appreciate my circumstances, I beg of you. I need a little more time."

"Do I look like someone who gives a damn about your problems?" Putin will scoff at him. "You're such a damn loser, Trump. . . . OK, I'm feeling generous today. Three. . . . make it two more months. That's all you gonna get from me. Start delivering the goods, or else—you know me. I have the tapes, the videos, the invoices, the wire transfer records—the works. If you can't make good on the promises you gave me last year, then what in hell would be the reason for me to keep you in the White House? Ask yourself that. I have three words for you: President Pence. Let that sink in."

"That's two words," Trump will mutter, discombobulated.

"Three, if I say so," Putin will tell him coldly.

And then, grinning broadly for the cameras, the two will shake hands.

July 7, 2017

The world is anticipating with bated breath the historic meeting of two ignorant, unsophisticated, intellectually lazy, brutish, thuggish, limitlessly amoral crooks: one—the supreme mafia boss of a giant failed state with a tanking economy, low living standards, and listless and demoralized populace; and the other—a malignant narcissist, sociopath, and feeble-minded, ignorant buffoon with the impulse control of a child (which leaves him eminently blackmailable by various interested parties), the elected president of the world's most powerful country by the resentful and also largely ignorant minority of its populace, with the crucial help from the more wily first ruler. The summit of the century: Putin and Trump, two criminals who by all rights should be communicating instead by knocking on the wall between their adjoining prison cells.

July 7, 2017

The Trump-Putin meeting is running longer than scheduled: it's been over an hour so far. All the Trump aides, left out of the meeting, are having a collective panic attack. H. R. McMaster has been able to peek in—and recoiled from the crack in the door at once, turning crimson in the face. Immediately thereafter, both Lavrov and Tillerson rushed out, ashen, shaking their heads, followed a second later by two visibly distraught interpreters.

July 9, 2017

 Donald J. Trump
@realDonaldTrump

I strongly pressed President Putin twice about Russian meddling in our election. He vehemently denied it. I've already given my opinion. . . .

6:31 AM – 9 Jul 2017

My cat stole a bologna sandwich off the kitchen counter. I strongly pressed the cat twice about stealing said sandwich, which I actually saw it stealing. My cat vehemently denied it. I know my cat and I believe it. I consider the case closed. I'll continue leaving bologna sandwiches lying around the kitchen counter. It's time to move forward. I don't suppose my cat thinks I'm a moron.

July 14, 2017
In a few days, it will be revealed that in addition to those already known to us, also present at that fateful meeting in Don Jr.'s office were 5 high-ranking FSB operatives, 7 top-notch GRU hackers, Putin's chief personal food taster, 3 stoned Russian pop stars, 2 fire-eaters, 1 German shepherd, 2 Pekingese, 2 Siamese cats, 3 Orthodox bishops, Roman Abramovich, and Dennis Rodman, with Putin Skyped in briefly from his private submarine somewhere in the Gulf of Mexico. Still, that would change nothing, since—sure, the room is a bit smoky, but where's the fire? Still no clear proof of collusion.

July 16, 2017
Once upon a time, there was a country called, meaninglessly, the Soviet Union. It was so large compared with any other country on Earth, it represented a virtual self-contained world unto itself. During the seventy years of its turbulent existence, its successive rulers managed to destroy or forever cripple the lives of many tens of millions of its people. That's all there is to say about it, in a nutshell.

July 18, 2017
In response to a WashingtonPost.com article, "Trump had undisclosed hour-long meeting with Putin at G-20 summit":

An hour must be about the right amount of time Trump needed to divulge to Putin, in a one-on-one conversation, all the top-secret national-security information bouncing around pointlessly inside his echoing head.

July 21, 2017
Trump is totally and completely innocent, and he only is asking his lawyers about the possibility of pardoning himself because of his well-known lively interest in abstract and complex legal matters.

July 24, 2017
Wrote a piece about Santa Barbara in post-Soviet Russia, to accompany Misha Friedman's excellent photographs.

The author provided a link to his article that appeared in the July/August 2017 issue of Foreign Policy. *Below is the opening of that article.*

Санта Барбара Форева!—*Santa Barbara* Forevah!—was stenciled boldly in tall purple-chalk lettering on the side of my parents' apartment building in the southwestern part of St. Petersburg, Russia, when I returned to the re-renamed city of my childhood and youth—Leningrad, USSR—in 1993. It was the first time I'd been back since immigrating to the United States seven years earlier. There were other signs of *Santa Barbara*'s presence in the city—improvised tributes to the American soap opera in the historic downtown area: a hole-in-the-wall café called Santa Barbara here, a Santa Barbara strip joint there. On several occasions I was asked, typically by women, whether I'd been to Santa Barbara myself and, if so, what it was like. I hadn't, unfortunately. "You should go. That'd be the first place I would go if I could ever make it to America," a middle-aged salesclerk at the grocery store said to me with mild reproach.

Santa Barbara certainly sounded nice. . . .

July 24, 2017

A bright July afternoon. West Virginia, USA. Thousands of kids in boy scout uniforms, their faces red with midday heat and excitement, are listening to the unhinged rantings of the leader of the nation, as he excoriates his political enemies, sneeringly calls them all kinds of childishly derisive and hateful names, fulminates against the "fake media" and wonders whether it would be bold enough to report truthfully on the sheer size of the enormous crowd of kids in front of him. Shouting at the top of his vulgar nasal voice, he rambles on, wades into the weeds of murky nonsequiturs, issues dark warnings about the calamity certain to befall the nation if the health-care system bearing the name of his immediate predecessor is not immediately repealed and then perhaps replaced with something . . . or whatever. "Death!" he yells. "Kill!" The kids respond with spontaneous chants of "USA! USA!" They are not boy scouts at this moment—they are the child soldiers of his would-be private un-American army.

This is America today. Today: this afternoon. The parallels with "The Triumph of the Will" are undeniable.

He is a madman, of course. But that does not mean he is not also a fascist.

July 27, 2017

"With the exception of the late, great Abraham Lincoln, I can be more presidential than any president that's ever held this office," Trump said.

That may well be true, but I still could think off the top of my head of a few individuals from among those never to have held the exalted office who strike me as, potentially even more presidential than him: Pee-Wee Herman, Britney Spears, Jonas Brothers, Scooby Doo, Paris Hilton, Ace Ventura, Dennis Rodman, and the entire cast of *Jersey Shore*, among others.

July 27, 2017

In response to a TheGuardian.com article, "Putin: Russia will retaliate if 'insolent' US lawmakers pass sanctions bill":

Was it worth it, Vova? All this trouble? Expending all this energy, all this money, all this criminal ingenuity on installing the harebrained clown Trump in the White House—only to find out now that Trump, all by himself, is unable to deliver on any of his bombastic pre-election promises and, quite to the contrary, is uniting instead all the institutional political forces in America in their intense loathing of and determination to punish you? As always, you've overplayed your hand. Ah, Vova. And now you're reduced to issuing empty threats against America and the West. Too much hubris, too much wounded pride, and not enough realistic assessment of your actual place in the world. You've never been able to grasp or accept your natural limitations. Once a KGB rat, always a KGB rat, with a KGB rat's outlook on and understanding of the world.

July 30, 2017

Some of the asymmetrical ways in which Putin would be likely to retaliate against the US over the new economic sanctions:

Close down every McDonalds, KFC, and Pizza Hut in the country; get rid of every last drop of Coke and Pepsi; ban the public use of the English language and make open wearing of American jeans illegal in Russia; expel every US citizen and stop issuing any new Russian visas to Americans; rename every roller-coaster in the land from "American Hills" to "Hills Like Russia-Hating White Elephants"; ban the export to the US of such quintessentially Russian products as pelmeni, balalaikas, matryoshka dolls, and kvas; forbid radio stations from playing American music of any kind; strip of Russian citizenship everyone married or engaged to a US citizen; drastically expand Russia's participation in North Korea's nuclear program; restart stringent military-level anti-American propaganda in kindergartens and elementary schools; stop paying pensions and selling prescription medications to those over the age of sixty-five and claim this is all America's fault; and many other such measured responses.

July 30, 2017

Russian people, men in particular, throughout history, have led relatively short—and at times, en masse, brutally truncated—lives; but the rulers of Russia, in their overwhelming majority, always tended to cling to power for as long as possible, even unto their final breath. Thus, one of Vladimir Putin's most potent advantages over the democratically elected leaders of the Western world until now has been his unchecked political longevity: they came and went, were elected and voted out of office, and he continued to abide forever, patiently waiting for his next Berlusconi or Gerhard Schroeder to bribe and corrupt and outplaying them all by outlasting them.

But now—ironically, as a direct result of what only a few days ago he and virtually everyone in Russia and beyond considered to be the most spectacular triumph of his vertiginous political career, his incredible life's crown of achievement—his luck appears to have run out, as he finds himself trapped in a political dead-end of his own creation.

Indeed, from the very outset of his ascent to power, some seventeen years ago, Putin dreamed of being viewed by America and the rest of the arrogant Western world as America's equal. Sure, Russia's GDP was, back then, and continues to be at present, a small fraction of the US's—but then, GDP is not everything: Russia has by far the world's largest landmass, vast reserves of oil and natural gas and, most importantly, a sufficient supply of intercontinental and medium-range nuclear missiles to destroy the entire world (and itself along with it, but oh well, so be it) many tens of times over. It also, despite being on the whole a desperately poor country, has dozens of multibillionaires and other, smaller oligarchs with trillions of dollars' worth of dirty money stolen from the Russian people and in dire need of being laundered. Humiliatingly enough, however, none of the three US presidents Putin has outlasted to date—Bill Clinton, George W. Bush, and Barack Obama—was willing, in the end, to treat him as an equal geopolitical partner, the ruler of one of the world's two great superpowers, one with its own, appropriately massive zone of sovereign political and military influence in Europe and Asia. He was allowed to get away with much, admittedly, but not everything, in terms of his increasingly aggressive and authoritarian behavior at home and abroad, especially during the Obama years, but the US periodically and in coordination with that brazenly disrespectful European Union would have the gall of punishing him and his inner circle (as if he and them, his merry band of childhood buds and megathieves, were misbehaved children) with targeted economic sanctions, for actions he considered to be strictly his own and no one else's business, such as the prison murder of whistleblowing lawyer Sergei Magnitsky or the annexation of Crimea and the subsequent, undeclared, "hybrid" war in Ukraine. Not only did the West consistently refuse to recognize in him the rightful lifelong ruler of the world's second superpower, but it also more and more treated him as an international pariah, and this annoyed Putin to no end, real bigly.

But then, in due time, as it always did, fortune smiled upon him, pushing out onto the roiling American political stage a shameless demagogue and inveterate grifter, thoroughly amoral and air-headed and prone to sexual perversions (those Moscow tapes do exist) and up to his laundering gills in dirty Russian money: someone, were he somehow to become president, whom Putin could control and manipulate, and manage as his personal asset in the White House. No wonder Russia, on Putin's orders, went all out in a concerted effort to make the Trump presidency happen.

And, of course, happen it does. Putin always outplays by outlasting. The Russian political class cheers wildly. In the Russian fake parliament, the Duma, they pop champagne and toast to Trump's astounding victory. Now Putin has his man installed in the most powerful office in the world. America, unbeknownst to itself, lies prostrate at his feet. He, Putin, a former street hoodlum-cum-KGB drone-cum–de facto tzar of Russia, has the president of America in his pocket. Pretty damn dizzyingly awesome!

Well, where does he begin? Where does he, Putin, even start reaping the benefits of such a mind-blowing development? Probably with having his man Trump lift those damn humiliating sanctions on his, Putin's, childhood buddies, right? And then repeal all the rest of those stupid sanctions, and pronto, because Russia's economy is tanking and people, especially the young, are getting restless and becoming the ardent followers of that annoying anticorruption crusader, Alexei Navalny, in droves, by tens and hundreds of thousands. So he tells Trump to go ahead, as per their previous agreement.

And then, in a matter of just a few weeks, it happens: Putin gets permanently defeated in his way of dealing with America—and by osmosis, with the rest of the West. The American political system, Congress and whatever else they claim to have in America—something he, Putin, always thought to be but a hypocritical token to the empty notion of so-called American democracy, merely an ephemeral, inconsequential adornment on the country's real power structure, like a cute flower wreath on one of White House doors or something— suddenly begins to assert itself, coming to life big-leagues and, what do you know, taking away from the new, Putin-besotted president the power of lifting those sanctions. Moreover, that heretofore suitably pliant and now rebellious, Republican-controlled Congress, for good measure, goes ahead and makes those sanctions effectively permanent, in place until such time that Putin gets out of Ukraine and at the very least starts negotiations with Ukraine regarding the status of Crimea— which is to say, for years to come, or never, because Putin's regime cannot survive without that interminable "hybrid" war in South-Eastern Ukraine and anti-Ukrainian hysteria in the media. "We don't trust your judgment when it comes to Russia, Mr. President, and so we take away from you the ability to reward Putin for his interfering with our elections," the Congress essentially says to Trump with its unprecedented near-unanimous bipartisan vote.

What does this slap across Trump's face mean to Putin? That Russia's economy is going to deteriorate at an accelerated rate, thus hastening an open rebellion of Russian people against his kleptocratic regime. And that, most importantly and devastatingly, he, Putin, will never again get to outplay any Western leader by outlasting him or her: the world has wised up to his one-pony trick. Never again will he be presented with a more favorable opportunity to influence from within, directly from the White House, American policy toward Russia. There is no further point for him in waiting for another American president: this guy was it, this was his golden chance—and that chance is gone now, for all intents and purposes. He has no way of undoing the damage done, of ingratiating himself somehow with the American political system and, through it, with the majority of Americans—not in the absence of his willingness to reverse himself completely, cross out his past, and reinvent himself from scratch, become someone else entirely, and give up in a wholesale fashion on the very basic nature of his criminally and aggressively corrupt authoritarian rule. He cannot change. He won't change. He has finally outplayed himself, maneuvering himself and his regime into the dead end of his own creation.

Mikhail Iossel
August 2017

August 1, 2017

Trump is just a crass, amoral, shameless and massively corrupt demagogue, a carnival barker. The real danger to democracy in America is presented by the 35-40% of Americans who are stuck in the past, have lost themselves in the morass of bitterness and bigotry and prejudice and xenophobia, have no use for democracy, don't know what democracy is and why one might need it in one's life; who are proudly ignorant and consider education to be a major source of societal evil; who cling on to a simplified, black-and-white, us-vs-them picture of the world; who are unabashedly greedy and egotistical and view compassion for their fellow citizens as a manifestation of human weakness. The real danger to American democracy comes from within.

August 4, 2017

We—all of us together—have been fortunate, so far, to be watching this inescapable insane round-the-clock reality show, *The Most Astonishingly Grotesque Presidency in American History*, in the relative absence (knocking on wood) of any major national or international crisis, when the country would actually find itself in dire and urgent need of a real president, rather than the whining, sniveling, massively ignorant, amoral, and corrupt empty husk of a human being currently residing in the White House. Still, the world, unimpressed with the fact that America (courtesy of the procedural anachronism called the Electoral College) has decided to take temporary leave of its senses, is a dangerous, tumultuous place, full of infinitely multiplying critical challenges to humankind's very existence—and sinister clouds are gathering on the American horizon. America cannot afford continuing to be immersed in that surreal Trumpean idiocy for much longer. The noxious reality show must be taken off the air, and as quickly as possible.

August 5, 2017
Since early this morning, I've seen the image of newly and regrettably shirtless and lasciviously Botox-grinning Putin, with an obviously dead fish he supposedly caught while vacationing in South Siberia, about two million times on "Russian" Facebook and elsewhere in cyberspace. I am not reposting it here, because, good grief, this is the stuff life-marring nightmares, the monstrous mares of the night, are made of. I would've loved nothing more than to be able to "un-see" it with my mind's eye—that Goyaesque torso and Boschian face of a severe sixty-five-year-old case of arrested development, a cunning and cruel teenager with the capacity for destroying the entire planet ten times over—but alas. . . .

August 7, 2017
Trump's phenomenon may be the most fascinating story of our time, because in him, we see a complete absence of recognizable humanness, replaced instead with a giant black hole of howling need that sucks into itself the multifarious resentments and grievances of tens of millions of people and devours the time and existential energy of many millions

more. He is the magnetic vortex of everything that is wrong with American society, in its sheer anguished superficiality; the bottomless gravitational receptacle of American darkness— and he currently occupies the world's most powerful office. If this is not a scary moment in modern history, I don't know what is.

August 8, 2017

Strong nations, let alone world's economic and military superpowers, don't talk the way Trump talks. His is street thug talk, the overblown bluster of a failing casino owner.

August 10, 2017

Water and stone and darkless sky. A child of four or five years, I was walking with my parents along the Neva's embankment for the first time.

Decades later, this would turn out to be the last such occurrence also, but that's not what I want to think about now. I have no recollection as to why, given that we lived in a whole other, much less lovely, midtown neighborhood, we were there that early summer or late spring night—where we were coming from or, for that matter, where we might have been going. Our stroll had no purpose, no beginning and no end.

That, of course, is memory's preferred way of functioning.

My parents were holding my hands on both sides. (I wish this sentence could be more interesting. It's late and I'm tired.) There were other people out for a walk there, too; there had to be. The river, wider than ten Nevsky Prospects put together and full of roiling silver, was to the left of us—and the rare cars, mainly fancy Volgas and posh ZIMs, were speeding by smoothly on our right. I remember feeling happy, but that's not saying much.

Luminous silver water and gray stone and the dusky sky glowing from within. My parents were looking at the river, because it was impossible not to look at it, for at the moment it exceeded everything in relative importance, even me.

"I know how to make it so that every bad person in Leningrad becomes a good one," I said loudly, partly in order to remind them that unlike the river, I could talk and, indeed, even say meaningful things on occasion. "All it would take for that to happen would be to bring all bad people to this place, right here, every night, and have them do nothing but look at all this—this, like, staggeringly harmonious confluence of stone, water, and sky—and in a very short time, willy-nilly, inescapably, they would just find themselves constitutionally incapable of continuing to be bad people. No human evil, I am convinced, can survive any prolonged exposure to this here panorama. As a general matter, it probably must be pretty difficult to be a bad person in this city. Too much sublime beauty around, in places."

Of course, I did not say that: I knew I couldn't possibly be expressing myself quite in those sophisticated turns of phrase, by the deployment of that sort of poetic grownup vocabulary. I do, however, remember saying something along those lines— in a normal, small-child's way, that is—or at least, wordlessly thinking something similar.

I looked up at my parents. (I don't recall doing that, but so what.) They exchanged quick glances, if only in my imagination. My father chuckled gently, inaudibly. My mother, while still holding my hand and looking at the river, put her cool palm on my head and said, even without saying anything, "You're absolutely right. That's such a beautiful thought. You are such a smart boy."

Does that make any sense? It's OK if not.

Stone, river, sky. We were walking along the river's embankment. I remember that—and whatever you remember is not yet finished.

I remember feeling as though my entire future rushed at me at that moment, and filled the moment to dangerous overflow with its presence. I didn't know what to make of that strange, almost unbearable, keen feeling back then, needless to say. I still don't.

August 12, 2017

Right now, live on CNN: violent clashes in Charlottesville, Virginia, between white supremacists, Nazis, and the KKK with pro-Trump slogans, swastikas, confederate flags, guns and baseball bats, and groups of counterprotesters. There should be no illusions with regard to this: Trumpism is American fascism, and the fascists of America comprise the hard core of Trump's base of support. And now he has emboldened and legitimized them.

Trump, in the meantime, is golfing in New Jersey. He and the likes of Bannon and Gorka and other such trash are the ones to blame for this ugliness: 2017 America as 1930s Germany.

August 13, 2017

Here is why Trump's failure today to condemn the neo-Nazi rampage in Charlottesville, his apparent organic inability to utter a single word of disapproval when it comes to the white-supremacist segment of his core base, is qualitatively different from all the other presumably fatal outrages of his grotesque political career up to now: from this moment onward, every self-identified Trump supporter automatically, by extension, also becomes a neo-Nazi sympathizer, a willy-nilly ally of hateful armed hoodlums parading around with swastika banners and baseball bats and sporting t-shirts emblazoned with Hitler quotes—and that may prove a bridge too far even for some of the most hard-boiled among his devotees. It's one thing to shout "F*ck your feelings!" and flip a middle finger at them leftwing snowflakes, cheering or looking the other way when your orange-haired idol mocks disabled people, repeatedly exhibits weird fascination with Putin, or brags on tape about being a sexual predator—and a whole different one to be seen by everyone as someone un-American to the point of siding with unabashed fascists. Supporting Trump has long ceased being merely a matter of political opinion and become instead a distinct marker of one's cultural values and moral judgment (or lack thereof). Now those values and that judgment, such as they may be, are going to be put to the most severe test to date.

August 13, 2017

We thought, back in 2016, that the Trump presidency would be unimaginable, but it turned out to be even more unimaginable than we imagined. The speed with which it has unraveled is quite astonishing. Over the last week alone, Trump has managed to manufacture a potentially catastrophic nuclear crisis with North Korea and effectively to side with newly emboldened and greatly energized white supremacists intent on restarting and refighting the results of the Civil War. At this point, the country is a rudderless ship adrift in a rising storm, listing precariously in the waves, and we can only hope that its self-righting mechanism is still in working order.

August 14, 2017

Just think about it, though: an American president finding it hard to condemn Nazism. Really? What then is an easy thing for him to do: insulting everyone who is not a Nazi—or Putin? Apparently so.

All he had to do was to say: "I condemn Nazism, period." Super-easy! But no. Too difficult. Too soon. Still not ready.

August 16, 2017

Trump likes Nazis and racists because they never said anything bad about him. They like him. They made him president. On the other hand, the violent anti-Nazi crowd, the nonracists— they say nothing but bad things about him, all the time—and never say anything good. They don't like him. They really don't. And he resents them for that.

Trump likes people who like him, and he doesn't like people who don't like him. He is only the president of the people who like him, and he is enemy-in-chief of the people who hate him. He truly is an enemy of the people, bigly—but only of the people who don't like him. If they hate him, he hates them back, tenfold. He always is and always will be on the side of those who don't say anything bad about him.

Putin, for instance—he never said anything bad about Trump, he only said good things about him, so why would Trump say anything bad about Putin? That just wouldn't make any sense. If Hitler or Stalin were alive today and never said anything bad about Trump, Trump wouldn't be saying anything bad about them, either. And if they started saying good things about him, he would go out of his way to be nice to them, too.

It's a no-brainer, really: Nazis and white supremacists like him, and anti-Nazis and anti–white supremacists hate him, so they are the bad guys, by default. Same with the Fake News media: the newspapers and TV channels that say bad things about him are fake, and the ones that praise him—those are the real stuff.

Forever he is an unloved, unappreciated child, the poor man. Nothing he ever does is good enough for his father . . . arrested, incidentally, during a KKK rally in Queens, New York, in 1927.

August 16, 2017
The Trump White House has started resembling the old Soviet Communist Party, in that people who want to join in or continue to be within close proximity to power must suspend their ethical norms and essentially say goodbye to their human dignity, smothering to death their sense of decency, because they know going in that they will be defined and dirtied forever by this one fateful step. It's the oldest trade-off in history: stay true to yourself or sell out for power and money, betray yourself and destroy your good name forever, and be aware that your grandchildren will be ashamed of you.

August 17, 2017
In response to Trump's contribution to the debate surrounding the removal of statues in the South to Confederate leaders:

Following Trump's logic, uncountable thousands of Soviet-era Lenin and Stalin statues still ought to be standing in Russia.

August 22, 2017
My thoughts as I'm watching the completely unhinged and manifestly demented Trump in Phoenix tonight: Nikita Krushchev on speed.

August 22, 2017
In Russia, the Soviet Union is back in full force, in that the country's rulers are completely at liberty now to treat ordinary

Russian citizens in any way they see fit: they can kill those they don't like or even entirely random people at will, have them beaten up half to death, throw them in jail for however long they choose, allow or disallow them to leave Russia, or else let them be for the time being, ignore them altogether with a yawn: there is nothing they could not do to anyone there—an ever-widening black hole of death in the middle of the country's living space.

August 23, 2017

"I really think they don't like our country. I really believe that."
Trump talking tonight about the US media.
This is what fascism looks like, people.

August 23, 2017

Khrushchev, Brezhnev, Andropov, Chernenko, Gorbachev, Reagan, George H. W. Bush, Bill Clinton, George W. Bush, Barack Obama: the Soviet and American leaders I lived under. Very different people, with very different (and in the case of the first four, at least—unequivocally, unabashedly, reprehensibly inhumane) political beliefs. This one, however, is the first downright crazy, stark raving mad one—an immensely bitter loser, just a total basket case.

August 23, 2017

Responding to a few questions I was asked yesterday and generally have been answering for years:

- I am nowhere near being bilingual. What I am is a native Russian speaker and writer who was fortunate enough to learn English fairly well, both on my own and with a couple of private tutors, as a teenager and young man, back in the Soviet Union. I came to the

US at the age of thirty, being able to read and express myself in basic terms in English, but not to write or comprehend anything said at normal conversational speed.

- I don't think I think in any specific language. I think I think in thoughts.
- In their dreams, people tend to speak every language known and unknown to humans.

August 24, 2017

Before social networks, we had the luxury of not knowing how much sheer ugliness dwelt in the hearts of quite so many ordinary people all around us.

August 24, 2017

The lowlife in the White House keeps braying about "fake news" and impugning American journalists' patriotism, Stalinist-style, repeatedly calling decent hard-working American citizens the enemies of the people and calling them horrible, dishonest individuals who don't like their country and work against its interests, trying to prevent America from becoming great again—yet he never once, even remotely, even in the mildest of terms allows himself to criticize Putin, dictator of the country where journalists the ruling regime doesn't like are routinely killed or maimed or jailed. That, of course, is old news, but it never quite gets old in one's mind, and by now America and the world have reached the point of psychological oversaturation with this unfortunate human being's surreal mendacity. Isn't it time for the mainstream media to start treating him accordingly, calling him out for what he actually is—an extremely dangerous, vile and breathtakingly ignorant, dictator-loving, limitlessly amoral and corrupt, thoroughly un-American, treasonous madman who needs to be removed from the White House as soon as possible, by any legal means available? Stop pussyfooting around him, stop calling him "president." This is a national emergency of the very first order.

August 24, 2017

This is how it was back in the Soviet Union: unless this was someone from your well-defined circle of friends and good acquaintances, you never knew what was in another person's head—but you knew better, of course, than to try and find out. You never talked about politics with strangers, obviously—all the more so, there was nothing much to discuss there, in that department: everyone was always assumed to be on the same page with everyone else, we were the hope of all of progressive mankind, ours was the most humane and future-bound society in the world, Lenin was eternally alive and the greatest man ever to be born of a mortal woman, the entire Soviet people were united like never before in history around their Leninist Communist Party and its Leninist Central Committee with its Leninist Politburo headed by the truest of true Leninists, Comrade Leonid Ilyich Brezhnev (Andropov, Chernenko), we were the super-luckiest people in the world to have been born in the Soviet Union, communism was our radiant future, imperialism and its battered bulwark the United States of America were historically doomed and belonged on the ash-heap of history, we were the most peaceful nation in the world but at any moment were fully prepared to defend unto planetary destruction the sanctity of our boundless borders and the borders of our brotherly Warsaw pact allies, we had something that no ordinary American or any other person unfortunate enough to live in the world of capitalism had: the total safety and security of our wonderful tomorrows . . . etc.

Of course, everyone, more or less, knew all that was a bunch of BS and hardly anyone in his or her right mind took it seriously—but then, it was also a well-known fact (if that's what it was) that millions of ordinary Soviet citizens were voluntary KGB informants and supported everything the Party told them to support and hated everything and everyone they were told to hate, because why not, what's wrong with you, comrade, you think you're different from us, are you some kind of anti-Soviet element or something, are you maybe unhappy with the way things are in our country, which is the only country all of us have ever known and would ever know, the best country in the world, in which case you should have your head examined, quite literally so, because what the hell is wrong with you, are you an enemy of the people or whatever, or are you just someone who can never be happy with his lot in life, one of those people, we know what kind of people, kinless cosmopolites and stuff, also perhaps bothered by the fact that you don't live on Mars or can't go camping on the Moon? Or would you like to live in America? Well, daydreaming is free. . . .

In short, who the hell knew, who could tell what was going on in other people's heads. You were not a mind reader. And besides, you were no different from anyone else, anyway. You were just an ordinary Soviet citizen, and other people also probably were wondering, in a nonwondering kind of way, what the hell was cooking in your head . . . if anything.

But this is not the old Soviet Union, this is America, and it hasn't been like that here before, or at least not lately; not since the McCarthy era. Up until now, one could tell, by and large, where other people stood, no matter their political views and ideological stances. You could be a Democrat living in a heavily Republican area, but you didn't ordinarily have the pervasive feeling that you were surrounded by virtual aliens. People have the right to have different political views in America, and to air those openly. That's the essence of a free society. Your neighbor has the full right to listen to Rush at full blast on his old-school portable radio on his lawn. It's a free country. Free country is as free country does.

Nowadays, however—in the era of Trump . . . things, somehow, have become perceptibly different. People are getting harder to read on the surface of their interaction with public spaces. We are not talking here about the burly mulleted dudes announcing themselves to the world with fat swastika tattoos on their forearms or the excellent folks wearing or having their trucks draped in Confederate flags, as if saying, in effect, "Yeah, I think slavery was in fact a pretty cool idea"—or else, just a bunch of rowdy guys in MAGA hats yelling something unintelligibly menacing as they fall out of a dive bar. No: things are quantitatively less obvious now. That kindly old gentleman at one's local McDonalds, talking animatedly with his equally benign-looking friends over a steaming cup of questionable coffee: can you know for certain he was not hooting and hollering the other night, red in the face, mad with evil glee, when Trump was sneering, in his cowardly passive-aggressive manner, at the unnamed senior senator from Arizona, who denied Trump his vaunted Obamacare repeal, and who also happens to be a war hero and is currently battling the deadliest form of brain cancer? You probably cannot. Or those nice, clean-cut young men with an idealistic glint to their bright eyes: would it be completely out of bounds for one to suspect in them a small part of the rowdy crowd of Tiki-torch bearers chanting with great energy and conviction "Jews. Will. Not. Replace. Us!" the other weekend in Charlottesville? Alas, it likely would not. And millions upon millions of other Americans one thought one knew, even without ever meeting them in person?

Not anymore, sadly. You don't know what they think. And they—well, they don't know what you think.

Wolf Messing was the name of Stalin's personal medium, seer, and prognosticator of the future, psychic and mind-reader extraordinaire. Hitler himself was afraid of him, apparently. A poor kid from a Polish shtetl. Wolf Messing. He could see right through one's cranium. He would come in handy in America today.

August 25, 2017

Breaking news: In the face of a massive hurricane bearing down on Texas, Trump issues pardon to former sheriff Joe Arpaio

August 27, 2017
What we talk about when we talk about Trump: nothing. Brightly colored emptiness. He has turned the US presidency into one nightmarishly endless, nauseating *National Enquirer* reality show. Trump represents America's willful temporary avoidance of its own reality.

August 29, 2017
"Place of birth: Russia," the burly middle-aged customs officer with a crewcut on the US side of the Canadian border said pensively, leafing through my US passport. "Russia, Russia . . . Putin. . . . Don't know much about it, personally, but my daughter took a class on Russian literature at State. Lots of

talk about death there, from what I gather. . . . Would that be an accurate perception? Are Russians more preoccupied with death than most other people?"

"Not really," I said, trying to suppress a yawn. (The hour was late: close to midnight.) "If anything, they think less about it than lots of other people. They just tend to die more often."

"More often—than who?" He raised his tired, red-rimmed eyes at me.

"Than lots of other people," I explained.

"Isn't it interesting," he said with sudden liveliness and a faraway look on his rough-hewn face, "isn't it funny, even, that, you know, we constantly worry so much about how people would remember us when we're gone, as if the purpose of our living was to become a good memory—but after we die, we don't give a damn about any of that, right? You know what I mean? . . . This is what I think: we die every time we think about dying, because there's no death after death, but there sure is being afraid of dying and being dead while we're still alive. Death is here and now, at any given moment—not after death, *comprenez?*"

"Right here and right now?" I said, wishing he'd be done with me already.

"Right here, right now!" he confirmed in an emphatic voice. "So, to be honest, I don't really know what all this fuss about being remembered when we're dead and all that is about. I personally, if you ask me—I'll only miss a few people when I'm dead."

"I'm guessing I wouldn't be one of them," I said, half-smiling to let him know this was a joke.

"No," he said simply, and handed me my passport back. The night was dark, but what else is new.

August 30, 2017

If only a couple of years ago one were to have written a dystopian novel, or even a novella or short story, set in the United States and featuring as the nation's president a Trumplike character, it almost certainly would've been turned down by every self-respecting literary agent, to say nothing of publishing house editors: Americans, the argument would go, would never elect someone so hyperbolically grotesque, so staggeringly ignorant and clinically narcissistic and pathologically self-obsessed, so openly vile and shameless and relentless in appealing to the worst angels of human nature, someone so totally void of any notion of patriotism—someone, in short, quite so one-dimensional in his rottenness, someone with not a single discernible redeeming quality. One has to have faith, after all, in the American mind's general collective soundness. But here we are and there you have it: the real-life confirmation of the well-known fact that realistic fiction, even at its most daring, can take a lot less strangeness than the actual daily reality of our lives.

 **Mikhail Iossel**
September 2017

September 4, 2017
In response to Trump's decision to rescind the "Dream Act," or DACA, which had offered protection for some 800,000 non-US citizens brought to America as children:

A useless man born into wealth, who hasn't done a day's worth of honest work in his life and has never sacrificed anything for anyone in his relentless lifelong pursuit of pleasure and less fortunate people's envious admiration, should not be in a position, with one ugly gothic scrawl of his signature, to destroy the dreams of eight hundred thousand young men and women who came to the US as little children, know no other homeland, and have done nothing but worked and studied hard throughout in order to make something good of their lives and be beneficial to society.

He shouldn't be, but he is, and that is the true American tragedy of our time. He is, but he won't be for long, and the evil done by him will sooner or later be undone.

September 5, 2017
After today, if someone looks you in the eye and tells you, "I support Trump, but I am not a racist," you can say in response to that, "Sure, and I eat meat, but I am a vegetarian."

September 12, 2017

A bit more on the stunning recording of Trump's 9/11/2001 call-in TV-interview, given just a few hours after the tragedy, in which he rejoices at the fact that now, according to the specific sources he goes on to cite, his building is the tallest in New York.

This, of course, is the behavior of a clinically narcissistic individual, a sociopath with not an iota of empathy with other people—or else, a sworn enemy of America. I am pretty certain no one among those reading this now knows personally anyone whose first response to the events of that day was even remotely akin to Trump's.

But as always is the case with Trump, his every reaction is a direct projection of his own character traits and personality characteristics.

Indeed, when he lied about witnessing from his rooftop hundreds of Muslims dancing and celebrating in New Jersey on 9/11, he was in effect talking about himself.

Every time he shouted "Crooked Hillary!" at his rallies—he was talking about himself, a professional crook and lifelong conman.

"Lyin' Ted"—being himself a self-admitted serial liar.

"Li'l Marco!"—well, his obsession with the size of his hands, obviously.

Whenever Trump is accusing someone of something, he is talking about himself.

September 22, 2017

Pious Trump supporters, soft-spoken and brimming with heavenly grace, fairly overflowing with kindness and calling upon everyone to love each other, including our president, because he is doing the best he can to solve the problems not of his own making—and feeling sorry for those unable to find it in themselves not to be angry in response to their Hallmark homilies: I will be banning your sanctimonious kind without warning on my timeline. Humbly and devoutly. With lots of love in my heart.

September 23, 2017

Trump is a fine person to lecture anyone on patriotism. Some of the memorable stepping stones of his life's path:

- Banning black people from renting apartments in his buildings.
- Receiving five (5) deferments from service in Vietnam: bone spurs in his heels—extremely debilitating, although he still, heroically, was able to dance his way through the 1960-70s nightclub scene, and without contracting an STD, too—the fact he later on referred to with understandable pride as his "personal Vietnam" on the *Howard Stern Show*.
- Declaring bankruptcy six (6) times, never releasing his taxes at any point since entering the presidential race.
- Having strong, long-lasting, and well-documented Russian mob ties.
- Spending five (5) years trying to delegitimize the country's first African American president, claiming Barack Obama was born in Africa and never went to Harvard or Columbia (because black people wouldn't be bright enough for that, presumably).
- Declaring John McCain was not a hero, because he, Trump, personally, liked "people who weren't captured."
- Trying to obtain Putin's permission to build Trump Towers in Moscow, even while already running for US president.

- Never once uttering a single word even of the mildest criticism with regard to Putin—the ruthless godfather of the giant oil-and-gas mafia corporation called "Russia," to whom Trump in large measure owes the very fact of his surreal presidency.
- And so much more. This is just scratching the surface. Robert Mueller is hard at work now putting together the repugnant mosaic of Trump's life.

All this by way of saying, again, that Trump is just the right person to lecture other Americans on patriotism.

America has never had an even remotely less patriotic president in its history, let alone an unmitigatedly traitorous one.

September 24, 2017

Published at NewYorker.com on October 19, 2017, as "Welcome to the World of 'Soviet' Feelings":

This, by and large, is how it was back in late Soviet Union: parents, at least in the intelligentsia families, would never discuss the country's rulers with their children. It was understood by default that the country was ruled by bad people, presumably in the service of some crazy ideology no one but the really old Party members and downright dotards (yes indeed) happened to believe even remotely. At nights, parents listened—or rather, attempted to listen, in big cities, through the howling and ululating of short-wave radio-signal-jamming KGB installations—to the "enemy" radio-voices on their portable VEF-Spidolas: the Voice of America, the BBC, the German Wave. Their kids, in turn, were normal Soviet children, the same as anyplace else in the world, ordinary high-school students (if we limit ourselves to that representative age group), keenly interested in fun and games and, above all else, love and sex (or at least, the latter's theoretical possibility). They were Komsomol (Young Communist League) members, because almost all of them, 90+ percent, were—and because without that nominal membership it was exponentially more difficult to be admitted in an institution of higher learning (and not being a college student by the age of eighteen carried, for boys, the unlovely certainty of being conscripted into the army), but they didn't give any great thought to all that Komsomol stuff. The teenage Soviet children also knew the country was ruled, not to mince words, by a bunch of old degenerates—but that's how it always had been in their country, at least since 1917, which meant forever in the context of their lives; so what was there to think too hard about? Thinking about all that pointless depressing stuff was a waste of time, no more useful than thinking about why the weather was cold in winter and warm in summertime. Things were the way they were because that's how they were.

Parents wouldn't speak to children about the kind of country they lived in, because for one thing they didn't want to complicate or darken the cast of their children's young lives, and also (and importantly) because the children, as a result of listening too intently to their parents' talk, out of the pure young and innocent lack of caution, were liable then to let it slip in their teachers' presence about their parents' harsh and entirely unacceptable words about the country's rulers, and that wouldn't be good for anyone. Silence, silence. Everything was understood tacitly, by implication. Similarly, high-school teachers mouthed only the ideologically correct platitudes and expressed their (yawn) boundless love for the country's rulers and all that stuff out of the sheer sense of strict ideological obligation, without an iota of conviction behind those words.

There was nothing to be done about it, on the whole: you were born where you were born, and at the time when you were born there, and there was no changing anything about the life you were going to live then and here as a child . . . or as an adult, for that matter, in most instances. It snowed heavily in winter in Leningrad, say—what was one supposed to do about that? Just dress warmly, layer up. There hardly was any daylight in Leningrad between mid-December and mid-March—well, so what, deal with it. You were born where you were born, and not someplace else, where the days are light and the breeze from the ocean is soothing and refreshing.

We were born where we were born, and therefore we couldn't have been born anywhere else. Some people were able (lower your voice) to emigrate from the country, which was pretty unimaginable, but we were not among those people, for a variety of reasons. So we just have to deal with it, and so too will you. The country was the way it was. It was our country, and yours. You could never leave it. That was just a fact of life. The country was ruled by moral degenerates. OK. Well, so what are you going to do about it? Deal with it. Pay them no mind and keep your damn mouth shut as much as possible, or else you'll be apt to land everyone in a heap of trouble.

The same is taking place in Russia now, too—at least, in intelligentsia families: what's the point of discussing Putin? Putin is as Putin does. Putin is. Putin is the street boys we grew up with. The majority of the country's populace support him, that's a fact of life, but they also supported the Soviet Politburo as well, and all the rest of them, all the rest of it all. They'll support anyone who's above them. Their rulers are their weather. They'll accept anything in their lives as a given, weather-wise. They'll support anything coming from above, without giving it much thought, the way they would support summer or winter, or a rainy day, or a cloudless one. Putin is evil, sure, and surrounded by fellow megathieves and (if necessary) murderers, and he is making normal Russian people ashamed once again of being Russian citizens, the way Soviet people used to be vaguely ashamed, deep down, of being citizens and, by dint of that circumstance, virtual prisoners of the USSR—well, what's to be done about it now? Some people—lots of them, but still very few, in terms of their overall percentage—are leaving the country for good, emigrating, and bully for them, but not everyone can do something so decisive and bold, or put together the kind of money one would need to have in order to make that happen: not by a long shot; very few people actually can pull off something like this. The gravitational pull of Russian mundanity is real, and it is extremely hard to overcome. So it probably would be best, if you are a parent there now, to suggest to your high-school (for instance) children not to talk too much about Putin and all the rest of them in grown-up strangers' presence. Who the hell knows who one or more of those strangers might turn out to be? And, certainly, don't say anything within earshot of your school officials, unless you want to land everyone in a heap of potential trouble.

Silence. Silence.

And what about the US these days? For as long as their country has been around, American children, en masse, were taught to look up to country's presidents, even if in many instances those children's parents had nothing good to say about any given president of the moment, considering him (not incorrectly, perhaps: but that's not the point) a war criminal and a shill for corporate interests. Still and all, that was within the normal scope of societal discourse, no matter how extremely heated and vitriolic at times. It was understood, generally, or at least it was grudgingly accepted and admitted, that the US president, whether right or wrong, smart or stupid, had the country's best interests at heart, to the best of his, frequently warped as all hell, understanding of the country's good.

The Soviet propaganda machine—through its main tool, the official Soviet literature of the party bent—had relentlessly pounded into Soviet people's heads the notion that American presidents were the mere meek and will-less (though never quite as incomprehensibly vulgar as would be Trump) pawns in the hands of the military-industrial complex and its shadowy rulers, underground billionaires, often hooked-nosed of appearance (yes, the eternal George Soros of timeless and geographically nonspecific barbarian mind), but that was the Soviet propaganda for Soviet people.

But Trump? Trump is a whole separate matter altogether, a distinctly ugly thread in the narrative of the American presidency, a human disaster unto itself. Yes, sure, it's clear that he is breathtakingly ignorant, no question about it, and that he is uncommonly venal and vile, yes, OK, but—he also, rather incomprehensibly, behaves like an enemy of most people of America, too. Is he an un-American American? He is indeed, although he also is as American as the belladonna berry pie. He clearly, for instance, admires dictators of various stripes and would like to be one in America. ("I alone can fix it!") He also, alas, is dirty up to his gills in criminal money. And, as seems likelier by the day now, he happens to be an illegitimate president, too, one brought to power as a result of his campaign's criminal collusion with Russian intelligence.

What are responsible American parents supposed to say to their children about Trump? "Sorry, kids, America has screwed up bigly this time around"? This—a national calamity of such immense magnitude—wasn't supposed to happen in America. This is the Soviet kind of narrative, if you will: the rulership of the worst among people—the reckless, the ignorant, the avaricious, the lethally indifferent, and the downright bad people all getting together and, even while still constituting a minority of American voters, managing to make an unabashedly bad and absolutely amoral man their president, just as the rest of the citizens let it happen, willy-nilly, by being outnumbered by smaller numbers, or by abstaining from voting altogether.

Yes, that—something possibly to tell one's children. And to tell them also that it might be best not to talk about any of that with strangers. This is the end of American-bound innocence for the new generation of America's children—and for their parents, too.

Welcome to the world of "Soviet" feelings.

September 26, 2017

Life in old Soviet Union was positively idyllic, in that no bad things presumably happening there from time to time, even in theory, ever were allowed to be reported in newspapers or on television and radio. Hurricanes, mass murders, train collisions, airplane crashes, and especially any open manifestations of popular discontent, however major or minor—all of that terrible stuff took place solely and exclusively in the historically doomed Western world of rotten capitalism. We were all supremely lucky to have been born in the safest and happiest place on Earth.

September 29, 2017

In response to an MSN.com article about the Department of Homeland Security headlined, "DHS planning to collect social media info on all immigrants.":

No problem, Big Brother. I am one of 20 million naturalized US citizens, and I, for one, welcome the DHS to my social-media information.

As a matter of fact, in the interest of saving the permanently overworked agency's time, as a friendly preemptive gesture, I would be glad to summarize for its benefit the rough totality of my social-media output:

- I loathe and despise Donald J. Trump and the kind of America he represents.
- I despise and loathe V. V. Putin, ruler of the re-renamed country whose citizen I used to be for the first thirty years of my life.

You are welcome, DHS.

Mikhail Iossel
October 2017

October 2, 2017

In response to the Las Vegas mass shooting:

Picture an ordinary, nondescript, law-abiding sixty-four-year-old American man. He is reasonably healthy for his age, has some money in the bank, to the tune of several million dollars, maybe a few income properties, and he generally is friendly to everyone, holds a private pilot license, likes his guns (but what red-blooded American male doesn't), lives with his girlfriend in a nice retirement community in a land of eternal sunshine, and enjoys periodic outings to nearby Las Vegas for a bit of gambling and some shows. If he may be increasingly terrified of his looming mortality, if he ever sits up in bed with a start in the middle of the night, covered in a cold sweat, his heart thumping away in the hollow of his chest, and moaning inwardly in a sudden excess of despair, saying to himself in a hoarse whisper, "Oh my God, what have I done with my life, what was the point of it all, how did it all pass so quickly, and now it's too late for everything, oh God, I've wasted my life! Please, no! So unfair!"—he, understandably, doesn't share those hypothetical moments of existential horror with anyone.

One day he goes and buys himself an extra bunch of souped-up semi-automatic weapons and enough lethal, bullet-armor-piercing ammo to sustain a siege of some small city by a mid-sized garrison of determined insurgents—he lives in a state with virtually no gun laws, so that doesn't take him long at all to accomplish—and then, filled with cold steely rage camouflaged by his gregarious outward demeanor, all that cornucopia of murder paraphernalia stashed neatly in ten (yes, ten) oversize bags ("No, thanks, I don't need any help with these, I'll carry 'em myself"), he checks into a spacious suite on the thirty-second floor of one of Las Vegas's largest and most famous hotels, whose windows offer a spectacular, unobstructed view of the open-air performance space where a massively popular annual music festival is about to commence come nightfall . . . and then he sits on the edge of one of the two ludicrously opulent and pointlessly gigantic beds in there, hands on knees, eyes half-lidded, and starts waiting.

October 3, 2017

This effectively is the official position of the Republican Party on the gun issue, in slight paraphrase: Living in constant fear of becoming a victim of a mass shooting is the price of freedom every American has to pay.

So very true! If you don't run the risk of being shot up by a maniac with forty-three souped-up semiautomatic weapons and thousands of rounds of military-grade ammo, you don't happen to live in a truly free country. Canada? No freer than Russia. Australia? Less free than Belarus. The UK, Norway, Denmark, Switzerland, Japan? Just a bunch of different-sized North Koreas.

I don't know how these people can sleep at night.

(Republicans to America: "We sleep very nicely, thank you.")

October 4, 2017

Trump is right: His secretary of state did not call him a "moron." His secretary of state publicly called him a "f*cking moron." That's a whole different thing.

October 5, 2017

The president of the United States is demanding a government investigation of the free press. These are dangerous times for American democracy.

But there is one country where his message of nonfreedom is met with enthusiastic official approval: Russia.

October 6, 2017

Vladimir Putin turns sixty-five tomorrow.

Well, what can one say?

The most obvious and glib thing to say about this would be that Russia and the world writ large would've been a whole lot better off if his parents had abstained from sex that dark and wintry night back in 1952 (when, incidentally, Stalin was still alive and abortions were strictly illegal in the USSR). But the simple truth of the matter is, if not this Putin, some other generic one inevitably would have come along, because Putin is not quite a sui generis persona, but rather a certain widespread subtype of big-city "homo Sovieticus"—one might call it "Putinus Vulgaris"—easily recognizable to everyone who grew up side by side with its representatives. In a word, this is the genus of an ultimate scrappy survivor, an indestructible human cockroach, limitlessly voracious and just as ruthless in pursuit of his immediate and long-term objectives.

Vice President Biden recalled in a speech the other day how, during his meeting with Putin in the latter's Kremlin office, he told Putin: "Mr. President, I'm looking in your eyes

and you have no soul"—and Putin seemed to have taken that
as somewhat of a compliment, by responding, "We understand
one another."

Of course he doesn't have a soul. Why would he need
something that cannot be monetized?

October 7, 2017

One of world's most prominent philologists of the modern
era, Russia's leading public intellectual, paragon of personal
rectitude and the ultimate moral authority, Vyacheslav Ivanov,
died today, on the date marking the sixty-fifth birthday of
Russia's limitlessly corrupt, criminal, and grotesquely amoral
ruler of the last eighteen years—someone whom Ivanov himself,
upon meeting him in person for the first time, immediately and
publicly termed an extremely dangerous hoodlum and thug.

History sometimes is prone to such unlovely conjunctions.

October 7, 2017

Imagine how many hundreds and thousands of books and
hundreds of thousands of magazine articles and untold
millions and billions of Facebook posts and Twitter tweets
concerning the dire state of the American society in all its
aspects, would NOT have been written if even half of those
fateful 114,000 Trump voters in three states had changed their
minds on a whim on the spot in the voting booth; or if the
state of Wisconsin's voter ID law had not suppressed 200,000
legitimate votes; or if 50,000+ of Wisconsinites alone had not
decided to cast their votes for Jill Stein; or if James Comey had
not taken it upon himself unaccountably to interject himself
into the campaign less than two weeks before the election;
or if Russian intelligence with WikiLeaks as its informational
outlet had not been able to find numerous individuals inside

the Trump campaign to collude with in its efforts to prevent the election of Hillary Clinton.

Imagine how many billions of combined hours' worth of composing all those books and articles and posts and tweets would have been saved for other pursuits by millions of people. We would be living in a whole different world now.

October 8, 2017

Why do assorted Nazis and white supremacists, greatly invigorated by Trump presidency, keep chanting "Russia is our friend!" at their tiki-torch rallies? What causes them to believe that? After all, the overwhelming majority of Russian citizens, subjected as they are to torrents of virulently anti-American propaganda poured on their heads around the clock by state-controlled television and print media, are firmly convinced that far from being its friend, America is Russia's sworn enemy. What, then, do those moral mutants reemerging again last night in Charlottesville—among whose hate-filled ranks, according to Trump, there are many "very fine people"—know that most Americans and Russians do not?

They know the same things, in point of fact, as do most Americans—they just interpret them differently. They know, first and foremost, that Russia helped make Trump president—and they don't need no Senate or Special Counsel investigations for them to be convinced of this—and for that alone, they are eternally grateful to Russia, and to Vladimir Putin personally.

That's why Russia matters as a crucial factor in Trump's election.

The American Nazis and white supremacists also happen to hate the same things about America, the same aspects of American life, that Putin and his nominal "electorate" hate about it: that America, by its own idealistic modern design, is a free and open, democratic, kaleidoscopically heterogeneous, multicultural, and quintessentially tolerant society. The American Nazis and white supremacists—and, more broadly, Trump's core base of support—hate that America with a passion, and they see nothing wrong with the idea of nonfreedom being America's governing system. What's democracy to them? What does it mean to them? Freedom for others, such as blacks and Jews and Muslims and Mexicans and women, to consider all Americans equal among themselves? No, neither Trump's nor Putin's core base of support care one bit for that kind of freedom. As far as Trump's America is concerned, if a totalitarian foreign ruler, the primary enemy of the democratic America they loathe, helped put democracy-despising Trump in the White House, so much the better: Thanks, Putin! Greatly appreciated!

In that sense, too, indeed, Putin's Russia IS Trump's America's unwitting friend.

That's why Russia matters as one of the deciding factors in Trump's election.

Yes, of course—it was American citizens, not the faceless army of Putin's trolls from Savushkina Street on the outskirts of St. Petersburg, who cast their votes for Trump on November 8, 2016. But they did so in a distinctly "Russianized" election: one premised on the deep, ignorance-fuelled, falsehoods-driven contempt in which tens of millions of Americans hold the very notion of democracy; and one, at the same time, severely tainted by the coordinated joint efforts of Russian intelligence and massively unscrupulous and de facto antidemocratic Trump campaign operatives effectively to render the free expression of people's will meaningless, by fairly drowning American democracy in a sea of lies and distortions. The US presidential election of 2016 was, in large part and for the first time in the nation's history, orchestrated by a hostile foreign power; it was heavily "Russianized."

That, among other, similar factors, is why Russia's essential role in bringing about the disaster of the Trump presidency is, unfortunately, anything but a conspiracy theory.

October 10, 2017

It is not being "Russophobic" to point out that in 2016, Putin in effect succeeded beyond his expectations at "Russianizing" the US presidential elections, by doing the only thing he really knows how to do well—the same thing he's been spectacularly successful at in Russia: relentlessly appealing to the very worst angels of human nature.

October 11, 2017

Trump is coming undone with such ominous acceleration, it's hard to imagine the kind of mental space he's going to occupy in another nine months, let alone another three years. It also is impossible to imagine the amount of global damage this deeply deranged and mentally incapacitated man could cause in that time. At some point in the near future—hopefully as soon as possible—even the congressional Republicans, lots of whom presumably have children, will have to recognize the self-evident: Trump poses a clear and present danger to the US and the world.

October 12, 2017

"It is frankly disgusting the way the press is able to write whatever it wants to write. People should look into it."

—President Donald Trump, 2017

"If freedom of speech is taken away, then dumb and silent we may be led, like sheep to the slaughter."

—President George Washington, 1789

October 14, 2017

Trump zealots are a Dostoyevskean lot: they love him for his ill-concealed contempt for them.

October 17, 2017

In response to Trump's Tweeted warning to Arizona senator John McCain, who was suffering from advanced stage of brain cancer at the time, "Be careful because at some point I might fight back":

Yes, Trump, McCain is going to be very afraid of you. He was tortured for five years by the Viet Cong and had refused his tormentors' offer to be released as the son of US admiral while his comrades still remained in captivity—all while you were cavorting the war away in Manhattan night clubs, doing your utmost heroic best not to contract an STD (your "personal Vietnam," in your words), despite your five deferments from Vietnam on account of extremely painful bone heel spurs— but he is going to be very afraid of you. Senator McCain is looking death squarely in the face right now, but his greatest fear at this point is to be mentioned in one of your moronic adolescent pathetic tweets.

You are a sick, deranged, shameless, heartless, and soulless man, Trump, in addition to being a moron. You and your supporters are America's disgrace.

Words cannot express how contemptible you are.

October 26, 2017

Only a fool can ever say, "I'm a very intelligent person."

October 27, 2017

It was like this: Russia committed an act of war against the US.

It happened, right? It did.

Those who say, "Oh, sure, but that did nothing to alter the results of the election"—I would suggest those breezily nonchalant people make public, for the whole world to see, the entirety of their private e-mail correspondence; then it will become clear whether or not other people's opinions of those brave individuals would be altered at all as a result, even if only slightly.

Donald Trump does not want to investigate or as much as admit the fact of Russia's aggression against the US, because he has been the beneficiary of it, and almost certainly colluded with Russian intelligence in this act of war against the American democracy. In other words, he almost certainly is a traitor.

The Republicans in Congress do not want to investigate Russian aggression against the US because their party has become the Party of Trump: the party of white grievance and racial resentment.

Just stating the fairly obvious.

Still pretty mind-boggling, isn't it?

October 29, 2017

It appears that the full dead weight of his terrible barren life of relentless shamelessness and interminable corruption is about to come crashing down on Donald Trump. If so, what a sad waste of a life. To quote from one of Chekhov's most poignant stories:

> His life had gone by without profit or pleasure.
> It had been lost for nothing, not even a trifle.
> Nothing was left ahead; behind lay only losses,
> and such terrible losses that he shuddered to
> think of them. But why shouldn't men live so

as to avoid all this waste and these losses? Why, oh why, should those birch and pine forests have been felled? Why should those meadows be lying so deserted? Why did people always do exactly what they ought not to do? Why had Yakov scolded and growled and clenched his fists and hurt his wife's feelings all his life? Why, oh why, had he frightened and insulted that Jew just now? Why did people in general always interfere with one another? What losses resulted from this! What terrible losses! If it were not for envy and anger they would get great profit from one another.

Mikhail Iossel
November 2017

November 3, 2017
All the forty-four former US presidents combined did not produce half of the whining and complaining, kvetching, and self-victimizing Donald Trump has been engaged in nonstop, virtually around the clock, ever since his installment in the White House a mere ten months ago. What a remarkably pathetic human being.

November 5, 2017
Jesus would be nauseated by your sick love of guns, America.

November 6, 2017
In response to a church shooting in Texas

It is not a mental health issue. It is a gun issue. Period. It is a uniquely American issue. Enough of this reign of stupidity.

November 11, 2017
"Obama," Trump said to reporters on Air Force One a few hours ago, "did not have the right chemistry with Putin."

It is indeed regrettable that President Obama did not have the right chemistry with a man who hates the US with a passion and who has committed the most brazen act of aggression against the US in modern times.

But Trump, luckily, does have the right chemistry with that man. Moreover, the chemistry between the two of them is so strong that the man who hates America with a passion and has committed an unmitigated act of war against the US went out of his way last year to put Trump in the White House, out of the sheer goodness of his heart. So strong is the chemistry between Trump and that man, indeed, that Trump considers that America-hating man to be much more of a credible person than all the recent heads of the CIA and FBI combined. He believes that man, who hates America with a passion, to be a better human being and a greater patriot of America than all those "political hacks," in his words—those deeply decent and patriotic men who have served their country for a total of well over one hundred years . . . unlike Trump, who hasn't served his country a single day in his remarkably hollow life—but who keeps the score.

November 11, 2017

"Every time he sees me he says, 'I didn't do that,' and I really believe that."
—Donald Trump on Vladimir Putin, en route to Hanoi, November 11, 2017

Why, Trump? Why do you believe him and don't believe every single intelligence agency in the country of which you happen to be president? There is absolutely no excuse or even a farfetched justification for that anymore!

That, of course, is a rhetorical question. We know why. The large majority of Americans know, by this point: because you and your associates have sold America out to Putin, for the sake of your winning and subsequently monetizing the US presidency. Because, Trump, not to mince words, you are a traitor.

It is imperative for America to get Trump out of the White House as soon as possible. He is the greatest existential danger the country has faced in many decades. Hurry up, Robert Mueller, before Trump, doing Putin's bidding, has gotten all of us, America, and the entire world into a nuclear war on the Korean Peninsula.

November 11, 2017

Trump at press conference in Vietnam: "I believe that Putin believes that Russia didn't meddle in US elections . . . and that's what's important."

So then, Putin kinda sleepwalked into meddling in US elections. He is an honest man, as former KGB agents tend to be, and he cannot tell a lie, especially not to an American president, so he honestly just doesn't remember. He MAY have meddled, but that was not intentional and he was not aware of doing it while doing it. And that's what's important.

Trump's core base of angry diehards may stick with him until the bitter end, but the inflection point seems to be near. This level of public idiocy is unsustainable even by someone like Trump.

November 14, 2017

It is an interesting experiment America is conducting upon itself: its president is a hand puppet of its worst enemy, its secretary of state is in its worst enemy's pocket, and so are most individuals in its president's inner circle, including his son and his son-in-law.

There is a word for this kind of behavior on the part of the current American president and his flunkies: treason.

America's democratic institutions are undergoing an extremely perilous stress test imposed upon them in the main by the authoritarian-minded, poorly educated, bitter, xenophobic, racist minority of its citizens—with the active help from its above-said worst enemy and courtesy of the hopelessly outdated constitutional oddity called the Electoral College.

Resistance is essential.

November 15, 2017

Trump's address to the nation this afternoon:

A child comes out on stage, tells everyone he's their president, rambles on for about an hour about how he got to go on an all-expenses-paid trip to Asia and how everyone he met there, all those important grown-ups and other people, totally loved him and told him how amazingly smart and incredibly cute and unbelievably great he was. Every single one of his sentences starts with an "I," and there are a couple of personal pronouns thrown in the middle of every sentence, too, for good measure. At times, however, he switches to referring to himself in the third person, as two-bit, Mussolini-size dictator. wannabes have been wont to do throughout history. Feeling thirsty, he spends a bit of time fumbling for a water bottle underneath his lectern. Then, finally, feeling and looking bored and completely out of his depth, seemingly uncertain as to where exactly he is and what he is doing there, he says he's done and doesn't want to talk anymore—and he leaves, taking no questions from thoroughly puzzled reporters.

November 16, 2017

Dictators tend to end badly.

Mugabe could've stepped down two decades ago and lived out the rest of his earthly existence in peaceful luxury, sipping pina coladas on the ocean shore at sunset. But he just couldn't give up power. At ninety-three, it is easier and more dignified to die surrounded by your loved ones, rather than by a detachment of scowling soldiers who hate your guts.

Putin, take heed. Remember also Stalin spending his last night on earth in a pool of his own urine on the floor of his Kutsevo residence, with every one of his servants too terrified of him to approach his prostrate dying body. It still may not be too late for you, Putin, to vanish without a trace, to just disappear from under the dense canopy of a Moscow night and, a few days later, reemerge in some undisclosed, solitary tropical location. You are the richest man in the word, Putin— what do you need all this money for while staying in power and surrounded by cameras on a daily basis? Put your billions to a better use than trying to throw monkey wrenches in the wheels of America's electoral process. Leave America alone. America is stronger than you and you don't want it to get really pissed off with you when Trump vacates the White House—which, as you must know, is going to happen sooner rather than later.

Look, Putin, you have no joy in your life. You don't drink or smoke, you are no connoisseur of fine cuisine, nor are you a paragon of male virility—you are a permanently bored, sleepy-eyed, bald little man with thin bloodless lips and a tremendous amount of hatred and anger in your heart. You have dozens of palaces and retreats all across Russia and abroad, you have oceanic yachts and a flotilla of private planes. There is nothing you don't have except the ability to enjoy life—Putin, get yourself some small measure of totally undeserved happiness, while the going is still good. Escape to some undisclosed tropical location, live in a palace by the ocean, or else relocate to some beautifully severe, austere island in the North Sea and spend your remaining years communing with the stars of eternity and contemplating your destiny. You are—spoiler alert!—still mortal, Putin.

That's what I would do if I were you.

But I'm not you, and you, of course, are going to try and hold on to power until the bitter end, because there is nothing else you know how to do—and you are going to end badly, Putin.

November 17, 2017

Alabama governor Kay Ivey a minute ago at a press conference, saying in essence: I have no reason to disbelieve the women accusing Roy Moore, but I still plan to cast my vote for a pedophile. Because, see, a pedophile is better than a Democrat. Because he is OUR pedophile, not theirs. If Roy Moore also were a Russian neo-Nazi AND a pedophile, I still would cast my vote for him. Because I am a thoroughly confused and, sadly, rather despicable human being. Because I think we should've won the Civil War, if you want to know my opinion. Thank you very much and have a blessed day.

November 19, 2017

Just a quick mental note:

This year marks one-hundredth anniversary of the Bolshevik Revolution in Russia—and three decades since the KGB (now FSB) had started collecting *kompromat* on the visiting vainglorious American businessman Donald Trump, with the ultimate goal of turning him into an asset.

November 20, 2017

Imagine yourself being Putin. You are a . . .

OK, you don't have to if you don't want to, and I don't blame you if you don't, because who would; but purely for some gloomy fun's sake, let me imagine you imagining yourself being Putin. (I would've imagined myself, but that wouldn't be interesting, because I've done this before, so the bloom is off the old rose.)

If you are Putin—an outwardly healthy and athletic sixty-five-year-old tsar of Russia / godfather of the world's largest mafia corporation; a shortish balding man with the pale eyes of dying pond fish and a forgettable thin-lipped face pumped full of Botox; an unimaginably rich man (nobody knows how rich exactly, except for Putin himself, but we're talking very many billions of dollars here), someone who almost literally has everything (for starters, the largest country in the world, landmass-wise, with everything that's on and beneath its surface, plus the unquestioning, if somewhat tepid, devotion of the great majority of its people)—what is you strongest desire?

Your strongest desire, if you are Putin, is to stop being Putin. You would like to continue being Putin, that is, but without being Putin. Because being Putin as Putin means being stuck with yourself as Putin for the rest of your biological life.

And your second-strongest desire is to have just one desire that would be stronger than the first.

Because you are bored and tired. You are bored and tired of being the tsar of Russia and the godfather of the world's largest mafia corporation. Your vast country is rather desperately poor, and in theory you wouldn't mind doing something that would improve the lives of its people, so as to be remembered as a good tsar by the generations to come or whatever . . . even though, in truth, you don't like people in general and the people of your country in particular, regarding them with benevolent paternal contempt, as children thoroughly incapable of being in charge of their own lives and only and invariably causing harm to themselves and those around them if left to their own devices. Still, you wouldn't mind it if their lives were a little easier, en masse. That'd be no skin off your surgically enhanced nose. Unfortunately, though, with the sky-high oil prices of the aughts unlikely to return in any foreseeable future, there is little you can do, because, obviously, a mafia corporation does not exist for the purpose of enriching everyone and their brother, but only that of its own members. So then, nothing doing. Sad!

You are tired and bored, yes, but also, not surprisingly, long in the grip of raging mania grandiosa. And who wouldn't be, in your position, given the vertiginously unimaginable parabolic trajectory of your life, from its Dostoevskian humble beginnings and through the miserable KGB career of a glorified fink and then an unlicensed cab-driver? You likely would lose your mental moorings also, in his shoes.

Well, then: what do you do with yourself, given all those factors, if you are a bored and tired and clinically egomaniacal Putin?

That's where your third-strongest desire, borne directly out of your delusion of grandeur, comes into play: you would really like to be recognized, and as soon as possible, as the most powerful ruler in the world. You would strongly wish to regather the former Soviet lands, to recreate the old Soviet Union, in all its ugly glory. You really do believe that might still be possible, although deep down you know it really isn't—not at present, anyway. Not with America and the rest of the old West standing in the way of your abiding dream and being so much stronger than your country, both economically and—yes, indeed, although not nearly to the same extent as the economic discrepancy—militarily. The Carthago of the West delenda est, but not literally so.

You know you cannot confront the West in any direct, frontal fashion—in the first place, because many, if not most, members of the mafia corporation of which you happen to be the godfather, have their lives all set up nicely there, in the West, what with all the luxury properties they own all over the place there and with their children going to Western schools and universities and all the rest of it; and secondly . . . well, because, see above. It's not rocket science. You are crazy but not insane. You don't so much hate the West, either, as you envy and despise it at once, along with virtually all the members of your mafia corporation. You would want to destroy it, the damn West, without quite destroying it—by corrupting and degrading it morally, rather; through poisoning it with massive doses of grade-A cynicism steadily being injected in its societal bloodstream. You would want to demoralize and confuse it, the soft gutless West, to weaken it psychologically, to help bring to power there the kind of people who, due to their copacetic inner rottenness, tend to share your belief that everyone in the world, with no exceptions, can be bought and sold for the right price—people, in other words, whom you could manipulate easily, through a combination of bribery, flattery, and blackmail.

You are not a tech-savvy guy, if you are Putin. Far from it. You don't use the Internet, and you don't even—how quaint, how tsar- and godfatherlike—have an e-mail account. But you happen to be aware that there are some highly skilled . . . what's the word—hackers? yes, hackers—hackers in your country. Hackers, yes. You remember your former personal chef— and, later on, one of your mafia corporation's most influential members—telling you about the so-called "troll factory" he set up on the outskirts of your native city. Well, that's a promising idea. The West, as per Lenin's timeless prophecy, has sold you, along with the rest of the world, the rope with which it will be hanged. And that rope is called the Internet.

So you summon to your main residence near Moscow the heads of you intelligence services and other such smart people, and you tell them it's time to go to work. Time to start helping the West self-destruct by devouring itself from within in a big way. "Bigly," as the word has it.

And of course, you start with America.

November 21, 2017

A slightly edited version of the original post, now with a title:

BOILING POINTS

Like millions of other Soviet kids of my time, my friends and I used to boil condensed milk in a large pan of water on the gas stove. It was an extremely popular thing to do back then, even though, generally speaking, the resulting tan-colored viscous mass, sweeter than sweet and tasting vaguely like toffee, was no more (and as far as I personally was concerned, less) delicious than the starting product. Needless to say, we were completely unaware that we were, in effect, preparing the popular Latin American dessert called *dulce de leche*—and it wouldn't have made the slightest difference to us if we knew that. It was, I suppose, primarily the very process of altering, through boiling, the physical nature, visual aspect, and essential consistency of the unseen contents of an unopened metallic container that was fascinating to us.

We did this after school, in the space of the three or four hours we typically had before my parents came home from work, in the kitchen of my family's apartment on Cosmonauts Avenue, in one of the dozens of then-new *micro-district* neighborhoods on Leningrad's rapidly expanding outskirts. (But then, admittedly, those latter historico-geographic details are of no real significance here.)

It was not a quick operation: in order to have its contents cooked through properly, thoroughly enough, to an obvious degree of their having become something else, the 400-gram metallic cylinder of the *sgushonka* can needed to spend between an hour and a half and two hours in boiling water (and the longer the cooking time, the darker the former condensed milk's eventual color and the more solid its consistency were going to be); and so, after the first sizable bubbles started gurgling up to the surface, we would lower the fire to medium heat and decamp to the living room, to play our rowdy horse games there, or to listen to the endlessly re-redubbed tapes of the great singer-songwriter Vladimir Vysotsky's unofficial concerts on my parents' massively heavy Dnieper-14A *magnitofon*, because when you are a young teen, watching water boil for two hours in the kitchen is not something you are or should be capable of doing. From time to time, however, one or more of us would return to the kitchen, to check on the can in the boiling water, because it was a well-known fact that if the former was not fully covered by the latter, it could, and very likely would, explode.

Still, sometimes, entirely at random and with no visible warning signs, the can would explode even when being completely submerged in boiling water—and that, of course, was the darkly dangerous "Russian roulette" quality of the whole undertaking and, if I were to venture a dully cerebral guess from the remove of all these intervening decades, the unspoken main reason for our engaging in it.

The terrible, booming sound of the can's detonation would shake the floor and rattle the windowpanes in the apartment, filling our fluttering hearts with horrified ardor.

The kitchen, when we would enter it cautiously a few long seconds later, would present a predictably dolorous sight: the quivering stalagmites of pale-brown goo hanging from the ceiling, angry live splatters of the same protoplasmic substance everywhere on the walls, diarrheic sprays of it across the window. . . . Nothing for the parents, upon their return from work, to rejoice over.

The can, a twisted gaping wound of its former self, would be lying empty on the floor, bereft of purpose, and the condensed milk it used to contain would be free of its constraints, finally out in the open, but at the expense of having been transmogrified permanently into some different substance, and hot as hell.

Yes, those were the days. . . .

I am now going to resist the easy temptation to throw the flimsy footbridge of a needlessly extended metaphor between that accidental distant recollection and the increasingly dangerous condition America is in today. (A can of condensed milk in rapidly evaporating boiling water it may or may not be. But it sure could explode at any unpredictable moment.) You, of course, should however feel free to draw your own parallels, if you'd like.

November 25, 2017

In response to Trump's tweet that Time *magazine had called him to say he would "probably" be Person of the Year again and wants a photoshoot, but that "probably" isn't good enough.* Time *denied it.*

Steven Spielberg just called me to say I'd PROBABLY be picked to play the lead character in his new film about the Russian mafia but I'd have to agree to wear a Donald Trump sweatshirt and Borsalino hat in every scene. I said "probably" is no good and took a pass. Thanks anyway!

November 25, 2017

In response to a headline reporting a Winthrop University poll: "Nearly half of white Southerners feel like they're under attack":

. . . under attack by the modern age. By foreign languages. By works of literature. By the existence of other countries in the world. By liberals. By them educated types. By the idea of democracy. By people who look or sound unlike them. By black people. By gay people. By Mexicans. By politicians standing in the way of building the Wall that Mexico will pay for. By Muslims with their sharia law. By them wily Jews in Hollywood. By fake-news media. By women who think they can be president. By you. By me. By themselves.

November 26, 2017

Someone I know—a Trump voter—wrote recently on his/her Facebook page something to the effect that although Trump may not be a great president, at least "he is a good man."

That took me momentarily by surprise, as human goodness does not seem to be the kind of quality ordinarily ascribed to Trump. I am not being facetious when I say that I cannot find a single trace of goodness in him; not one discernible redeeming quality.

Asked at the conclusion of one of last year's presidential debates to say something positive about her opponent, Hillary Clinton, after a pause, praised his children. But his children— the three of them constantly in the limelight—are manifestly terrible people. As for Tiffany and Barron—they, thankfully, are just the ordinary anonymous human beings, a young woman and a child, clearly immaterial to Trump from the standpoint of his endless self-love, and thus spared by the immense gravitational forcefield of his public awfulness, as far as the world writ large is concerned.

What an arid desert of humanness his long and exceptionally loud life appears to have been.

But perhaps I'm overlooking something. That could easily be the case. Well, then, can anyone think of something, anything at all Trump has ever done or said that might to some extent justify referring to him as a "good man"? Please do tell. Inquiring minds want to know.

November 27, 2017

American politics no longer is about the juxtaposition between conservatives and liberals. Now the choice for the country to make, going forward, is between decency and indecency, honesty and dishonesty, faith in knowledge and self-proud ignorance, hope and fear, future and backwardness.

November 28, 2017

Wouldn't it be nice if, just in a dream world perhaps, there could exist a country called Trumpland, where all the ardent Trump supporters could live in perfect harmony! There a pedophile would be an infinitely more valuable member of society than a civil rights hero, for instance, to say nothing of them educated types; where one could, to one's heart perfect content, spout all manner of ugly racial and homophobic and misogynistic slurs from dawn to dusk; where even small children would be armed to the teeth; where there would be no big cities with them arts museums or bookstores and stuff, or any real universities, but plenty of churches for explaining to the Lord why pedophilia is less of a sin than freedom of choice for women; where people would love the dictator of Russia, say, or the Grand Wizard of the KKK much more than any member of the Democratic Party in neighboring, Trumpless US.

Because, in all seriousness—do you see any great chance of finding common ground with people like that . . . the pedophile voters?

I don't, in truth. Committed Trumpists cannot be won over. They can only be outnumbered at the polls—again, but this time everywhere it counts and watching the voting process itself very closely.

November 28, 2017
What both America and Trumpland need is an amicable separation.

Mikhail Iossel
December 2017

December 1, 2017

The vile clown in the White House shouldn't be president. It looks increasingly certain by the day that he was elected illegitimately, with the help of a foreign adversary. He shouldn't be signing any bills. He should instead be thinking of resigning—or else, fleeing to Russia under the cover of night, to avoid inevitable impeachment and subsequent prosecution.

How many people do not yet know what, in essence, took place here? It was a classic quid pro quod: Putin helped Trump get elected, Trump was supposed to return the favor by lifting the economic sanctions on Russia. It was as simple and straightforward as that.

December 2, 2017

There is only one person in Russia, at this time, whom Putin and his regime genuinely fear. His name is Alexei Navalny, a forty-one-year-old lawyer, anticorruption crusader, prolific blogger, highly charismatic political opposition leader, and remarkably gifted and efficient political organizer. If he were allowed to participate in upcom ing 2018 presidential elections in Russia, he'd give Putin a serious run for his money—for all those megabillions stolen from the Russian people by Putin and his fellow kleptochekist mafiosi. But Navalny is not allowed to participate in presidential elections, as someone previously and repeatedly indicted on openly absurd charges in clearly fabricated cases, specifically with the purpose of providing the regime with a quasilegal pretext for precluding Navalny from being able to register as a presidential candidate.

Navalny and his associates at his Anti-Corruption Fund are under constant pressure from the government; they regularly are thrown in jail for weeks and months on end, are physically assaulted by FSB-employed hoodlums (Navalny himself recently underwent vision-restoration surgery abroad, after having acid splashed in his face), are followed and filmed everywhere by FSB snitches, have their phone conversations intercepted by the so-called "Center 'E'" (counterextremism) FSB department, and so on.

Putin is reluctant to have Navalny sentenced to a lengthy prison term (like Mikhail Khodorkovsky) or simply killed (like Boris Nemtsov) because of his massive popularity in Russia— millions of dedicated, mostly young followers—as well as his broad international renown. The situation, for Putin, is somewhat similar to that which the Soviet Politburo was facing back in 1970 while trying to decide what to do with Aleksandr Solzhenitsyn after the publication of *The Gulag Archipelago* abroad. They were reluctant either to jail him or have him liquidated, because of the international furor that would have been certain to follow. (Eventually, under the cover of darkness one night, they just kicked him out of the country, putting him on a charter plane to Germany, where Heinrich Boll had expressed eagerness to be his host.)

It would, however, be difficult now for Putin to strip Navalny of his Russian citizenship and put him on a West-bound charter plane; so for now the waiting game continues.

Navalny keeps on traveling the vast country, drawing thousands of enthusiastic young people everywhere he goes, despite local officials' determined mulish resistance; and Putin, in order to diffuse and dilute the protest electorate, has tacitly put forth a charismatic spoiler of a presidential candidate, in the persona of the famous socialite, TV personality, glamour-magazine editor, and onetime member of political opposition, Ksenia Sobchak, thirty-six, daughter of the former mayor of St. Petersburg and Putin's erstwhile benefactor and employer, the late Anatoly Sobchak.

That, for those possibly interested, is, in a nutshell, the situation around the upcoming presidential elections with a predetermined result, there, in that giant, economically stagnating, politically unfree, and deeply disheartened country.

December 3, 2017

Putin was KGB. Leningrad KGB, more specifically—the most aggressive and ideologically severe in the Soviet Union. A midlevel KGB operative. The KGB people were the lowest of the low, as everyone knew—much worse, on any human scale, than the ordinary, run-of-the-mill Party members, your garden-variety, generally nonbloodthirsty, cynical conformists and careerists. The KGB got off on being universally dreaded: they loved beyond measure seeing the dull flicker of fear in people's eyes, experienced gloomy arousal at knowing that ordinary people knew they, the KGB, could ruin anyone's life irrevocably at a whim, just so, just because they could, just because they had unlimited power over them lowly regular folks. Had Putin been born thirty years earlier, say, he most certainly would've been one of the untold thousands of NKVD torturers and executioners, beating supposed enemies of the people into signing tearful confessions of being imperialist spies and implicating their own spouses of being enemies of the people, too, for good measure. Every generation of Russian people, males in particular, yields an extremely high—at least 50%?—ratio of potential Putins.

December 5, 2017

On the banning of Russia from the 2018 Winter Olympics:

It is not the athletes' fault. It is Putin's fault, the fault of those currently in power in Russia.

However, I can guarantee you with 99% certainty that every one of these athletes believes Putin is bee's knees, brilliant, and faultless, the greatest political leader alive. And they are not going to blame Putin and his former-KGB cronies in charge of sports in Russia these days for ruining their Olympic dreams— instead they are going to blame the West, the Russophobes at the International Olympic Committee, the CIA, George Soros, you name it, anyone and everyone, but not Putin and his fellow lowlifes in power.

December 6, 2017

During the last ten minutes of his Jerusalem announcement today, Donald Trump sounded uncannily like the late Leonid Brezhnev circa the late '70s: slurring words, sounding gutturally thick and gummy, consonants sibilant, vowels dully resistant to being pushed out of his mouth. It was easy, back at the time, to imitate Brezhnev's bumbling, lowing speech in a harshly parodying manner, further exaggerating the sheer agglomeration of its defects—and a lot of people, my very young and immature self included, had a lot of fun doing just that. By then, of course, Brezhnev had already had a couple of strokes and seemed permanently uncertain about his surroundings. Hardly anyone, however, felt sorry for him.

December 7, 2017
100 years of Soviet/Russian history:
    Leonid Brezhnev: 1964–1982
    1982–2000: Brezhnev, Andropov, Chernenko,
    Gorbachev, Yeltsin, Putin
    Vladimir Putin: 2000–2064

December 7, 2017
In response to the president's recognition of Jerusalem as the capital of Israel:

Trump, who knows nothing about anything and generally is out of his mind by now, has just taken the US out of any future peace negotiations in the Middle East. The US no longer could serve as an independent arbiter in any potential Middle Eastern peace process, if and when the latter might resume, which at this point appears to be never. There is, to state the obvious, no peace process currently ongoing in the Middle East, and the two-state solution between Israel and Palestine is over now. Not a single country in the world has approved of Trump's decision yesterday. Not one world leader, other than Netanyahu. It is, in the meantime, an empirical certainty that Trump, in his infinite wisdom, is the stupidest and least informed of modern-era American presidents. One would be extremely foolish to rely upon his historical vision or geopolitical judgment.

    Now what? Eternal war?

December 7, 2017
At the close of the Constitutional Convention of 1787, as he left Independence Hall, Benjamin Franklin was asked by one of the people waiting outside: "Well, Doctor, what have we got, a republic, or a monarchy?"

Franklin famously replied, "A republic . . . if you can keep it."

Right now, what we are seeing is the American Republic trying to keep itself.

December 7, 2017

On the resignation of US Senator Al Franken, a Democrat representing the state of Minnesota, after sexual misconduct allegations:

There is a harshly cold Russian saying: "When a forest is felled the chips fly." (*Les rubyat—shchepki letyat.*) It was used to justify, in particular, the enormous wastage of many millions of human lives for the sake of building, ostensibly, the perfect socialist-communist society in twentieth-century Russia.

Cold and harsh—but it is true, however: the cause may be eminently just and urgently overdue for resolution (such as one manifested in the current process of silence-breaking and the felling of the forest of misogyny in the US, partly as a reaction to the ugly charade of having a self-admitted sexual predator in the White House and in the wake of Harvey Weinstein's decades-long criminal behavior finally coming under public scrutiny) or grotesquely unjustifiable (effectively, the entire history of the old Soviet Union and its very seven-plus-decade-long existence), but when the forest of the old societal order is being brought down, human chips will fly. They will, inevitably, and both fairly and unfairly. They will, for instance, at times, take the form of an essentially decent and bright, progressive senator with his heart in the right place but, in keeping with his past as an irreverent public comedian, possessed occasionally of the unfortunate and indeed inappropriate propensity for boorish behavior and scatological jokes: that chip will fly, along with many others, as society is making its way through the gloomy forest of its past, toward the dead but still powerful and seemingly indestructible trees of hatred in the heart of the heart of its darkness.

December 8, 2017

This is not saying anything particularly new, but a large part of Trump's support among the poorly educated poor white people in rural America stems from the fact that nowhere else in the word is it considered to be as shameful to be poor as it is in the US. Admitting, even to oneself, to being poor in America is tantamount to admitting to being the ultimate loser in life. And so the poor people, who believe themselves to be the rightful owners of America rather than some nonwhite folks, simply flat-out refuse to admit to being poor. They consider themselves middle class and potential future millionaires. They are not poor, it's the immigrants who are poor, and the black people who are poor and lazy, and the Mexicans who are poor—and we don't want poor people in our country of successful middle-class individuals. We don't need Democrats' promises to make poor people's lives better—we aren't poor ourselves, we're in the billionaire's camp, we are with Trump, he treats us as his equals, he is one of us, only a little richer at this point—and we don't need or want Democrats to be making life easier for them poor nonwhite, non-100%- American people, unworthy of the great American dream.

December 12, 2017

Trump's insanity is engulfing the entire country like some dark, toxic fog. The moment Trump is gone from the White House, the fog will start to lift.

December 20, 2017

In response to a WashingtonPost.com analysis, "In Cabinet meeting, Pence praises Trump once every 12 seconds for 3 minutes straight":

All these people—Trump toadies, the congressional GOP, Trump supporters—would've made model Soviet apparatchiks of all levels and varieties. Oleaginously obsequious to their worthless superiors, contemptuous of everyone below them in the nomenklatura hierarchy, they have the noxious virus of authoritarianism blooming from birth in their bloodstream.

December 22, 2017

I do not accept the notion that Trump, the first American president in modern history to be cherished and beloved by the American Nazis and the Ku Klux Klan and someone who believes that there were some "very fine people" among the Charlottesville tiki-torch marchers chanting "Jews will not replace us!"—is a good guy who loves Israel and respects Jews more than the leaders of France or Germany or the UK and 120 other countries do. I don't believe Trump and Micronesia with Guatemala and Nauru are greater friends of Jews. It would be insane to think so. With Trump's unprecedentedly low, rock-bottom approval ratings, he needs to shore up his evangelical supporters with their "rapture" nonsense. I think it pathetic to think of him as a decent person, and doubly and triply so for a Jew. If you support someone supported by the Nazis, well, maybe you should be supporting someone else. Yes, next year in Jerusalem, but this was a symbolic decision with zero practical import and potentially very serious and tragic real-life consequences. Yes, it is a terrible and intractable situation, a raging fire there, but you don't fight fire by dousing it with kerosene.

December 23, 2017

In a few words and broad brushstrokes, this is what I and more and more people in America and everywhere else in the world believe the situation we're all in now is like: the current president of the United States owes a lot of money to the Russian oligarchs, and Russian intelligence has a wealth of personally embarrassing *kompromat* on him. The current US president also happens to be an authoritarian by nature, and he admires tyrants and dictators the world over, Vladimir Putin being the foremost among them. To sum it all up, the current president of the United States works for Russia, representing the interests of Vladimir Putin in the White House.

December 24, 2017

Think of all the hard times you've been through in your life. Think of all the obstacles you've overcome. The sham presidency of an extraordinarily repulsive, vile man with no redeeming qualities is just another stretch of darkness in our lives. This too shall pass—and, probably, sooner than most of us would anticipate, understandably predisposed as we, the survivors of our own past, tend to be to a somewhat gloomy outlook on the future. The future, however, has a way of surprising us, time and again. A mere few months—indeed, weeks—before the purportedly invincible and presumably eternal Soviet Union's ignominious demise, nothing seemed to portend such a dramatic development. The rusty machine of the totalitarian regime rumbled on, if fitfully so. The overwhelming majority of Soviet people were apathetically accepting of the Party's ironclad rule and of their own miserable plight of kindergarteners in a boot camp, resigned to the notion of living and dying in nonfreedom, without ever being allowed to experience any other kind of life; and they were either downright hostile to or sneeringly contemptuous of the steadily persecuted few—the dissidents, the human-rights activists—who dared to challenge the regime's legitimacy. But, then, virtually overnight, everything changed. The very same lethargic and apparently content human masses of the faceless populace suddenly, instantaneously, and much to their own amazement, were transformed into many-million-strong, impassioned multitudes of self-respecting individuals. (It is a different story that, alas, having been handed that unprecedented gift of freedom by history, they, en masse, essentially threw it away in fairly short order, opting again for the comfortable familiarity of the criminally corrupt and endlessly cynical totalitarianism-redux rule of de facto moral degenerates.) We don't know when exactly Trump will go down, but it will happen before too long, and probably sooner than many of us would anticipate. And when it does, he won't be missed—not even by his current supporters, my guess would be. As it says in Nahum 3:19, "There is no relief for your breakdown, Your wound is incurable. All who hear about you Will clap their hands over you, For on whom has not your evil passed continually?"

December 24, 2017

For years I've been dreaming of the time when, though not a Christmas celebrator myself, I would be able, freely and openly and without fear of reprisals and repercussions and political persecution, to say to all my friends near and far, far and wide: "Merry Christmas!" But I was afraid. I am not a brave man, admittedly. I was afraid that even in seemingly placid and safe Canada, amid the boundless fields of grain and hockey rinks and whatever else, the long arms of Barack Obama's secret police would find me. And so I kept quiet, only daring once in a while to whisper the Russian version of "Merry Christmas"—"*S rozhdestvom khristovym!*"—in passing, without lifting my eyes and all but inaudibly, to random strangers in the street.

But now, finally, with a man of true Christian morals in the White House, who out of the Ten Commandments has violated only maybe eleven or twelve in the course of his event-filled and superupright life, our long national nightmare of not being able to say "Merry Christmas!" to each other in a public space, loudly and clearly, is over!

Merry Christmas, everybody! Or, better yet, boldly and freely and proudly—MERRY CHRISTMAS!

December 29, 2017

In response to a WashingtonPost.com op-ed, "Trump's 'No collusion!' cry is getting increasingly desperate":

"I am 7 feet tall and fabulously rich and immortal. . . . I am 7 feet tall and fabulously rich and immortal. . . . I am 7 feet tall and fabulously rich and immortal. . . . I am 7 feet tall and fabulously rich and immortal. . . . I am 7 feet tall and fabulously rich and immortal. . . . I am 7 feet tall and fabulously rich and immortal. . . . I am 7 feet tall and fabulously rich and immortal. . . . I am 7 feet tall and fabulously rich and immortal. . . . I am 7 feet tall and fabulously rich and immortal. . . . I am 7 feet tall and fabulously rich and immortal. . . . Trump is no colluder. . . . Trumps is no colluder. . . . Trump is no colluder. . . . Trump is no colluder. . . . Trump is the Large Hadron Collider."

"Frankly there is absolutely no collusion. . . . Virtually every Democrat has said there is no collusion. There is no collusion. . . . I think it's been proven that there is no collusion. . . . I can only tell you that there is absolutely no collusion. . . . There has been no collusion. . . . There was no collusion. None whatsoever. . . . Everybody knows that there was no collusion. I saw Dianne Feinstein the other day on television saying there is no collusion [note: not true]. . . . The Republicans, in terms of the House committees, they come out, they're so angry because there is no collusion. . . . There was collusion on behalf of the Democrats. There was collusion with the Russians and the Democrats. A lot of collusion. . . . There was tremendous collusion on behalf of the Russians and the Democrats. There was no collusion with respect to my campaign. . . . But there is tremendous collusion with the Russians and with the Democratic Party. . . . I watched Alan Dershowitz the other day, he said, No. 1, there is no collusion, No. 2, collusion is not a crime, but even if it was a crime, there was no collusion. And he said that very strongly. He said there was no collusion. . . . There is no collusion, and even if there was, it's not a crime. But there's no collusion. . . . When you look at all of the tremendous, ah, real problems [Democrats] had, not made-up problems like Russian collusion."

December 30, 2017

If you say you are a Trump supporter, I would dare you to read the transcript of his *New York Times* interview of two days ago. Aloud. In full. Word by word. If you can do this without cringing or saying midway through, "No, to hell with it, I give up"—**congratulations**, you are a true hardcore Trumpist, entirely unembarrassable and unreachable to the voice of reason; and although I feel profoundly sorry for you, I wouldn't waste a second of my time arguing with you.

December 30, 2017

As a child, you see some impossibly old-looking man, say, smiling in the street blissfully and for no apparent reason—and for an instant you are taken aback, puzzled and feeling sorry for the poor deluded fellow: What is wrong with him? What is he so happy about? Doesn't he realize just how extremely close he is to dying and ceasing to exist forever?

An old man is not much wiser than a young boy, except in this one respect: he knows, if only on some visceral, nonverbal level, how to be quietly grateful for life's every passing moment.

December 31, 2017

In the year 2017—which, in a rare act of decency against the backdrop of its habitual braying shamelessness, is poised to leave us for good—all of us, separately and jointly, in the general balance of our lives, had our median fair share of success and failure, happiness and heartbreak, elation and despondency, love and lovelessness, joy and joylessness, fame and fortune, hardship and anonymity, companionship and lonesomeness, living to the fullest and merely existing, subsisting. Above all, however, whether or not every one of us was realizing as much, in 2017 we were preoccupied with the oppressive business of merely surviving it, this terrible year, waiting it out, outlasting it. Consciously or not, willingly or reluctantly, we do know, separately and jointly, that America—and, with it, the world writ large—is facing the greatest threat to its democratic institutions in modern history.

And so we are gazing with hope at the hazy nascent outlines of the incoming year: yellow dog of 2018, sort us out, set us right, fortify our spirit of resistance, make us stronger and more determined still to fight, help us defeat the dark entropy of cynicism and ignorance, racism and xenophobia, wanton greed and moral degradation!

Happy 2018, everyone! Let it be the year to end the bitter winter of our discontent.

December 31, 2017

2018 will be the most important, pivotal year in modern American political history. Either America beats back the plague of Trumpism, or Trumpism will throttle American democracy to death.

December 31, 2017

Less than six hours remaining, here on the Eastern Seaboard
of North America, until the end of the most corrupt, tainted,
and humiliating year in US modern history. History and its
agents—the majority of Americans—will eventually take care
of the cancer of Trumpism, I believe. But at this time, along
with some of my friends, I am thinking of, and will raise the
first glass of the New Year to, the good and kind people in our
lives, the ones always brightening our days, who no longer are
with us, whose light has been extinguished in the course of this
long and difficult year. They are and will always be loved and
missed.

Mikhail Iossel
January 2018

January 2, 2018

>
>
> **Donald J. Trump**
> @ realDonaldTrump
>
> North Korean Leader Kim Jong Un just stated that
> the "Nuclear Button is on his desk at all times."
> regime please inform him that I too have a Nuclear
> Button, but it is a much bigger & more powerful
> one than his, and my Button works!
>
> 4:49 PM – 2 Jan 2018

That insane Tweet alone should be grounds for immediate
impeachment.

January 3, 2018

Forget for a moment about the country and the world and
just think of how infinitely better it would've been for Donald
Trump himself never to have become the accidental TV
president of the world's unending shared nightmares whom

fate, working alongside the cold-blooded Russian dictator and the angry masses of poorly educated white people and tax-cut enthusiasts, has forced him to be. Now his whole life is going to come crushing down on him, turned inside out, in all its stunning unsavoriness—all the sheer ugliness of his existence, in which there has not been a single day of simple untainted decency. His very name will go down in history as the synonym of vulgarity, bigotry, incompetence, graft, nepotism, authoritarianism, moral turpitude, and stunning lack of patriotism, if not outright treason. His supporters, as well, will come to be viewed by future generations of Americans as the dead-enders of the stubbornness of undead past, bigotry, xenophobia, and vile ignorance—or else unbridled greed causing otherwise seemingly sane people to put their tax cuts above their conscience and the common good of other people and the nation at large. Trump, Trump. . . . All he ever wanted to be was the most famous man in the world, and a superstar of his own TV show playing on a loop 24/7. And now this. . . . He didn't want this, wasn't asking for this. He already is in the bloom of rage-fuelled dementia; in a year he won't know where or who he is and what he is doing in this cold, unfamiliar house. . . . How careful must one be in one's pursuit of insincere, lying dreams.

Time to go board my connecting flight.

January 4, 2018
The Trump presidency is a bad joke gone way too far.

January 4, 2018
The Republican Party is never going to cleanse itself of the taint of is original sin of 2016: pretending that a lifelong crook and conman, pathological liar and clinical narcissist,

demagogue and charlatan, ignorant buffoon, racist, and sexual predator, emotionally stunted and exhibiting telltale signs of early dementia—its nominee for the presidency—was in any way, shape, or form mentally or psychologically fit to occupy the world's most powerful and consequential office. The GOP leadership has betrayed the American people and covered itself with everlasting shame, by putting its political agenda of catering to the wealthy above the good of the country.

January 5, 2018

Future historians will have a hard time writing about the surreal current moment in America, when, due to a unique combination of highly unfortunate domestic circumstances and illicit outside influences, the power in this country has fallen into the hands of a seventy-year-old child beset with a whole host of psychological and emotional deviations, mental deficiencies, and rotten character traits.

January 5, 2018

Everyone in Trump's world knows Trump is an idiot, a child, and the worst human being ever to hold any elected office in the US, let alone the Oval Office. They know he has no more business being president than does an actual ten-year-old child, and they despise him with a vengeance, deride him behind his back, mock and badmouth and laugh at him privately. Yet they keep working for him, enabling him, and publicly praising him to the skies, singing hosannas to his face. . . . They are pathetic, and they certainly do not have America's best interests at heart.

They are no better—and in many ways they're worse—than the Soviet apparatchiks of late Brezhnev era, praising to the skies and showering with superlatives (the wisest! the shrewdest! the most perspicacious and blazingly patriotic!

the truest of Leninists!) an obviously demented, confused, and disoriented man who'd had multiple strokes and with a semiparalyzed brain, the general secretary of the Central Party Committee, the entirely insensate and incognizant supreme totalitarian ruler of more than two hundred million people, a thoroughly pitiful, wretched man who had difficulty walking, speaking, or reading, much less understanding, the texts of his endless, lifeless, deadeningly formulaic speeches printed in large font on the rustling pages laid out for him on the podium.

People working for Trump now, his enablers, are no less representatives of the Homo Sovieticus breed than the Soviet apparatchiks surrounding Brezhnev in the Kremlin back in late seventies. You don't have to be born and raised and brainwashed and morally warped in a totalitarian state, in the condition of ultimate nonfreedom, to be a cynical cad.

January 6, 2018

I am not stupid! I'm, like, really smart! I went to the best colleges and got the best grades there! I went into business and made billions and billions of dollars! I got through five bankruptcies and ruined the lives of lots of people! I've laundered more money for the Russians than any other American! Where is my Roy Cohn? Roy Cohn, where art thou? There are two things I love in this world: cheeseburgers and Putin! I was a tremendous TV star! I am not mental! I am not deranged! I'm not demented! Fake media! Fake media! No collusion! No collusion! My mind works like a well-oiled . . . where was I? Who am I? O God, I've screwed up my life, totally! I am a waste of fake hair! There is nothing but the cosmic chill of eternal nonexistence awaiting me! I . . . I . . . Ah! Yes. I am a very stable genius! I have, like, the world's largest penis! The last thing I am is a moron, which is something I'd like to expand more on!

January 8, 2018

Reading Michael Wolff's *Fire and Fury*. Without praising or disparaging it, let me just say there is no doubt in my mind it will end up being the defining book of the ugly charade of the Trump presidency, much in the same way Woodward and Bernstein's *All the President's Men* became the ultimate encapsulation of and history's judgment on Nixon's rule.

January 11, 2018

In response to news that Trump attacked protections for immigrants from "shithole" countries during an Oval Office meeting:

You voted for this vile, bigoted cretin, Trumpland.

January 12, 2018

The US president is an open racist. In 2018. It takes a minute for that to sink in.

January 14, 2018

What does Putin's Russia want, first and foremost?

To be feared by the rest of the world, the way the Soviet Union used to be feared. In Putin's system of values and that of his mythical 86% of his supporters, fear, of necessity, is synonymous with respect. Since they know they cannot, and never could, have the latter (to be feared the way the Soviet Union used to be), they have no other recourse but to opt for the former. Only through making other, more successful nations fear it, in their instinctive judgment, can Russia reclaim its illusory honor.

Everything else—all this endless blather about moral sovereignty, Russia's vaunted, uniquely "Russian" pattern of spirituality, and the sheer glorious singularity of its tortuously twisted path through the misty plains of Middle Ages–bound history—is secondary and, indeed, entirely meaningless. Envy-based bitter resentment: that's the one reliably true emotion behind its current modus operandi.

January 14, 2018

After we are done arguing whether Trump is a racist, let's have an equally lively discussion as to whether Stalin was a Stalinist.

January 14, 2018

I recall a conversation I had with a distant relative, an older man, lifelong Party member, back in Leningrad, as a teenager, very many (well, obviously) years ago.

He said, "Sure, Stalin did kill millions of people, but that's not the whole story."

NOT THE WHOLE STORY? I remember feeling stunned, incapable of imagining the sheer scope of the story in which the senseless wholesale murder of millions of innocent people was but one of its narrative components.

January 14, 2018

On this day twenty-seven years ago, 500,000 people came out onto the streets and squares of central Moscow to protest the invasion of Soviet tanks in Vilnius, Lithuania, sent in there by the Politburo in a last-ditch effort to stave off the dying Soviet empire's inexorable disintegration.

In the following decade, hardly anyone in Moscow came out to protest the Russian invasions of Georgia and Ukraine. The people of Russia, en masse, had by then returned, of their own free will, to their comfortingly familiar, apathetic prefreedom, "Soviet" state of being. Russia had failed the test of freedom.

January 15, 2018
The pretend president is honoring the legacy of Martin Luther King Jr. by spending the day marking the great American's memory on—where else?—one of his, Trump's, golf courses.

January 17, 2018
The only excuse Trump conceivably may have for repeatedly referring to US journalists as "enemies of the people" is his infinite, vertiginous ignorance. He simply has no idea of the horrific historical context in which that phrase was used some 70–80 years ago in the Soviet Union, signifying death sentences for millions of innocent people.

Trump would've loved Stalin, of course: he admires tyrants, the more unbounded and homicidal the better.

Stalin, in turn, would've ordered Trump's execution, as an enemy of the people, minutes after their first meeting, based simply on the obnoxious braying sound of Trump's voice.

January 17, 2018
In response to news reports that the FBI is investigating whether Russian money went to the National Rifle Association to help the Trump campaign:

The ultimate freedom-loving American patriots from the NRA appear to have been in receipt of large sums of money earmarked for Trump's presidential campaign from a top Russian banker and political functionary with equally close ties to Putin and the international mafia. It goes almost without saying—yet still needs to be said, the better to be processed by one's boggled mind— that if presented with an existential choice between Putin and say, Obama or Clinton, the NRA would immediately side with the America-hating dictator of Russia. He may be the world's foremost enemy of freedom, but he is good for the NRA—and therefore, in the NRA's view, he is good for America.

January 20, 2018

For the first time in its history, America has an openly anti-American president, someone who does not believe in and actively undermines democracy and its basic institutions. Today marks the first anniversary of his inauguration. He is celebrating it with a government shutdown. It was an exhausting and terribly humiliating year. Let 2018 be the last one of this unprecedented national disgrace.

January 20, 2018

In response to a WashingtonPost.com article, "In the crowd at Trump's inauguration, members of Russia's elite anticipated a thaw between Moscow and Washington":

All them various, infinitely corrupt, thoroughly mobbed-up Putinesque oligarch and suboligarch human trash so happily in attendance of Trump's inauguration one year ago, all aglow with excitement—indeed, *gospoda*, finally, after eight years of an arrogantly unbribable and unfriendly black man in the White House, well, at long last, one of their own ilk, a bird of their crooked feather, someone on whom the Russian secret services have tons of *kompromat*, someone kept afloat financially for decades by dirty Russian money, has come to play ball on the Kremlin's terms, to lift those painful and humiliating economic sanctions, to flood the Russian mafia's coffers with murky rivers of corporate American dough, and generally to transform America into a larger, more prosperous version of Putin's Russia, with Putin naturally becoming its de facto shadow ruler, Trump's gray cardinal!—how deeply disappointed, heartbreakingly downhearted they're feeling now, one year later. Nothing of what they dreamed of and hoped for last January 20 has remotely materialized. The sanctions have not been lifted. In fact, they've been tightened further. Russia, the only country in history ever to be run by a giant mafia corporation, is universally viewed throughout Europe and North America and beyond with loathing and disgust—an international pariah of a rogue state whose sole function in the world at this time is to wreak havoc and subvert democracy in as many parts of the planet as possible. And indeed, many of them, last year's celebrants from Russia, are likely to end up soon on the US State Department's "persona non grata" list, barred from entering the country where, mind you, they have luxurious properties (purchased frequently via Donald Trump's money-laundering services), where the children of some of them go to school, where their wives and mistresses like to spend way more time than they do in Russia. . . . How and why did all this happen? Well, they have no one but their own *capo di tutti i capi*, Don Vladimir, to thank for this ugly situation. Once again—only this time on the grandest scale of all—he has outwitted everyone, beginning with himself. As ever, a passable KGB tactician, and a truly crappy strategist. One can take the boy out of the KGB overcoat, but . . . one can never actually succeed at doing that. Because he does not and never has believed in democracy as a remotely viable mode of governance—deeming it to be just an old bourgeois pablum deployed by Western imperialists to keep the inherently stupid and eminently dupable human masses in a state of relative contentment with regards to the (largely illusory, of course) degree of their personal freedom to chart the course of their own little lives—he naturally assumed that if he, Putin had been able to subjugate every potential source of political independence in Russia, turning himself effectively into a modern-day Russian tsar, then why wouldn't Trump be able to do the same, despite his being obviously as stupid as hell, with his, Putin's help? Why wouldn't he be able to arrest and imprison his political opponents, take full control of the main channels of American television, put out of business all large-circulation outlets of the print media, abolish the institution of the independent judiciary, turn both chambers of Congress into an assembly of his paid marionettes . . . and so on? Of course he would! Why wouldn't he?

Well, but then, ultimately, it is not all that surprising that Putin still views the world through the narrow-slitted prism of his pathetic mindset of an eternal KGB snitch. What's funny—and by "funny" I mean not funny at all—is that Trump, too, due to his never having read anything, including the US Constitution, also believed, on the day of his inauguration, that he would be able to become in essence the Putinlike king of America, its benevolent crook in chief, someone for whom America is the sovereign domain of his lifelong sleazy conmanship.

Well, guess what.

This January 20, Putin and his minions are sending no congratulatory cablegrams to the White House, breaking out no champagne.

January 21, 2018

It would, of course, have been much better for the US and the world at large if in 1885, a poorly educated sixteen-year-old Bavarian named Friedrich Drumpf, dashing off across the ocean in a bid to avoid fulfilling his military service (this last tendency being one that seems to run in the family), had not been admitted to the United States, as per the Donald Trump administration's current specifications, as someone with nothing but a set of decidedly murky moral principles to offer his prospective new motherland—and had not subsequently gone on to pave the way for the current White House inhabitant's wealth by opening and operating a string of brothels in the Klondike during the Gold Rush.

But alas.

January 22, 2018

When I was in high school, the entire Soviet nation raged against Aleksandr Solzhenitsyn. There were days when all one could hear on the radio or on television, from dawn to dusk, or read in every newspaper, were the shrill, vitriolic denunciations of that traitor, that contemptible lowlife, yellow earthworm, rabid dog of international imperialism— Solzhenitsyn. Hundreds, thousands of ordinary Soviet people's letters were printed in newspapers and read on the radio on a daily, weekly, monthly basis: throw him in jail, kick him out of the country, kill him, we don't want to breathe the same air with him, we would kill him ourselves with our own bare hands and our own teeth if we were allowed to do so or knew where to find him; he is repugnant, a reptile, the lowest of the low, even his last name is rooted in the word "lie" (the latter statement technically true—MI), do something about that Judas, our dear Soviet leaders and competent authorities, or we can't promise we won't take matters into our own hands! Etc. There were days when one felt one was fairly losing one's mind amid those boundless murky torrents of infinite zoological hatred. One felt scared, frightened. The occasion for the well-orchestrated insanity of the anti-Solzhenitsyn campaign, back at the time (for there would be another and even more vicious one, too, a few years later, when *The Gulag Archipelago* came out), was the publication in the West (well, obviously, not in the Soviet Union) of his novel *August 14*, about the defeat of the tsarist Russian Army in one particular battle in Prussia at the outset of World War I. It seemed, by the sound of it, like a rather innocuous subject: after all, wasn't the tsarist regime the epitome of everything evil in the world? Wasn't its defeat by anyone and anywhere an a priori good thing? Well, apparently not. Apparently, it was the very fact that someone had dared to write an unsanctioned novel about the presumed weakness of the eternal Russian military and Russia's matchless fighting spirit and, infinitely worse still, to manage somehow surreptitiously to have the manuscript smuggled abroad and published ipso facto by some anti-Soviet print outlet, first in Russian and then, in an exponentially greater number of copies, in English translation—this was what drove the Soviet leadership crazy. How dared he? Who did he think he was? . . . And so, there was this vast, unending boiling rage, from morning to night, seven days a week, month after month, set off by a novel no ordinary Soviet citizen had read or even knew much about and why it was so terribly bad and treasonous. People raged because they knew they were expected to be enraged. They hated for hatred's sake. They felt good raging and hating away, too. If they had been allowed to kill Solzhenitsyn with their own bare hands and their own bared teeth and had known where to find him, they would indeed have done so—that was no joke, no hyperbolic figure of speech. They couldn't rage about anything else in their lives, or at least not openly so, so they raged against Solzhenitsyn, a man no one had seen, whom hardly anyone in the country had read beyond his 1962 novel *One Day In the Life of Ivan Denisovich* (which by then had long been banned and removed from any library open to ordinary Soviet people).

It was quite something, this nationwide orgy of rage. Inevitably, it was taking its toll on people, even in my own little, tiny world. One girl in our class went ashen pale and fainted when the geography teacher mentioned Solzhenitsyn's name in class, seemingly out of nowhere. I, for one, one evening in the dark bedroom of a classmate's parents, once saw Solzhenitsyn's face growing darkly and terribly in a mirror illuminated only by the trembling flame of the candle in my hand..

Briefly: The girl's parents had gone off to Moscow for the weekend, and so there was a party in her apartment, with six of us, high school classmates, in attendance—three boys and three girls. Nothing out of the ordinary: weak white wine (Rkatsiteli, I believe), Salvatore Adamo's suffering voice ("Tombe la neige"), Engelbert Humperdink, Mireille Mathieu, Tom Jones, Raphael, Karel Gott, Edita Piekha, Janos Koos, Lili Ivanova, Valery Obodzinsky, and so on. We slow-danced awkwardly, and then someone came up with the idea of playing the game whose supposed purpose was to discover and confront one's greatest fear in a darkened mirror while standing in solitude in front of it with a lit candle in one's hand. It was a stupid idea, of course. We were all more high-strung and screwed up in our hearts and minds than we knew. The hostess went in first, and just a couple of minutes later she fairly fell out of the bedroom, deathly pale and unable to utter a word or stand on her own two feet. She stuttered and sputtered, and dared not say the name of the someone or something she'd seen in the mirror. (Later it was revealed that it had been Mao Zedong.) While others were fretting over her, ministering to her, bringing her water, and cooing over her, I took the candle from the table and went in, closing the bedroom door behind me. There I stood, in the crimson light of the candle's trembling flame reflected ominously in the mirror, and at first I saw nothing but the pale outlines of my own frightened face in it and was about ready to return to the living room with a dismissive announcement that the whole thing was a stupid hoax—but then, all of a sudden, a black-and-red cloud started rising from behind my face in the mirror, slowly and inexorably, swelling, growing, undulating, mushrooming out of the dead lake of the amalgam's surface, and gradually acquiring a semblance of facial features, and . . . Oh, it was an abominable, devilish face, full of unspeakable vileness and cruelty, its eyes burning with venom—and right away, then and there, I knew beyond a shadow of a doubt that this was Solzhenitsyn, yes, Solzhenitsyn and none other than him, even though I'd never seen his face before. With a cry of pure horror, I fled not only the room but also the apartment, barely finding the presence of mind to place the candle back in its cast-iron holder on the table in the living room first and then to put on my winter coat and shoes. Others stared at me wordlessly. I said nothing. Solzhenitsyn! I'd seen Solzhenitsyn's face in the mirror! Now I knew what he looked like—and now HE knew what I looked like, too, it suddenly dawned on me. That thought filled me with infinite fear and despair. As I ran through the empty spaces of our "microdistrict" on Leningrad's southwestern edge in snow-bound darkness—through the narrow passageways, where every square centimeter was familiar to me, between the identical-looking five-story cinderblock buildings where all of my friends and classmates lived, yes, as I ran through my entire little world, I knew my life was over, lost beyond the point of no return or salvation. Solzhenitsyn was going to find me, now that he knew what I looked—and he was going to kill me. That's what he was going to do. I knew I was going out of my mind, but there was nothing I could do about it in those moments. My mind was occluded, eclipsed. My heart was galloping in my chest.

Already nearing my apartment building, I stopped for an instant to catch my breath in front of the one next to it, the only tall, nine-story building in the microdistrict and the only one made of brick. It was cold, but I felt as hot as hell. The starless, moonless night was brightened darkly with the glowing whiteness of snow and the muted yellow and bluish light falling from the countless windows in that giant building, where lived ordinary Soviet people, ones just like me. Luckily for them, they'd never seen Solzhenitsyn's face. The *fortochka* (a small ventilation window in . . . oh, just Google the word) in one of the first-floor windows was open, probably because of the smoke rising from something being cooked with rancid margarine on the gas stove in the kitchen, and I heard a comfortingly upbeat, quietly confident radio announcer's voice issuing from it—a shred of program-concluding sports news: ". . . and the bronze medals in the ice dancing competition at the world championship in Lyon, France, went to the American athletes Judy Schwomeyer and James Sladky. . . ."

Judy. James. Judy Shoo-meyer and James whose last name meant "sweet" in Russian. Americans. Ice dancing. Sweet! Our dancers had taken first place, of course: Lyudmila Pakhomova and Alexandr Gorshkov, who else? She, in particular, was the pure genius of ice dancing. . . . Oh! All at once, a blissful sense of peace and serenity came over me. Ice skating! Evening news! Bad margarine! Life, life! Life as I knew it, my Soviet life, one in which there was no place for Solzhenitsyn with his monstrous wickedness. All was well with my world, and Solzhenitsyn had no dominion over it. He could do nothing to me while I was within the safety of its cocoon. My world was tiny, and it was beautiful. I felt safe, protected. He could do nothing to me. Nothing. Tender and kind was the night. All was well with the world.

January 26, 2018
1st Red Army (Krasnoarmeiskaya) Street.

A five-minute walk from where I was born—just not in 1946—and spent the first eight years of my life. In the metaphoric shadow of the Trinity (Troitsky) Cathedral.

But, of course, I remember those wooden streetcars of my childhood very distinctly.

January 29, 2018

No, Trump is not making all of us "a little more like him," as some argue—he, instead, is making it plain for all of us to see that between 30-35% of all Americans don't give a damn about democracy, wouldn't mind living in an authoritarian society, are poorly educated, ignorant, none-too-bright or else enormously greedy and cynical, tend to be strongly hostile to everyone who doesn't look or think like them; and, generally, are glad finally to have a president who actively encourages them, by his own example, not to be ashamed of exercising and presenting to the disgusted world their worst selves. He liberates them from that silly psychological rudiment—the sense of shame. Trump is a walking empty vessel of darkness, and, like a powerful magnet charged with an inexhaustible amount of demagogic ugliness, he draws in those whose hearts and souls, similarly, are filled with darkness.

January 29, 2018

I know and fully appreciate the fact that the majority of people potentially reading this are not quite interested in any of that overt political stuff, Trump, shmump, because what's the point and what would be the use and how naive is that, and all politics is crap and whatever for and what does it have to do with the daily grind and flow of one's own life, politics is tacky and idiotic, there are books to read and movies to see and places to go and stories and essays and rhymed and nonrhymed poems to write and all that, one's job is demanding and time-consuming and money is tight and life is hard, I wish I had your problems, what a massive waste of time and emotional energy, etc.—but right now, in my humble personal opinion, could just be the moment to become interested, if maybe just a little bit, and maybe even to become a bit vocal, because, um, stuff is getting real and things are accelerating and this is a seriously dangerous moment and the prospect of the loss of American democracy no longer is but an abstract mental construct or some snappy shred of empty verbiage . . . especially, you know, if one has children and wouldn't want them to have to live in some dystopian novel of a society—but even if not, even if one doesn't have children, still and all, life in a dystopian novel or movie of a society is no life . . . like Alcatraz, no good for nobody—or, indeed, like the old Soviet Union.

January 30, 2018

Such a very exciting night! The nation is positively a-tingle with anticipation as to whether the justice-obstructing, money-laundering, dictator-worshipping racist, bigot, sex predator, and traitor living in the White House courtesy of Vladimir Putin and a minority of American voters is going to look presidential and not engage in his characteristic, crudely nonsensical ad-libbing, while dutifully and dully reading off a teleprompter a self-congratulatory speech, written by someone else, about the State of the Union he is actively seeking to divide and destroy.

January 31, 2018
FBI TO TRUMP: Don't release that bogus memo you cooked up at the White House and then handed over to your stooge Devin Nunes to present as his own handiwork: it uses classified information in order to falsify reality and would be damaging to our national security. We have grave concerns about it.

TRUMP TO FBI: Security, shmecurity. I don't give a damn. I don't work for the American people, I am here to do my master Putin's bidding. And he tells me I must subvert American democracy as much as possible in the process of trying to save my butt from impeachment and subsequent prosecution. Haven't you seen millions of "releasethememo" hashtags launched by Russian bots? Go take a hike, FBI.

January 31, 2018
It is a strange feeling for a former Soviet subject to be watching American democracy being steamrolled by a Russian asset in the White House.

February 2, 2018
. . . reminded of myself back in '85 in Leningrad, outside my apartment on Frunze Street, by Sergeui Artiouchkov.

Toy Colt gun and empty plastic bag, for bread and stuff.

February 2, 2018
Good, decent people who have lived in the US for 30–40 years, brought into the country as children, including those who have fought for the country in Afghanistan and

Iraq and those with green cards, are being torn away from their families and deported to the countries of their birth, where they have no one and nothing awaiting them. What Trump has unleashed in the US, with his vile anti-immigrant rhetoric and his open encouragement of xenophobic foulness among his supporters, is nothing short of ethnic cleansing. He doesn't want brown people in the US. He wants Norwegians.

Yes, indeed: ethnic cleansing in twenty-first-century America.

February 2, 2018

It's hard to see how this rapidly and uncontrollably accelerating madness and mushrooming clustermuck AKA so-called "Trump presidency" can be sustained, in the very best of outcomes, beyond a few short months from now. The orange burger-muncher, having crashed through all the guardrails of essential sanity, to say nothing of the basic norms of American democracy, is in total freefall.

February 5, 2018

The Berlin Wall stood for 10,316 days. February 5 marks 10,316 days since it's been gone.

Its presence in the world was temporal, its nonexistence eternal, but its shadow is still with us, and someone somewhere always keeps trying to bring it back to life.

February 7, 2018

In response to news that Trump has asked the US military to plan for a grand military parade in the nation's capital:

Sure. Grand military parades. What's not to dig about those? He admires dictators and would love to be one. A Kim Jong-un, say. He also would strongly prefer for his official designation to be His Excellency Generalissimo Super-President Donald J. Trump. A souped-up military uniform befitting the first American generalissimo would be a must for him: a giant high-peaked visor cap similar to those worn by banana republic strongmen or the late Muammar Gaddafi, enormous golden tasseled epaulets, and dozens of golden medals and orders made of precious stones covering every inch of available space on his tight-fitting tunic.

February 7, 2018

That sprawling gray building near Leningrad's southwestern edge in which I spent the last six years of my life in the Soviet Union, that building with a massive granite foundation—it had been put up in the late Stalin era by German POWs and featured uncommonly thick and sturdy outer and inner walls. Not once, in all that time, did the ageless middle-aged woman with a perennially tired, kindly face, whose apartment was the only one sharing the sixth-floor landing with mine, complain or otherwise express even mild displeasure about the loud voices and boisterous laughter or discordant singing and poetry-reciting or guitar- or flute- or tambourine-playing and whatever other kinds of noises were produced by any of the hundreds or thousands of my, mainly young, daily and nightly visitors: hard-drinking underground writers, poets, actors and actresses, engineers and mountain-climbers, dissidents and internal émigrés and Party members, Jewish refuseniks and Siberian secessionists, childhood- and school friends, American and European students of Russian, guests of the city on the Neva from Moscow and Vladivostok, Vilnius, and Khabarovsk, assorted ne'er-do-wells and ambitious up-and-comers, random acquaintances and total strangers, friends of friends and friends of friends' friends and friends of friendless friends' friends' friends . . . and oh, so many others.

She was an ideal neighbor, that woman, whose name I never got to know; and whenever we would cross paths outside the building or run into each other on the landing or share the old and clanky elevator in our entryway, she would always smile and nod at me, and I would reciprocate in kind.

But when, finally, in the end, at the apogee of Gorbachev's desperate efforts to improve the Soviet Union's relations with the surprisingly deathless Western world (a world of undeserved plentitude), having suddenly and along with tens of thousands of other such lowly outcasts of society been informed that I was free to get the hell out of the country on a permanent basis in three weeks or less, I had walked out the door of my apartment for the last time, two suitcases with books and clothes in tow, feeling entirely overwhelmed with a complex mix of sadness, fear, and elation, she—that friendly neighbor of mine—unlocked and unlatched her door across the landing, poked her disheveled head out and, contemplating me with sheer hatred and disgust, sad venomously in a loud, hissing whisper: "Thank God I won't have to breathe the same air with you anymore, you kike bastard, with your endless synagogue's worth of anti-Soviet-trash friends and sluts. I hope you die there!"

To which, though understandably taken aback, I replied something along these lines: I too hoped I'd die in a country I wouldn't have to share with her, and my wish, contrary to hers, would be that she'd end up living five thousand years more right there, in that very apartment, without ever getting any older or younger or richer or poorer or any happier or unhappier. Eternity would be her punishment. She spat on the landing and slammed the door shut. My parents and a few of my friends were waiting for me downstairs.

While getting into the old clunky elevator for the last time, I thought it might be a cool epitaph on one's gravestone, etched in angular lettering in two languages, English and Russian: "Here lies one who was born in one country and died in another." Five or however many thousand years later, the budding archeologists of the future—provided humankind was still going to exist then with most of its faculties intact—might stumble upon that broken-up sliver of darkened stone, my putative gravestone, and one of them would say, "Oh, look, another Sumerian tablet. One language is English, clearly, but the other one . . . Russian, I guess? So this goes all the way back to when Sumerians still spoke Russian? They had a kingdom called the Soviet Union, a terrible place, if I'm not mistaken." And the other one would look at the first with admiration and say, "It's incredible, how you manage to keep all these tremendous amounts of totally obscure, useless information in your head."

February 10, 2018

Too much investment in righteous, self-congratulatory rage in North America right now. There is something essentially, and disturbingly, "Soviet" about it.

February 12, 2018

It would have been impossible, back in 1938, to explain to the majority of Germans that Nazism would lead Germany to ruin.

It would be impossible nowadays to explain to the majority of Russians that Putinism is leading Russia to disaster.

And it would be impossible, too, to explain to current Trump supporters why democracy is preferable to tyranny.

February 14, 2018

On Valentine's Day, a young man—a teenager, apparently—walks into a high school in an upscale suburban neighborhood in southern Florida, carrying a gun, and starts shooting indiscriminately at boys and girls his own age: his schoolmates, most likely.

17 dead. 20 wounded.

17 dead. 20 wounded.

The fifteenth school shooting of this, still very young year.

What happened here? A broken heart? Some deeply held grudge, a long history of humiliation at the hands of resident bullies?

It doesn't really matter. I shudder at the thought of what would it would have been like if, back in my day, all of us, kids at my school—elementary-to-high school #511 of Leningrad's Moskovsky District, on Yuri Gagarin Avenue—had had any realistic access to lethal weapons. It would've been a bloodbath. There was lots of bullying. And plenty of heartbreak.

But this is twenty-first-century America, the land of the free, where every eighteen-year-old can walk into any gun store in a state like Florida and quickly and legally purchase a deadly weapon, where 3% of the population owns half of all the uncountable millions of guns in the country, and where millions of seemingly reasonably sane people, members of an all-powerful organization fairly owning the lowlife in the White House and dedicated to oversaturating the country with guns on a permanent basis, are fully prepared to have any number of children's lives sacrificed for the sake of their repugnant gun-sickness.

February 15, 2018

Remember Trump's inaugural address?

"This American carnage stops right here. . . . I'll be able to make sure that when you walk down the street in your inner city, or wherever you are, you're not going to be shot. Your child isn't going to be shot."

This was spoken by the most pro-NRA president ever, someone whose campaign had received five times more financial support from that gun lobby organization than any other in history; and someone, too, who had to know full well that the $30 million of NRA money his campaign had benefitted from was the money the NRA had received from the shady Russian lawmaker with equally close ties to international organized crime and Putin's inner circle.

"Your child isn't going to be shot."

February 16, 2018

"Mr. President, do you have any comments about today's indictments of the thirteen Russians guilty of interfering with our elections, apparently on direct orders from Putin?"

"No collusion! No collusion, no collusion. NO COLLUSION! You know it, and I know it. And no obstruction. They may have meddled, but that didn't change the outcome of the elections. I am a legitimate president, with the largest inauguration crowd in history. This whole Russian investigation is a hoax cooked up by Crooked Hillary as payback for her stunning loss. There was no collusion. When I asked Russians to find Crooked Hillary's missing e-mails, that was a joke. And when I kept saying I loved WikiLeaks, that was irony, and I had no idea where that guy, what's his name, was getting that information I kept reading out loud at my rallies."

"But Mr. President, aren't you even a little bit outraged by Putin's meddling in our elections?"

"Look, it's not like we're not meddling in any other countries' elections ourselves, OK? Like we're so innocent. And Putin is a real leader, one who wants the best for his country. He is a patriot, and he sure is a stronger leader than Obama was, and a million times better than Hillary would've been. When he looks me in the eye and says he had nothing to do with it, I know he believes what he says, and I know he is sincere. If I have to choose between his word and the so-called findings of this Russian hoax, this Democratic witch hunt, I'll know who to believe. Listen, he's a great man, Putin is, and we'd be lucky to have him as our own, American secretary of state or attorney general, I'll tell you that."

February 17, 2018

The sheer volume of *kompromat* the KGB-FSB has managed to collect on Citizen Trump over the last three-plus decades must, I would imagine, be at least ten times the size of *War and Peace*. And sooner or later—and likely before too long, too—a good deal of it will come out in the open. And America will shudder in horrified disbelief.

February 18, 2018

I've never witnessed a less dignified, more pathetic behavior on the part of any politician—and that includes all manner of two-bit Party functionaries back in the Soviet Union—than the one Trump is exhibiting right now. He knows the great majority of the country is on to him by this point, realizing his so-called presidency is a fraud and that he is an illegitimate—a modern-day Boris Godunov. A remarkably humiliating spectacle. His tweets this morning—It's not me! It's not me!—are, in effect, the written equivalent of a terrified chihuahua's barking.

February 20, 2018

 Donald J. Trump
@realDonaldTrump

I have been much tougher on Russia than Obama, just look at the facts. Total Fake News!

8:38 AM – 20 Feb 2018

. . . and I have always been a much better ballet dancer than Mikhail Baryshnikov. That's just common knowledge. I know it and you know it and so does everyone else. Just look at the facts.

What an embarrassing spectacle this is—a frightened, endlessly self-humiliating empty shell of a human being in the White House.

February 22, 2018

Since assault rifles tend to be school shooters' preferred weapon of choice, it would stand to reason to have teachers armed with AR-15s as well. Indeed, what can a tiny little handgun do against a firearm designed for speedy reloading in combat situations and capable of shooting off dozens of rounds in seconds? I also would suggest equipping teachers with a couple of hand grenades, for good measure—to provide them with a bit of tactical advantage over the insane attacker.

School children also probably should be armed—not all of them, of course, but only the gun-adept and firearm-talented among them. Having 20% of schoolkids designated class countershooters, armed with smaller-sized AR-15s, probably would suffice.

Those would just be the first sensible steps on the long and thorny path toward making American schools the perfectly safe places they deserve and need to be.

February 23, 2018

Bright and hopeful high school students against the ragtag army of NRA-bound, gloomy-eyed "gun enthusiasts." This is the modern-day children's crusade against the superannuated America of embittered aging adults with empty, meaningless, wasted lives, clinging to their grotesque arsenals of monstrously lethal firearms as the only remaining means by which they believe, the sad sons of guns, they still can exercise a measure of control over the inexorable passage of time and the pitiless world of tomorrow that has left them behind for good.

February 23, 2018

Ask any Trump supporter from among the ranks of reasonably successful, well-adjusted, well-read, worldly, and sophisticated former Soviet Jewish immigrants in the US—rather than any number out of hundreds of thousands of our oft-older and less "Americanized" former compatriots, denizens of nominal Brighton Beach, who don't know much English and tend to watch nothing but Russian television in their homes and automatically consider to be Fake News everything that's not Putin news or Fox News—why they support Trump, despite his glaring deficiencies, to put it mildly, as a sentient human being presumably familiar with the concept of *right* and *wrong*, and in most instances you likely will hear: "Because he is good for Israel. Because he's tough on Muslims."

Oh, sure. Totally. So very true. He's really good for Israel. He is the king of assorted bigots and programmatic anti-Semites, idolized by neo-Nazis and white supremacists, extolled by the Ku Klux Klan coterie, David Duke's all-time favorite . . . and of course, the absolute hero of your ordinary, garden variety, NRA-loving, all-American Jew haters.

When deciding which political candidate or leader to support, I would suggest the rule of thumb for a normal person generally should be: "Look at whom neo-Nazis are supporting—and support someone else."

My friends, are you out of your damn minds?

"No, Mikhail, it's you who's out of his mind. No matter what you say, he's good for Israel and tough on Muslims. He gives us a liberating opportunity to say openly and without shame things like: 'Because he's against Muslims.' He mainstreams and legitimizes our prejudices. That's very therapeutic. He's good for us."

February 24, 2018
Paul Manafort was indicted for "conspiracy against the United States" yesterday.

Let that sink in.

The chairman of the president's election campaign.

February 24, 2018
Someone asked me the other day, referring to the current state of affairs in the world, "So what do you think is going to happen in the end?"

One of two things are going to happen, I would suggest:

1. Nothing.
2. Something.

Of course, it could be argued that Nothing is but a variety of Something and Something frequently (and indeed, almost always) leads to Nothing—but either way, in the end, Everything (which, of course, is but another name for Nothing) is going to be fine. The world (if not us personally) has been here before.

February 24, 2018
On the frozen Neva. St. Petersburg, ca. 1910.

Trump? Putin? Internet? Soviet Union? Lenin, Stalin, Hitler? FOX News? Lady Gaga?

Life is life. Death is death. Without the former, there can be no latter, and vice versa. Or maybe not. It's a brutally cold day today, but what would you expect. Winter is winter. Russia is Russia. Life goes on. We've all been dead for a long time now. The ice on the Neva is strong.

February 24, 2018

Two-thirds of Americans view Trump—whose presidency by now looks like fifty shades of certain illegitimacy—in starkly negative terms. His rock-ribbed base of support is but a sliver of the country's electorate. In a democracy, the majority of people do not resist the tyranny of an illegitimate, antidemocratic president and the authoritarian-minded and largely ignorant minority of backwood bitter-enders backing him primarily (though not exclusively) for existential reasons, because of his having legitimized and validated them in their inner darkness. The majority of people in a democracy should not call themselves The Resistance. To the contrary: it is the antidemocratic and likely treasonous president and the distinct minority forming his cultist base of support that are the resistance (with a small 'r')—an ultimately doomed resistance, in this case, to the rule of democracy in America.

It is not the majority of American people resisting Trump—it is Trump resisting the majority of American people.

February 25, 2018

The general Russian attitude toward the West could be described partly as a combination of the following: contemptuous envy, spiteful deference, timid resentment, hostile self-abasement, friendly condescension, furious anger, faked indifference, avid curiosity, true soulfulness, and genuine warmth.

February 26, 2018

The official state motto of the Soviet Union was "Proletarians of all countries, unite!" *[Editor's note: From the original German of* The Communist Manifesto, *this was popularized in English as,* "Workers of the world, unite!"]

The unofficial state motto of Putin's Russia could well be, "Corrupt politicians of all countries, unite!"

Putin and his flunkies, such as former Ukrainian president Viktor Yanukovych, have been buying the corruptible, amoral Western statesmen for many years—frequently, employing as intermediaries the mercenary likes of entirely conscience-free Paul Manafort. Nothing personal—strictly business. If Western democracy stands in the way of the business interests of Putin's mafia, Western democracy must be destroyed.

In Trump, Putin has found his kindred spirit. It was love at first sight—on Trump's part. This forever will remain the greatest success of Russian intelligence: a former two-bit KGB functionary was able to install his personal asset in the White House.

February 26, 2018

This is the innate weakness of the US media: whatever the president says must be covered seriously, thoughtfully, as if his every word had some inherent value. But Trump is not a typical US president—and not a president at all, strictly speaking: he is a demagogic, fascist-minded impostor—and when that clown says something moronic, as in the latest case with this harebrained "arm the teachers" proposal, the only appropriate response on the responsible mainstream media's part should be open derision, mockery, or simply an out-of-hand dismissal.

February 27, 2018

Trumpland is not the "real" America. It is the worst of America: the past-bound America of racism and xenophobia, ignorance and small-mindedness, unbridled greed and cynicism.

Trumpland, desperate to keep itself from extinction by the advent of the future, has vomited up the grotesque figure of Trump, an ignorant sociopath and fascist demagogue, for the real America, the America of decent people, to awaken to the realization that democracy cannot be taken for granted—and, ultimately, to consign Trumpland to the ash heap of American history.

February 27, 2018

 Donald J. Trump
@realDonaldTrump

WITCH HUNT!

7:49 AM – 27 Feb 2018

Witches hunted down, so far: Papadopoulos, Flynn, Manafort, Gates, thirteen Russian trolls, Putin's personal chef-cum-dirty billionaire, and some sleazy dude from California.

Witches in waiting: a baker's dozen thereof, headed up by the madly panicked author of this insane tweet.

February 28, 2018

In response to a NYTimes.com headline, "Anti-Semitic Incidents Surged 57 Percent in 2017, Report Finds":

This undoubtedly is a direct consequence of the Trump presidency. White supremacists, neo-Nazis, and just your ordinary, garden-variety anti-Semites all across America view Trump as their unequivocal ally, someone who pointedly would not disavow their support of him, and who winks at them with clear approval and praises the unnamed many of them as "fine people." They salute him, fascist-style, shout "Heil Trump!"—and they believe they've been given the green light to be perfectly open about their deep loathing of Jews.

Last night I was "unfriended" on Facebook by a fellow former Soviet Jew—a reasonably smart man, a talented and accomplished musician—who took offence at my mocking the demonstrably vapid and pitifully opportunistic Jared Kushner as potential Middle East peacemaker. I have zero objections, to put it gently, to having a Trump supporter remove himself/ herself from the ranks of my "friends" or followers—but I continue to be saddened by the degree of delusion that has taken root in the minds of otherwise decent and none-too-stupid Soviet/Russian Jewish immigrants in the US.

I can hardly think of anything more obscene than a Jew supporting Trump, no matter how strongly they believe that clown might be "good for Israel." (Jared Kushner, a slumlord

and dim-witted scion of a failing New York real-estate family—
in the capacity of a Middle East peacemaker and de facto
secretary of state: that's how great for Israel Trump is.) Doubly
shameful is infatuation with Trump on the part of former
Soviet Jews who, en masse, have had personal experiences
of dealing with direct manifestations of anti-Semitism, both
institutional and grass-root level, in the old country.

But oh well. There is no point addressing them now.
They've been lost to the voice of reason, for the time being,
having allowed the worst of their instincts to take over their
hearts and minds.

Difficult and unpleasant will be their eventual awakening.

Mikhail Iossel
March 2018

March 1, 2018

After almost thirty years of trial and (mostly) error, the Russian people have decided they would like to be Soviet people again.

March 1, 2018

In his message to the so-called Federal Assembly earlier today, Putin boasted about a new secret nuclear weapon capable of penetrating any and all US anti-missile defenses, and effectively threatened the West with total destruction, unless. . . .

Unless what, though? What is Russia—read: Putin— purporting to defend so strenuously, with such suicidal self-abandon? Unlike the late Soviet Union, with its indigestible ludicrous abstract hodgepodge called Marxism-Leninism that hardly anyone in the country believed in, Russia does not have a governing ideology, other than one of brute strength, triumphant cynicism, and shameless corruption. What is Putin talking about when he talks about defending Russia's national interests?

He is talking about the interests of the oil-and-gas mafia corporation called Russia, of which he is the CEO/ Don Vito Corleone. He insists on Russia's right to be a country with medieval social values and a total contempt for human rights. He insists on his and his corporation's right to continue plundering Russia's wealth and corrupting and subverting Western democracy for the said purpose of their unchecked self-enrichment. He essentially says to the West: stop meddling with our business affairs as we re-annex former Soviet countries' territory, bribe Western politicians, and install the kind of president who shares our antidemocratic values in America. If you don't, we . . . we'll destroy you, with our new wonder-missile, even at the cost of certain death for ourselves. I am crazier than you, as young hoodlums used to say to their opponent before a fight in the dangerous cavernous interior courtyards of midtown Leningrad circa his unlovely childhood.

OK, well. . . . Let's see. Putin is a sixty-five-year-old man who likes luxury, misses no opportunity to take his shirt off in front of the camera, and has a face repeatedly pumped with Botox. He is just as insanely vain as Trump is—only in a smarter, more covert, quiet, KGB-like way. People of that sort are not given to suicidal behavior. Putin would like to live forever: his emissaries from among the inner circle of his favorite oligarchs reportedly have been quietly traveling the world in search of an elixir of eternal youth, a recipe for immortality, for years now. If there is one thing Putin is not it is crazy.

But he is greedy—insanely so. And ambitious. And bored. And forever tolerated, if tepidly so, by the largely apathetic and increasingly impoverished and ever-more "Sovietized" populace of his giant land. And now he also has a useless orange stooge sitting like a blob in the White House, unable to lift the economic sanctions on his, Putin's, close friends. He needs to occupy and entertain himself somehow. . . .

And so he goes and gives a belligerent speech to his pretend Federal Assembly—an obsequious claque of yes-people—in which he brags, Kim Jong-un–style, about the super-powerful nuclear weapon in his possession, capable of destroying the West . . . the West, where most of his pocket oligarchs and other members of his mafia corporation own luxurious properties and educate their children and intend on living out the remainder of their useless lives.

March 1, 2018

Putin has turned himself into another Kim Jong-un, only one who doesn't really mean it. He just wants to be feared and loathed even more than he is now. Is that so wrong?

Which makes Trump a confused orange-haired clown in the pocket of a pretend Kim Jong-un.

Now might be a good time to check oneself into some remote monastery nestled in some less accessible corner of the Himalayas.

March 4, 2018

Let me restate a few simple truths, for clarity's sake:
- Russia is not a free country.
- Putin is not a democratically elected president. There are no democratic elections in Russia.
- Russia, overall, is an impoverished country, despite its vast size and immense mineral riches. Its population, en masse, is getting increasingly poorer by the year.
- The absolute majority of Russian journalists working in the US are not actual journalists: they are employees of the state, paid Kremlin propagandists.
- Putin is not an exceptionally bright man. He is a KGB-bred intellectual mediocrity, a narrow-minded tactician and lousy strategist. He also is a vile, vengeful sociopath full of unresolved adolescent complexes, firmly in the grip of raging megalomania and batting way above

his weight, as far as his military fiascos in Syria and the Ukraine and the general thrust of his wet, warlike dreams of world dominance are concerned.

- He does indeed have Trump by the balls, but the current spike of his helpless spite against America is the result of his dawning realization that having addlepated Trump by the balls is nowhere near tantamount to having America in his, Putin's, pocket.

March 4, 2018

In response to a CNN.com headline, "Trump tries self-deprecating humor at Gridiron dinner":

No, dear mainstream journalists laughing at this repugnant man's "self-deprecating" jokes at last night's "white-tie" event— it is not OK to treat Trump as if he were just an ordinary, normal, legitimately elected, and patriotically minded American commander in chief: he is a minority president elected due to a no-longer-defensible constitutional anachronism called the Electoral College and with massive help from an enemy power, he is a lifelong tax evader and crook and con artist and money launderer, and he is an enemy power's asset in the White House, a traitor, as well as a fascist-style authoritarian who ardently wishes he could put many of you "enemies of the people" in jail, and he is a self-admitted sex predator, and . . . the list goes on—and you, the media establishment figures, chuckling and laughing obsequiously at the jokes his flunkies wrote for him, you are normalizing him and his so-called presidency, you are shirking your responsibility to serve the public good, you're covering yourself with shame, and this behavior of yours is one of the prominent reasons why the majority of Americans believe the country's political system to be broken.

The similarity between Stormy Daniels and Vladimir Putin is that they both have *kompromat* of graphic sexual nature on the 45th president of the United States.

However, Stormy Daniels never attempted to rig the US presidential elections. Stormy Daniels never annexed the Crimean Peninsula. Stormy Daniels never instigated a "hybrid" war in Ukraine. Stormy Daniels never downed any passenger planes or ordered the lengthy imprisonment or outright murder of independent journalists or opposition politicians. Stormy Daniels never sent troops to Syria, just in order to spite the United States and the rest of the West there. Stormy Daniels never financed any profascist political parties in Europe. Stormy Daniels never vetoed Mitt Romney's candidacy as would-be secretary of state, to insist successfully instead on appointing a Stormy Daniels–friendly oilman from Texas.

The personal lawyer of the 45th president of the United States paid Stormy Daniels $130,000 in hush money. Vladimir Putin, on the other hand, got a free gift of the White House from the 45th president of the United States.

March 10, 2018

Putin's message to the West: I'll be poisoning people with super-deadly nerve toxins indiscriminately in the middle of your cities, I'll be scaring the bejesus out of you with my crazy talk about some undetectable and unstoppable nuclear missiles with feathered tails I supposedly have at my disposal and aimed at you at all times, I'll be telling your journalists about my total preparedness to destroy the whole planet were the evil West to provoke me into believing I was about to be attacked because the world in which there'd be no Russia would have no reason to exist, I'll be meddling with much more than just your elections, I'll be messing with your electrical grid and other such essential infrastructure, I'll be doing this and I'll be doing that—look, lift those damn economic sanctions on me and I'll become the most peaceful and lovable person you'd ever meet. I've got nothing to lose, because I know you know I'm bluffing and lying like a dog about everything, and I know I am going to end badly, just like every other two-bit dictator that attempted to blackmail you before I did . . . but—this is stronger than me and I can't help it, because I also am a sociopath and malignant narcissist, just like my poor puppet Trump, only a marginally smarter and less flashy one. Character is destiny, and so is self-induced insanity.

March 10, 2018

In response to a JPost.com (Jerusalem Post) *headline, "Putin: Jews might have been behind U.S. election interference":*

It was inevitable, Trumpland: your president's master, Russia's Al Capone, was bound to take a hard anti-Semitic tack in his insane crusade against the accursed decadent West with its modern, nonmedieval values. This is Russia, baby, after all. Many, if not most, of your citizens, Trumpland, will rejoice at the news: rank anti-Semites, along with other assorted racists and bigots of every stripe, constitute the unyielding, flinty core of Trump's support. Where would he be today without the anti-Semites, racists, and other such super-low-information voters?

It was Jews, then, Trumpland, who had interfered with the US presidential election, for the purpose of . . . But wait: for the purpose of electing Trump? How is that possible? Them devious Jews! In order to hurt America—which is what the very purpose of their existence in the world is, and has been ever since they crucified Jesus—they gave America Trump? That just doesn't make . . .

. . . Oh, but no matter. No need to overthink things. All's well that ends well.

March 11, 2018
In my old Leningrad apartment on Frunze Street

March 11, 2018
"The great events of world history are, at bottom, profoundly unimportant. In the last analysis, the essential thing is the life of the individual. This alone makes history, here alone do the great transformations first take place, and the whole future, the whole history of the world, ultimately spring as a gigantic summation from these hidden sources in individuals .In our most private and most subjective lives, we are not only the passive witnesses of our age, and its sufferers, but also its makers. We make our own epoch."

—Carl Jung

March 11, 2018
If somehow, miraculously (and God forbid that from happening) you were to be transported to the Moscow or Leningrad of my grandparents' youth, say—and, more specifically, to the short historical interval commonly known as the Big Terror years, 1937–39—you likely would find the surface of daily life there to be anything but terrifying, especially in spring or summertime. The streets would be crowded with energetic, businesslike-looking passersby and leisurely strollers in bright clothes of breathable fabrics, people would be smiling, buying ice-cream and thick-glass mugs of cold kvas from street vendors, cooing at their grandkids if old or flirting with each other and falling in

love in the case of those in the bloom of youth. People, in other words, would be going about the ordinary business of existing much in the same way we do today, with the only meaningful (if still purely insubstantial) difference between us and them being that they are all gone by now and we still happen to be around. Come postmidnight hour, however, inevitably, without fail, dozens of elongated hunchbacked black automobiles, the dreaded black ravens of the night, some with their lights turned off and some not, would come into undivided possession of the deserted, silent streets, growling along with a sense of terrible purpose and now and then swerving under an archway and into the interior courtyard of this or that apartment building; and coming to a shuddering halt there, in front of some unlucky stairway. The heavy black door of the darkened carriage would be pushed open from within, and three men would emerge into the hushed night air: two armed soldiers and their superior—a grotesquely self-important shortish character in a long black leather overcoat and wide-brimmed fedora hat (round steel-rimmed spectacles on the bridge of his nose were optional).

People inside the building, in the communal apartments up and down the staircase, would be watching with galloping hearts through the narrow conical cracks between the chintz curtains on their room windows and the edge of window frames, resigned to the helpless knowledge that the always hungry black raven, one out of dozens of its exact replicas tirelessly prowling the city in the dark, was about to claim the life of one of them tonight.

March 12, 2018

In response to British Prime Minister Theresa May's announcement that it is highly likely that Russia was behind the attempted assassination of a onetime Russian double agent and his daughter:

Trump on Theresa May's statement today: "Listen, maybe it was Russia. It also could've been China or some other country. Or it could've been some 400-pound guy sitting on a bed in New Jersey who spread poison gas in the UK. OK? The truth is, we'll never know for sure."

March 13, 2018
Theresa May: "Based on the positive identification of this chemical agent by world-leading experts at Porton Down, our knowledge that Russia has previously produced this agent and would still be capable of doing so, Russia's record of conducting state-sponsored assassinations, and our assessment that Russia views some defectors as legitimate targets for assassinations, the government has concluded that it is highly likely that Russia was responsible for the act against Sergei and Yulia Skripal."

The situation is as follows: Russia—and that, inevitably, means Putin—has committed a direct act of war against a NATO member country.

Is Putin prepared for all the potential consequences of such a breathtakingly brazen step?

I don't believe so.

March 13, 2018
The deadliest of nerve agents ever created by man bears the cheery, peppily optimistic name "Novichok"—rookie, greenhorn, newbie, in Russian. It is at least ten times more lethal than any other such infernal substance, and its formula is top secret, known only to its original synthesizers and their FSB minders.

Novichok. Another lovely Russian word for the West to remember now.

March 15, 2018

Why, people are wondering, did he do it? Why did he use the most lethal chemical weapon currently in existence, one bearing a mockingly cutesy Russian name and manufactured in Russia only, with such brazen openness on the territory of a large European country, a NATO member state, threatening the lives of thousands of people in a relatively provincial, small-size city, as if begging to be instantly identified as the perpetrator? What was the purpose behind it? To send some kind of sinister signal to the West, to the effect that he believes he can now do whatever he wants, wherever and whenever he feels like it, to those he considers to be his personal and the KGB/FSB's enemies? If so, that's just breathtakingly stupid: he can't in all seriousness hope to take on the entire Western world—Russia, after all, is an economically weak country with a large but generally substandard military force; plus, all the top members of so-called Russian "elite," the main beneficiaries of the mafia state called Russia, own luxurious properties and soccer and basketball and hockey teams and all that good stuff in the West, their children and grandchildren go to school and universities there, and thousands of them also reside permanently in London themselves, of all places. . . . What the hell was he thinking, then? Perhaps, you know, to scare the above-said Russian oligarchs in London and elsewhere abroad into returning to Russia with their money, to be on the safe side? If so, that would've been an entirely counterproductive and downright stupid way of trying to convince them, no? The whole thing is so dumb, so . . . irrational. Why on earth did he do it?

To that, I have a counterquestion: Why do fools fall in love? Or more pointedly still: Why are people the way they are? Why are there bad people in the world? Why is Trump a completely amoral conman and criminal, bigot and traitor?

Why did the snake from the only poem Trump has ever read—
the poem he was fond of bellowing out at every other one of
his Nuremberg rallies during the campaign and beyond—bite
the woman who saved it? Because it was a snake, that's why!
Because there were just as many good people in the old KGB,
Putin's spiritual . . . everything, than there must have been in
the Nazi Gestapo: that is to say, none. Because he is a lowlife
with his head full of Botox. Because he knows there is nothing
he could do at this point to change the civilized world's attitude
toward him, to be trusted again by any major Western leader
except his puppet Trump. Because he knows he looks strong
at home when he does this crazy stuff in the West and then
brazenly denies doing it, as if saying to the West and Western
journalists: "Yes, I know you know I'm lying—and so? So what?
What are you going to do about it? Roses are blue and violets
are red: you have any problem with that? My people like it when
I openly mock the West, via the likes of you, when I humiliate
you by making you look stupid and pathetic while trying to find
any kind of logic to my actions or truth to my words."

He did it because he did it.

March 15, 2018

"The first offensive use of a nerve agent in Europe since the
Second World War."

Wow, Putin. Impressive. You've come a long way, little
punk, from the dank interior courtyards of your miserable,
petty-crime-ridden midtown-Leningrad childhood.

March 16, 2018

It was suggested to me that I should write an optimistic, life-
affirming fairy tale, instead of vi . . . vituperating constantly
against the pretend president Trump.

Good idea!

Except I've never written fairy tales before in my life.

But OK. There's always a first for everything.

Well. . . . Let's see. . . .

Once upon a time, there lived an orange man with no redeeming qualities. He was a very bad man indeed, but lots of people liked him, because he was rich and had a TV show and no sense of shame whatsoever, and so they—those impossibly bright people—envied him and found his behavior refreshing and wanted to be like him.

Among the orange man's numerous and largely smarmy interests was staging international beauty contests, which he used as an opportunity to harass young women with impunity. One day he decided to bring one of his most incredible beauty contests to the giant faraway eastern land of No Holds Barred, ruled by evil potentate Vlad the Pale-Eyed Dead Fish. Once there, in that extraordinary land, our orange man, completely overwhelmed by its total no-holds-barred-ness, instantly lost the scant remainder of his presumptive marbles and threw himself with heedless abandon into a whirlwind of less-than-upright interactive pursuits.

Fast forward a bit. Awakening from uneasy dreams in his inexplicably damp triple-king-size ten-star hotel bed on the last morning of his stay there, in that wondrous, mind-bending land of the evil potentate Vlad Etcetera, that pallid underbelly of the enervated Western psyche, our orange man commenced the painstakingly slow and generally tortuous and extremely unattractive process of getting ready to present himself to the world and, already in the latter's final stages, discovered the mysterious disappearance of one of his shoes—a $75,000 custom-made Il Diavolo d'Oro loafer. One of his amazingly lovely and outstandingly fun-loving nighttime visitors must have made away with it, understandably viewing it as a priceless memento of their unorthodox encounter, he thought in not-unpleasant mild exasperation. He was about to call his trusted squire, Keith, long nondormant in the adjacent, austerely appointed squire's chamber, and order Keith to bring in another pair of shoes providentially packed for the trip, also incredibly expensive ones—when suddenly, mysteriously, and with a loud, crashing sound, as if obeying the brutal outward-vectored force of some invisible giant hand, the triskelioned window of his penthouse suite fairly flew open, and through the wind-filled aperture, in sailed, and subsequently landed on the tremendous ancient Persian carpet right by orange man's feet, a large, size 12 loafer of orange glass: the exact replica of the one that had gone missing, only . . . well, made of very classy, fantastic-looking orange glass.

Inside the orange glass loafer, the orange man found a neatly typewritten note: "Hello, my blueberry hill. I am glad you had a lot of thrill last night, as well as on many other nights and days here in my land of No Holds Barred. I want you to know that every second of this visit of yours, as well as every single moment of every one of your previous trips here, has been documented, on tons of videotapes. Lordy, do we have tapes. All kinds of incriminating materials. You also owe some dough to my guys, if I'm not mistaken, which I am not and never am. This means, my dear orange man, that you're mine now, all mine. You'll be my faithful servant from here on out, and I'll be the light of your life and, accordingly, the fire of your figurative loins. . . . Well, no, not that last part. Yuck. OK, then. Now you know where things stand. Breathe not a word about this to anyone, eat this note with your next Big Mac and chase it down with two Diet Cokes. Go back home and live your normal life there, for the present time: be famous for being famous, insult people for a living, cheat and con the hell out of them, launder our criminals' money—the works, the usual. We'll activate you when the time comes. You'll know. See you later, alligator. Hello, I love you, won't you tell me your name? . . . Sorry, never mind, that last line was from a different letter to a different person."

And so that's how it all transpired—at least in this, fairy-tale version of the events. The orange man went back home, to America, and resumed his normal life in New York—and then . . . We all know what happened then: we all started living happily ever after.

March 16, 2018

In one day, an obscene political travesty under the code name "presidential elections" will take place in Russia. It will have as much to do with democracy as I have with the Olympic-level biathlon. Congratulations to the overwhelming victor (85–89% of the vote), head of the world's largest mafia corporation, called "The State of Russia," former lowly KGB colonel (professional nickname: Pale Moth), Vladimir Putin.

March 17, 2018

I don't think Democratic Senators and members of Congress should be accepting Trump's invitations to the White House anymore. I don't think they should be shaking his hand—or at least, not before putting on rubber gloves or some other protective gear. Being in his presence is unhygienic. He is repugnant, and his condition is contagious. He should be ostracized completely, roundly boycotted. He is not a real, legitimate president, so having tea and bantering with him does not constitute actually "working with the president" on this or that item of the nation's agenda. The nation's agenda at this point consists of only one overriding plank: getting that rotten creep out of the White House, as soon as possible, along with all the rest of his crooked gang, and then fumigating and delousing the premises for a good long while, before the next president, a normal human being, can take up residence there and proceed to attempt healing the severely traumatized nation.

March 18, 2018
Remote historical connections:

If Boris Yeltsin, back in early '90s, had possessed the foresight or found the determination to drive a stake through the undead heart of the defeated, badly wounded, and temporarily incapacitated KGB, by declaring it a criminal organization (which it certainly was, and to no lesser degree than the Nazi Gestapo) and subjecting its past and present members to lustration (prohibition to occupy any government positions)—there would be no President Trump now.

March 18, 2018
When much-decorated, four-star Army generals, such as Barry McCaffrey, start saying on television repeatedly that they have come to the conclusion that the current US president is under the sway of America's arch-enemy, it may be high time for Republicans in Congress to come to their senses and revisit their notion of patriotism.

March 19, 2018
"It's not a question of pessimism or optimism. . . . It's just that ninety-nine out of a hundred people don't have any brains."

—to quote a Chekhov character

March 20, 2018

Make of it what you will, or nothing at all: this past Sunday, on the day of so-called presidential elections in Russia, one could see a kilometer-long line of Russian citizenship holders in front of the Russian Consulate in New York, up on East 96th Street. Periodically, in sporadic intervals, the various segments of that giant snake of human bodies erupted in powerfully discordant choral singing of the Russian national anthem. These, by overwhelming preponderance, were US citizens or permanent residents, denizens of Brooklyn and Queens, Staten Island and New Jersey, the island of Manhattan and Upstate New York, etc., waiting patiently for hours to cast their vote—again, by tremendous prevalence—for their beloved political leader and favorite autocrat, ruler of their confused, Soviet-bound minds, Vladimir Putin.

Back in November of 2016, those of them with the right to vote in US presidential elections also—likely, the large majority of them—almost certainly did so for (who else?) Donald Trump.

Oftentimes, people retire into insanity voluntarily, as though into a monastery . . . as Viktor Shklovsky wrote.

You, my friends, are pathetic.

March 23, 2018

If my grandparents, both long gone (he in 1974, she in 1981), were somehow able to see me now, from the boundless cosmic nowhere of their eternal nonexistence, as I am writing about them, in English—or rather, about a few minutes of one night of their life in the winter of 1939 in Leningrad—how might they react, what would they say?

Grandfather—an old Bolshevik, dedicated to the Party cause until the end—would be saddened and confused (I almost wrote: "heartbroken" . . . But no). "Why in America?" he would want to know. "Well, Canada, America, same difference. Why in the capitalist world? And why in English? How is that even possible? Why did you abandon our common ideals, your Motherland and your mother tongue? What happened to you?"

And Grandmother, peering into my eyes intently, would say, in a barely audible voice: "Is that really you, my little boy? It can't be."

March 25, 2018

Everyone, or almost everyone, born and raised into adulthood in a place of tyranny, such as the old Soviet Union, carries forever within himself or herself the cautious, self-aware heart of someone capaple of instantly adjusting again to a life in a condition of nonfreedom. Those who naturally tend to take liberty for granted, as the majority of Americans do (because why wouldn't they?), may not know or ever want to believe it, but they also, en masse, possess that ultimate survivor's capacity for learning, one way or another, to exist under a dictatorship. That final point of bare survival in a silent state of internal emigration, the point of the lowest human denominator, is an ugly, lonesome, soul-crushing spot to be. It is therefore (and this is not saying anything new, of course) more important than words could tell for everyone with an ounce of self-respect to resist to the full extent of one's moral strength the un-American wannabe despot in the White House, with his constant, relentless encroachments upon the essential territory of freedom and democracy; with his ceaseless concerted effort to appeal to the basest angels of human nature in order to turn us all into the worst versions of ourselves.

March 26, 2018

In response to a shopping mall fire in Russia that claimed the lives of more than fifty people, many of them children:

Unimaginable. Those kids in Kemerovo, dying in the fire in a locked-up movie theater at the shopping mall. Their trying to call or send one last message to their parents. Their parents. How are they going to keep on living now? Unimaginable. And yes, lots of people are directly and indirectly responsible for those kids' terrible death—from the megathief Putin himself down to the regional Kemerovo head of the Ministry of Emergency Situations driving around in a Toyota Land Cruiser that costs more than twice his annual salary and all the way down to that last security person at that movie theater whose idea it was to lock up the fire exits in there, lest other kids, ones without tickets, try to sneak in and watch those cartoons for free. But right now, this is not about them. It's about those dead kids. And about those dead kids' parents, whose lives for the rest of their lives I cannot imagine. Unimaginable. . . . And it is about the giant and largely indifferent country, too, spread out over eleven time zones, where most of the one hundred and forty million people of its populace keep going about the routine business of daily living as if nothing much happened: watching crime serials and sports events on TV, going to see movies, drinking, eating, sleeping, feeling angry at the pernicious West. . . . Unimaginable.

March 30, 2018

Russia is closing down the US Consulate General in St. Petersburg. Another old boxful of Leningrad-bound memories gets an iron lid put on it. At some future point, I would hope to reopen it and sift carefully through its contents.

The American Consulate, the only tiny purchase of US territory on the swampy soil of mad Tsar Peter's dream city, was, for the young people of the eighties like myself—the deliberate misfits voluntarily thrown out of the dull round of mainstream middle-class Soviet existence—the magnetic place of wonder and awe, nerve-tingling happy risk-taking, and impossible international imaginings. Once inside, having passed through the gloomy inspection of your official cultural-attaché's gold-embossed invite by two burly KGB officers in militia uniforms, you instantly ceased being who you were in reality—a virtual Soviet nobody with hopeless literary or some other artistic ambitions from the gray sameness of dolorous Leningrad outskirts, a security guard in the Roller-Coaster Segment at the Amusement Sector of the city's Central Park of Culture and Leisure or a night-shift boiler-room operator, etc.— and you became a free citizen of the world, a legend in your own mind, suave and sophisticated, a sampler of fine and oddly potent American drinks and highbrow Hollywood cinema, overwhelming in scope and sound, if largely incomprehensible because all the talk there was in English. (But the moment you got out of the consulate, emerging back into the Neva-silvered day, re-entering the reality of the world you lived in, all bets were off: you could potentially get picked up for public inebriation—a uniquely grave offence, to be sure, in a giant city overflowing with zonked-out zombies—by irate KGB plainclothesmen, or you could get bopped on the head a few times later in the evening, right in front of your apartment building, say, courtesy of the same omnipotent three-letter organization, just for good measure, sans any direct intent on the goons' part to maim or kill you, but merely in order to bring you back to your senses and remind you, ever so gently, of the actual reality of the world you lived in; just to let you know, in other words, or to remind you, rather, that they could do anything they damn well wished to you at any moment, and that you continued to lead your sorry life strictly on the sufferance of their benevolence. "Next time we'll fucking kill you," one of them could, and would, say to you in the end, with a good-natured chuckle over his massive shoulder.

Well, but in fairness, you knew, every time, going in, what the lay of the land was, so to speak; so it was all par for the course, by and large; no major complaints.

Whiskey and gin, and Hollywood movies, and long conversations about not much in halting English, and visits with cultural attachés in their spacious apartments with carpeted floors and giant foreign TV sets and all manner of foreign-made whatchamacallits everywhere. All that—and, of course, a whole lot more.

For a long while, from 1982 and on, up until the Soviet Union's postperestroika demise, the dinky basement headquarters of the Soviet Union's first official club of "unofficial," underground writers—a separate long story unto itself, also yet to be told—was located just a few doors down from the consulate on the upscale, posh Petra Lavrova (now Furshtatskaya) Street: barely thirty seconds' worth of a slow, uncertain walk away—and worlds apart, as the old saying has it. Those two nearly adjacent buildings could well be situated on two different planets: so close and yet so far indeed—or, if one prefers Metallica to Elvis, so close no matter how far. But far, very far. The frequently blitzed Leningrad samizdatchiks, ambling in and staggering out of the club's scruffy doors, couldn't help grazing the consulate's stately edifice on their immediate left or right with their blurry gazes, thus unwittingly generating multiple mini–force fields of vague, diffuse, yet still intense longing for another, different, cleaner, better life, for another world, another . . . everything.

Not one of them, us, back at the time, could remotely foresee that in a matter of a few seconds on history's invisible stopwatch, the seemingly eternal Soviet Union, ostensibly indestructible in its fearsome, ironclad ugliness, would collapse virtually overnight, with terrible and irreversible finality, and everything around us would change forever. We never saw it coming. But that's exactly what happened. The mighty USSR ceased to be, and now it's nothing but memory of its own memory, the lifeless Soviet Atlantis lounging on the silty bottom of the ocean of time. Sic transit just about everything. Every adult in our childhood was right: life does pass very quickly. Most of those among us who used to spend some memorable moments of their youth within the walls or in the company of the real live American people of the US Consulate General in Leningrad are either gone or far away by now, waxing nostalgic and dealing the best way they can with the stealthy onslaught of old age.

And now the old consulate, too, is gone.

 **Mikhail Iossel**
April 2018

(Sunday) April 1, 2018
First thing this morning Trump tweets: HAPPY EASTER!

Two hours later he tweets: NEED WALL! and NO MORE DACA DEAL!

That's the Easter spirit, Trumpland! Your orange Duce doesn't disappoint! How many rabbits did his motorcade run over on his way to church this morning?

Did Trump go to church today?

[Editor's note: In reply, one of Iossel's Facebook friends shared a picture of the president and two women, including Melania Trump, eyes concealed behind her sunglasses, going to church, and commented, "Yes to church. The happy family."]

April 3, 2018
"Nobody has been tougher on Russia than I have. I know you are nodding yes because everyone agrees." —**Donald Trump**

"Nobody has been tougher on newborn kittens than I have. I know you are nodding yes because you're afraid I'll come over and punch you in the nose." —**Mahatma Gandhi**

April 4, 2018

It is much easier to become one's worst self than one's better one, just as it takes infinitely less effort to be falling into a bottomless abyss than climbing up a never-ending steep slope. What a relief, what powerful release of energy one experiences stepping into that void, after having been granted permission by the supreme ruler to cast aside such ephemeral encumbrances as shame, basic morality, a sense of decency and the ability to feel compassion for others. All it takes is that one first, initial step.

April 6, 2018

Breathtakingly ugly remarks by Trump today, even by his own abysmal standards of a sewer rat: crazed immigrant rapists, millions of illegal voters in California—every word dripping with petty fear and cruelty, the absolute nadir of humanity. This is not surprising, of course—it's just routinely and nauseatingly disgusting.

And I am thinking now of a few smart and well-educated and otherwise decent people I know who continue to support him, even now, for reasons I don't want to speculate about. I don't speak to those people anymore, because there would be no context now for any such putative conversations between us, but I still would have liked to continue thinking of them as generally well-meaning and morally undamaged humans. I really would. But I no longer can. It saddens me, but there is just no way, at this point. One cannot be a good or even half-decent person and continue to support . . . all this ceaseless vileness and sheer repugnancy, no matter how deeply and sincerely one may love and appreciate music/poetry/visual arts/ballet/opera/photography/fine cuisine/wild nature/dogs/cats . . . and every other wonderful thing of this world. None of that uplifting and soul-ennobling stuff matters a whit in the face of the pure infernal darkness you've allowed yourself to be swallowed by, my good people.

My good people, you no longer are good. You are bad people now, at least in my book. You've been changed beyond recognition. I will never again be able to think of you as your former, pre-Trump selves. This may not be, and probably is not, any cause for you to feel even mildly upset—but it does sadden me mightily. Voting for that man may have been a mistake on one's part, if a really terrible one; but continuing to support him now is unforgivable.

April 8, 2018

Bashar al-Assad has killed scores more innocent people, lots of children among them, with poison gas tonight. He likes doing that: killing children in the most cruel, excruciatingly painful way imaginable. And why wouldn't he continue to keep at it, time after time? It works, and it works fast, and it makes him happy. His life is good: he has a loving wife and beautiful children of his own, and he has all the riches of his land at his disposal. He also has a big, strong friend named Vladimir, the world's most corrupt and dangerous man, who protects him from any and all of his enemies, both those right in his back yard and oceans away. Bashar al-Assad is one lucky monster.

April 8, 2018

Trump's tweets are the equivalent of his yelling at his TV. Granted, millions more people around the world hear his cranky outbursts than tends to be the case with the verbal eruptions of most other crotchety, lonely, and unhappy men in their seventies having no one but their idiot boxes to converse with—but still, the general mode of his relationship with the world is the same.

Which is pathetic, considering that he, at least nominally, is the world's most powerful man, having uniquely limitless access to more supersensitive information about every single corner of the world, no matter how tiny, than any other person alive. It is truly sad, indeed, yet also dangerous in the extreme, that the world's nominally most powerful and consequential and, at least in theory, most exhaustively informed man behaves like a hard-drinking retiree whose only source of information about the world is FOX News. There is only one conclusion to be drawn from this: he never wanted to be president, because he knew he was almost grotesquely incapable of being one. But Trumpland wanted him, or someone like him, so—what could he do? He is president in name and official status only—but in actual reality, he is a lonesome and confused seventy-two year-old man who has no one to talk to, in part because nobody likes him for his relentless meanness, and who as a result is reduced to screaming, in rage and frustration, at his TV screen in his barren room in an old, half-abandoned apartment building in a bad part of town.

April 15, 2018
When this obscene period in American presidential history finally draws to an ignominious end, many people would find themselves too exhausted, too mentally drained and emotionally hollowed out to rejoice, my guess would be. Some would immediately fall asleep for a few days. Awakening from a prolonged nightmare can be a difficult process.

April 17, 2018
Trump, there will be no Trump Towers in Moscow—much less in St. Petersburg. Just give it up. Live with it.

Putin will do nothing to help you avoid impeachment, trial, and subsequent prison time. Accept that. Internalize this thought. Resign yourself to it.

Do resign, actually. Just leave. Do something praiseworthy, for once in your life. What's the point of waiting? You are beyond the point of no return. Michael Cohen, Stormy Daniels, Robert Mueller are going to bury you, separately and jointly— and your entire long life, in which there has not been a single day without some kind of sleazy criminal activity, will indict you unto eternity.

And one more thing about Putin: you've dealt extensively for decades with mafia people, mob bosses, and other such excellent individuals: did they at any point strike you as being appreciative of your or others' gestures of supposed goodwill? What do they respect more: strength or weakness?

Do you want to know what Putin thinks of you? He finds you pathetic.

April 19, 2018

This is what, more likely than not, is going to happen in Russia in the foreseeable future:

The country, as per Putin's ominous recent suggestion, will be cut off from Facebook; the next step will have the "Russian" Internet, known as Runet, disconnected from the outside world. As for the rest—unfortunately, Vladimir Sorokin's *The Day of the Oprichnik* may well prove to be a prophetic novel. Russia will become one giant "estrangement zone," to use the Chernobyl terminology. Putin and his mafia corporation, quite simply, could not survive under any other conditions.

People—in the main, the young and ambitious ones— will still be allowed to emigrate from the closed-off country, however: a safety valve for the regime.

April 19, 2018

Trump talking to his own reflection in the mirror:

No collusion!

No collusion.

No collusion, no?

Collusion? No.

Collusion, no collusion.

No collusion. No.

Collusion!

No collusion.

No!!

Collusion!!?

No!

Collusion. . . . No . . . Collusion. . . . No . . . Collusion. . . .

No, Collusion! No!

Collusion. . . . Collu . . .

Sionno.

Col?

Lusionnoco.

Llusi?

Onnoc.

Ollus!

Ion. . . .

No.

April 21, 2018

In his latest tweets, Trump is hysterical with fear. He is downright panicked, as he realizes that his entire long life of unremitting criminality, relentless sleaziness, and ceaseless ugliness—a total and complete putrid waste of a biological existence—has all but caught up with him and is about to come crashing down on his indescribable head. When he is trying to convince himself, in his late-night and predawn tweets, that his "fixer" Michael "Ray

Donovan" Cohen is not going to flip on him, he effectively admits himself to being guilty as sin.

But to hell with Trump. His unraveling is now unstoppable. Garbage in, garbage out. He'll be forgiven when he is forgotten, to paraphrase one of Beckett's protagonists.

Except that he won't be forgotten, unfortunately. We will not be able to unremember this grotesquely vile and unspeakably vulgar stretch of America's modern history. We will always know that at one point in the first half of this century, the White House, the heart of American democracy, was occupied by a thoroughly rotten chunk of human protoplasm—one of the very worst individuals anyone would ever meet along life's sinuous sylvan path.

Nor will we be able to regain our fondness and respect for those among our acquaintances and (thankfully, less frequently) friends who, much to our repulsed dismay, had fallen for this man and continued to stick with him throughout—for any of the variety of equally unsavory reasons: because he liberated their inner racist, because his vulgarity thrilled them secretly with its heedless transcendence of any and all societal norms of decency, because they could relate to his cruelty, because he told them all but openly that it was OK to be a xenophobe, anti-Semite, Islamophobe, fascist, sexual predator, and whatever else no one in any position of authority had ever told them before it was OK and not in the least shameful to be; because he promised them tax cuts and that was all they could care about; because he was rich and famous and therefore quite likely indeed to be eager to "drain the swamp," because they wanted to send a signal to the "elites" and to shake things up but good in Washington, just for the fun of it, because they hated Hillary so much they would support a rank racist and lifelong crook and someone clearly in Putin's pocket and in the pocket of Russian mafia over her. . . .

Lots of reasons spoken and, more frequently, unworded.

At no point in an imminent posttraumatic post-Trump future am I going to ask people I once, on the whole, considered decent and good, as to why they had allowed themselves—and willingly and happily so, by all indications—to sink to the very bottom of indecency; what was the exact nature of that black hole of inhumanity deep within them that Trump, that walking aggregator of human darkness, had been able to access. There would be no reason for me to do that, for I would be no more interested in asking that question than they—in answering it. Dark and dirty is the water under the broken old footbridge.

April 23, 2018
In response to a WashingtonPost.com article, "Frustrated at visa holdup, Russians give up on American vacations":

Russians, in their majority, hate America—a pitiful sublimation of envy—and dream of American vacations.

Russians loathe the West, because Putin told them it was loathsome and because they resent it that the rest of the world no longer is afraid of their country (they tend to equate fear with respect), but in every large Western city one sees large flocks of Russian tourists.

Russians, it's not the West's fault that much of the world currently views you with suspicion and distaste. You've stuck with your putrid Putin for too long, and Putin has let you down big time, turning all of you, by extension, into international pariahs.

Start with yourself if you want to improve your image abroad. Take the first baby step in that direction. Stand in front of the mirror and say, loudly and clearly, in two languages: "Krym ne nash. Crimea is not ours."

April 25, 2018

A "very open and very honorable" man, said Trump of North Korea's Kim Jong-un yesterday, adding that he, Trump, hoped the two of them could "do something very special" together.

That's just very beautiful. Trump is such a lovely humanitarian. A regular Mahatma Gandhi.

In the same vein: Hitler was a very open and very honorable man. Had Hitler been alive today, he and Trump most certainly would do something very special together.

Stalin, too, was a very open and very, very honorable man. Had Stalin also been alive today, he and Trump would do something very, very, very special together.

Putin, of course, is a very open and very honorable man. Extremely open and, like, vertiginously honorable. Luckily for Trump, Putin is still very much around, so there's no doubt Putin, having already done something very special to Trump, will continue doing something very, very special special to him, and to all the rest of Americans.

April 29, 2018

When the enemy of democracy occupying the White House calls you, American journalists, "enemies of the people," "sick people," "fake news," and "the most dishonest people in the world"—that man is your enemy, too, rather than "Mr. President," and you should get yourself some dignity and start treating him and his flunkies accordingly, even at your posh annual black-tie event celebrating the fake spirit of nonpartisan bonhomie and camaraderie.

Mikhail Iossel
May 2018

May 1, 2018

In response to a news report that White House chief of staff John Kelly has called Trump an "idiot" behind his back "multiple times":

Is this really any kind of breaking news? I mean, seriously. How could he NOT have called Trump "an idiot" multiple times, if always behind the latter's back? That's just a statement of fact, akin to asserting that cats like to sleep and eat a lot.

Yes, brave general, your boss is an idiot, and you are an idiot's flunky and enabler. That's how you are going to be remembered in posterity, too—as a vile idiot's cowardly and ignoble flunky and enabler.

May 1, 2018

There is a slangish word in Russian: *bespredel'shchik*—literally, someone who knows no limits to his behavior, willing to engage in acts of *bespredel,* or the kind of conduct trespassing any conceivable moral or ethical boundaries. *Bespredsl'shchik* is a savage, fiendishly pathological man unbound, unfettered, unconstrained by any norms of humanity, bereft of any notions of decency or compassion, wholly unencumbered by any considerations of the possibly catastrophic consequences of his actions, and entirely, vertiginously shameless and completely unembarrassable.

That's been Trump's shtick all along: he is never ashamed of anything he does or says, and he is congenitally incapable of ever feeling embarrassed. In the game of "Who Will Feel the Pangs of Conscience Last," he would always be the winner, the last man standing. That's how he's been going through life so far: repeatedly flooding the zone of people's ability to cope with the sheer shamelessness of his outlandish persona, lying nonstop and so breathtakingly and with such natural ease that people just had a hard time believing someone might actually be capable of being so brazenly, shamelessly unbelievable.

But now the ultimate American *bespredel'shchik* has come to the end of that lifelong shameless, lying road of his: time to start answering some serious, specific questions posed to him by his nemesis, Robert Mueller, who already, along with most Americans, knows all the answers.

May 2, 2018

On this day several decades ago, at the conclusion of our high school contingent's nationwide celebratory four-hour May 1 walk across Leningrad—from our microdistrict on city's southwestern edge to Palace Square—I inconspicuously tossed, or let slide as though by accident into the Neva the large plywood stick–mounted portrait of abstemious-visaged, constipated-looking, Savonarola-esque Arvid Yanovich Pelshe, the oldest Politburo member, that decidedly uncool and ridicule-inviting load I'd been stuck with for most of the distance, since our first brief pitstop for some camouflaged booze and piroshki, in the immediate vicinity of our local Park of Victory metro station. It was there that it had found me, through my own lack of due vigilance and courtesy of our semideranged, war-damaged school director (nickname: "Tank Driver"), who had snuck up on me from behind on cat's feet with Pelshe in his paws.

"Oops, fuck, how very unfortunate," I said under my breath, sort of accidentally letting go of goddamned Pelshe over the roiling silvery water. Quickly and surreptitiously I looked about to make sure no one had seen me committing, ever so unaccountably and unexpectedly to myself, this serious and likely felonious and future-obliterating act of adolescent, anti-Soviet vandalism. Luckily no one had, it seemed, even though the area, obviously, was teeming with KGB plainclothesmen and their countless voluntary assistants—enthusiasts of ratting random people out and ruining the lives of total strangers.

That's all I have to say at the moment about this day worlds away and a lifetime ago.

May 7, 2018

Putin is now the longest-serving Russian ruler since Stalin. Serving no one but himself and his mob underlings.

On the eve of his fourth presidential inauguration, his special-police-force goons (OMON, popularly referred to as "cosmonauts," on account of their fearsome, space suit–style uniforms) and medieval-minded make-believe "cossacks" brutally, with unbridled cruelty, suppressed peaceful anti-Putin rallies in Moscow, St. Petersburg, and dozens of other cities across the country. They aimed to maim, to damage, to hurt. Their victims overwhelmingly were very young people—teens, children born in the twenty-first century who have never known any other motherland but the increasingly unfree, totalitarian, cynical, corrupt, isolationist, and virulently anti-Western Putin's Russia.

I lived "under Brezhnev" for eighteen years—the full length of his stagnant stint in the Kremlin. It felt like a lifetime—and it was.

Brezhnev was a narrow-minded, thoroughly ignorant, and none-too-bright Party apparatchik, steeped to the unibrow in the insanely inhumane and just plain insane, degenerate ideological dogma. But I doubt he would've personally sanctioned the mass beatings of children. Whatever he was, he was not a lowlife. Putin is a lowlife.

May 8, 2018

Trump is about to scrap the Iran nuclear deal.

Why?

There are a number of reasons, of which by far the most significant one is that he is a moron and a vile, ignorant buffoon, for whom keeping his hard-core base of largely ignorant and virulently xenophobic folks is infinitely more important than considering the repercussions of his rash and stupid actions for domestic and international security.

May 9, 2018

"Curiosity, I'm convinced, IS intelligence," the great Guy Davenport, my favorite, once wrote.

That observation is absolutely correct, in my modest personal experience: intelligent people, who already know much, always want to know more. Dull people generally are content with what they already know, which tends to be not a whole lot. When I first came to the US, I was struck initially by this clear discrepancy between the two kinds of Americans: those who had questions for me about life in the Soviet Union and all things "Russian"—and those who generally possessed no such curiosity. The first kind, by and large, already was familiar with Soviet politics or Russian literature, etc.—the second encouraged me good-naturedly not to be afraid to step into an elevator or use other such unfamiliar futuristic forms of advanced Western technology, derived a sizeable amount of their information about the daily life of Soviet citizens from the film *Moscow on the Hudson,* and periodically addressed me with a Boris-and-Natasha or Yakov Smirnoff accent, speaking very loudly and slowly, the way one talks to toddlers or mischievous dogs. St. Petersburg, Florida, was of greater interest to them than the St. Petersburg on the Neva, especially in wintertime (and I could understand them on that count). They didn't aim to upset or offend me, needless to say—on the contrary, they wanted to be helpful and supportive; and it is true that my comprehension of spoken English at the time left quite a lot to be desired. They were good, kind people—just not very curious ones.

But that was a long time ago. Lots of fast and slow water under all the bridges of the world.

May 11, 2018

Trump last night, greeting North Korean prisoners: "I want to thank Kim Jong-un, who really was excellent to these three incredible people."

And to the journalists: "So I want to thank you all. It's very early in the morning. Uh, I think you probably broke the all-time in history television rating for three o'clock in the morning. That I would say."

He is, without a doubt, the stupidest and shallowest president in modern American history. That I would say. It would be great to have a nonmoron in the White House again—that would be wonderfully comforting.

One doesn't even have to put him next to Barack Obama—that would be comparing apples and clumps of dirt. But just anyone who is not a screaming goddamn moron.

May 12, 2018

You start writing in a foreign language in order to become a foreigner to your own past, so as to see it more clearly and understand it better by having fewer words to account for it.

May 16, 2018

I like it when people on Facebook are calling for a more "polite, civilized debate" about the current political situation in the US, the way "we used to have." I agree. That would be great. My only question is: when? When exactly was it, that blessed time of civilized, polite political debate in America? Before the Civil War? During it? Immediately thereafter? Or perhaps during the Jim Crow era? Or maybe the Great Depression, was it?

The World War II years—that probably was the heyday of civilized political discourse. And also during and right after the annihilation of Hiroshima and Nagasaki. And the fifties, too, obviously. McCarthy, the Red Scare, Hollywood blacklists, the Rosenbergs, the nuclear arms race, nuclear fallout shelters— how idyllic; no major angry public disagreements there. Mayberry time, Father knows best!

The sixties also were quite serene, on every count, and the public political debate during that particular decade was soothingly civilized. JFK, RFK, MLK, Malcolm X. Also, Kent State. Stonewall riots. Also, Vietnam—that one definitely went over pretty smoothly, without any overtly and inappropriately rude public disagreements. What was there even to argue about?

And the seventies. Watergate. The energy crisis, "Carter, Kiss My Gas." Peaceful, lovely times.

The eighties, under Reagan: a highly harmonious span of time, too, from the perspective of public debate. AIDS. The Iran-Contra affair. Star Wars. The proxy war with the Soviets in Afghanistan. The EPA, the savings and loans crisis, the rigging of housing development grants, lobbying scandals—and that's just scratching the surface. As for the nineties. . . .

In the nineties, public political discourse was very polite indeed. Almost scarily so. No one ever called Bill Clinton any bad names. No one ever tried to impeach him over lying about an affair with an intern. Everyone was cool with that. He was universally beloved. The same, of course, goes for George W. Bush, the renowned public intellectual, with his hanging chads in Florida, his Iraq war, and—oh, where does one even begin? You name it.

Obama, also—well, Obama never provoked any strong negative feelings in America. He never was accused of having been born in Africa; of being a Muslim, a communist, an America-hater, an anti-Christ. He never was called a whole gamut of ugly racist names. Even when some of this did happen, it was all done in a polite and pretty civilized manner, and it never happened to begin with.

So then, why now, all of a sudden, are people saying harsh, rude, bad things about Trump, as well as, by extension, not infrequently, about people who support him no matter what? Why are his detractors and vilifiers—the majority of the country—calling him a racist, a conman, an infinitely immoral and corrupt grifter, a money launderer for the Russians, and generally, on balance, a fairly unique man without a single discernible redeeming quality? That just boggles the mind—such incivility.

I must admit, I happen to believe he is the human equivalent of a sewer rat. I do. That's rude of me, I know, but that's what I believe, and for the time being there still is such a quaint thing as freedom of speech in America.

People didn't have social networks before, and that's why everyone was so very polite and civilized back in the olden days. Facebook, Twitter—those vast amplifiers and multiplicators of each and every person's weak, individual voice: people didn't have those before. Hence, all this cacophonous noise of the terribly impolite public discourse going on now.

I can tell you when and where I, for one, experienced a period of extremely polite public political discourse: in the Soviet Union, for the first thirty years of my life. There was no public political debate, so it was all very quiet and polite. There were, admittedly, some half-insane, antipatriotic, anti-Soviet "underground" types with the audacity to disagree with the ever-infallible Party and its Leninist Politburo, but who cared about them, with their pathetic little "samizdat" flyers and leaflets and hand-sewn magazines, against the grand background of the infinitely unified, Party-loving, Lenin-adoring, but generally completely apathetic, hundreds of millions of Soviet people?

And going further back in time—isn't it quite amazing that under Stalin, there were no dissidents in the Soviet Union? None. Zero! No public political disagreements! Total and complete agreement, boundless adoration of the Great Leader! People were being shot in the back of the head by the hundreds of thousands and millions before any bad, impolite, anti-Stalin thoughts even had a chance to enter their minds, so there you have it.

This, I hope, has been a post filled with politeness and good nature toward everyone.

May 17, 2018

It doesn't matter whether Mueller can or cannot indict Trump. That's beside the point now. Sure, we, the majority of Americans, are repulsed and dismayed by Trump—by his stratospheric vulgarity, his limitless venality, his pathological narcissism and mean-spiritedness, his immeasurable crookedness, his racism, his rampant misogyny, his being the first bona fide home-brewed fascist to make it into the White House, and by the entire fetid swamp of his very being in which he's managed to submerge America comprehensively and, as he likes to brag on a variety of occasions, in record-short time—but we don't know one-tenth of what at this time is known only to Mueller and his team, with regard to the sheer staggering scope and number of variegated crimes and misdemeanors perpetrated by Trump and his gang. When all the facts are laid out for the whole world to see, America will be staggered into a massive shock of self-revulsion first, and then—when the initial numbness at the realization that this has been the greatest and certainly most shameful and sordid political disaster in modern American history starts to wear off—the shock will be transformed into a tsunami wave of anger, one that will wash away not just Trump himself, along with the inner and broader circles of his traitorous iniquitous flunkies and felonious abettors, but also wide swaths of the country's corrupt, money-mad political establishment, beginning with the entirety of the GOP. Only the most desperate and also prison-bound of Republican congressmen will dare to stand in the way of that giant wave.

So, no—it really doesn't matter whether or not Robert Mueller has the constitutional authority to indict Trump. Trump has already been indicted in the court of public opinion, and now the main order of business is to get him the hell out of the White House.

May 18, 2018
In a free society, one's integrity is defined mainly by what one WILL do. In nonfree one, primarily by what one WON'T do.

May 19, 2018
The official state television of Trump's America is FOX News. Trump supporters watch no other news channels on television.

The official state television of Putin's Russia is the entirety of Russian network television, extending its reach across the country's eleven time zones. Putin supporters—and that's a large majority of all Russians—watch no other television but Putin-owned ones, which effectively are all there is for them to watch on TV.

Most young American watch no television at all. The same applies to the majority of young Russians.

FOX News tirelessly and relentlessly seeks to instill and reinforce in its viewers a feeling of injustice constantly being done to them by arrogant left-wing intellectuals, coastal liberals, eggheaded academics in tweed jackets, progressives and feminists and social-justice warriors and the Black Lives Matter movement, as well as illegals, Muslims and Mexicans, all those rich, Soros-like owners of all the country's newspapers, all of Hollywood, and the identity-politics crowd, et al.—all of whom, separately and collectively, look down on and constantly mock and otherwise disrespect people like them, the FOX audience: ordinary, hard-working, nonintellectual, God-fearing, gun-owning, salt-of-the-earth Americans.

FOX News is a remarkably potent and efficient, round-the-clock generator and supplier of Trumpland's grievances.

Likewise, Russian television, tirelessly and relentlessly, blasts its viewers' brains with a sharply-focused message of anti-Western bitterness and anti-American resentment: dastardly America is the source of all evil in the world, along with its toxic sidekick the UK; most of Europe has been subjugated into meek obeisance by the US with its endlessly proliferating military bases; America is quickly running out of natural resources and therefore seeks to crush and eventually conquer and occupy Russia, the largest and most mineral-rich land on earth, making it one of its fifty or sixty or however many states with a capital in Siberia; Russia is the only remaining citadel of traditional morality and transcendental timeless spirituality towering amid the sea of degenerate bourgeois decadence, iniquity, moral turpitude, sexual all-permissiveness and degradation . . . and all the rest of that ugliness. That's why America, and the West as a whole, hate and fear Russia and her indomitable leader Vladimir Putin, an intellectual titan and unmatched strategist and tactician among the pitifully mediocre, dwarfish political figures on the world's political stage today. That's why America and the rest of the West constantly laugh at Russia and mock the supposedly backward Russian people, that's right, the West constantly disrespects the Russian people, unlike back in the Soviet days, when the whole bleeping world was afraid of us, which means everyone in the world respected the hell out of us too, because fear is the same as respect in international politics, as well as in life in general, but we'll show them yet, all those arrogant Westerners, how to mock and disrespect us, we've already demonstrated to America what we can do by electing their weak-minded president for them, and that's just the beginning. Americans are stupid and boring and soulless. They live longer lives than we do, but our lives, though shorter than theirs, are lived much more interestingly and with greater intensity; we don't value life as much as they do, which means we wouldn't think twice or three times about wiping America off the map with our nuclear weapons if it continues to disrespect and threaten us, even knowing that would lead to our own immediate reciprocal destruction also, but so what, who cares. They think they can disrespect us, but they're wrong, and they're going to pay dearly for disrespecting us, those sonuvabitches, they're going to pay, those stupid arrogant Westerners. They think they're better than us, but guess what . . . guess what . . . guess what. . . .

Grievance is the fuel both Russia and America are running on at this moment in history.

May 21, 2018

Trump's tweets are rapidly getting ever more moronic, incoherent, demented, shrill, hysterical, and terribly panicked. At this point, his Twitter output amounts essentially to one prolonged thin, piercing, pitiful howl of primordial despair. It is just an awful, deeply embarrassing sight. America, what have you done to yourself?

May 22, 2018

Trump is poison spreading through America's bloodstream. Millions of people are getting angrier, meaner, more despondent, and less shocked by the day by the fact that the illegitimate, accidental, vile, and ignorant occupant of the White House, a two-bit dictator wannabe, is quickly turning the country into a de facto banana republic. He is pure poison in the guise of a human being, and the only way for the country to start detoxifying from Trumpism before it's too late is to have that pernicious creature removed from the White House.

May 24, 2018

Dear Little Rocket Man, the Insane and Much-Respected and Beloved Honorable Homicidal Supreme Leader of Democratic North Korea,

I, Donald J. Trump, sadly, am not going to hold the preplanned and much-ballyhooed peace summit with you, which I already had commemorated with a special beautiful coin/bottle-opener, the best and most beautiful anyone has ever seen, because the United States will not be bullied or intimidated by the harsh words said about its vice president by some random flunky on your staff, and my heart is broken. Holding this summit would have served the interests of world peace and all that and, much more importantly, would have clinched the Nobel Peace Prize for me, which everyone is saying I should've been given a long time ago. Please call me? On my blocked number? I still would love to meet with you, you crazy little cruel dictator. Just the two of us, plus maybe Dennis Rodman.

Sincerely and with much respect and cold contempt, with love and squalor and half of my faculties intact, Donald J. Trump, Nobel Peace Prize Winner In Waiting

May 26, 2018

He keeps calling immigrants "animals"—and the ICE agents no longer find it impossibly hard to tear a screaming child away from his mother: after all, she is less than human, so her feelings don't matter. In 1930s Germany and Nazi-occupied East-Central Europe, Jews were called rats and cockroaches; in Stalin's USSR "enemies of the people" were branded rabid dogs, vermin, snakes.

America, 2018.

May 27, 2018

Losing your country means losing your faith in its essential goodness.

May 30, 2018

Russia is a giant mafia state and infinitely corrupt oil-and-gas corporation headed by the world's most dangerous criminal. It is, at this point in history, the ultimate cancerous growth on the body of humanity. This summer, it hosts the global soccer championship, the World Cup. Welcome, world, to the 2018 version of the 1936 Berlin Olympics!

May 31, 2018

If you really want to hurt a racist's feelings, call him a racist. Instantly you'll see a deeply wounded person in front of you: "Who, me? A racist? How dare you! I'll have you know I'm the least racist person you'll ever meet! Just because I happen to believe black people are lazy and predisposed to crime, or just because I happen to state the obvious fact that Jews own all the media in the country and don't have the best interests of America at heart, doesn't make me a . . . How dare you! . . . What? Trump? He may be a bit of a racist, sure, but so what? That's not why I support him. I'm on his side because he wants to shake things up in Washington, drain the swamp, make America great again and return it to its rightful owners—the forgotten little people like me."

Mikhail Iossel
June 2018

June 3, 2018

A lack of meritocracy leads to the deadening of society. One of the reasons the old Soviet Union came to its ignominious end: mediocre, ignorant, incurious people of subpar knowledge and creative capacity, finely attuned to the prevailing political winds and to their equally obtuse superiors' boundless appetite for flattery, people whose only real strength lay in their uncanny ability to toe the party line by mouthing the ideological dogma of the day with fiercely authentic conviction—bona fide frauds, not to mince words—had been grandfathered into nearly every position of importance and influence in the humanities sphere, in particular; in the fields of literature and education, to name but two. The humanities' blood system was completely, hopelessly clogged. Innovative thinking and ambition of a nonpolitical nature were strongly discouraged. New creative ideas were dismissed right off the bat. Dogma ruled supreme. Freedom of expression was virtually banned.

And then, one fine day, the society stopped functioning altogether.

June 4, 2018

The hit TV series *The Americans* is over, but the reality show *The Un-Americans*, starring Donald Trump and the rest of the Republican party, is still dragging on.

These are deeply unpatriotic people of bad faith and authoritarian mindset, greedy and cruel and bigoted, bent on dismantling democracy in America. To say that they are infinitely more dangerous to America than any number of KGB spy couples would be an understatement.

June 4, 2018

 Donald J. Trump
@realDonaldTrump

As has been stated by numerous legal scholars, I have the absolute right to PARDON myself, but why would I do that when I have done nothing wrong? In the meantime, the never ending Witch Hunt, led by 13 very Angry and Conflicted Democrats (& others) continues into the mid-terms!

5:35 AM – 4 Jun 2018

As has been stated by millions of legal scholars, I have the total Right to Pardon myself for being a money launderer for Russian oligarchs for decades, for actively seeking and accepting Russians' assistance in getting my ass installed in the White House, for being a traitor to my country, for being a grifter my whole damn life, for being a racist and a sex predator and an unfeeling and vile malignant narcissist, for being an ignorant buffoon, for having affairs with porn stars shortly after my wife's giving birth to our son, for paying hush money to scores of women I had affairs with, for having not spent a single day in my sorry life without being a dishonest and criminal bastard, for admiring dictators and loathing democratically elected leaders everywhere in the world, for being America's enemy's stooge, for wasting my life in a breathtakingly monumental way, and for many, many other such little transgressions—millions, billions of legal scholars unanimously (would I actually know the word "unanimously?" probably NOT, so let's just say "bigly"), bigly and totally agree I could PARDON myself. Totally. Whether God would forgive me when my time comes—probably not, but I'll worry about that when I'm there, at the Pearly Gates, not that I really know what those are, because I don't believe in God, plus I'm pretty sure I could make a deal with God also. God is not some holier than thou loser. I'd make him an offer he couldn't refuse. The art of the deal!

June 5, 2018
In response the US Supreme Court decision in favor of a Colorado baker who, on religious grounds, refused to bake a wedding cake for a gay couple:

I shall bake no cakes for sinners, for adulterers, sorcerers and idolaters; for gluttons, pornographers, tax evaders and tax collectors, grifters, chiselers, and embezzlers; for moneylenders and money launderers; for excessive lovers of the self, narcissists and sociopaths, potty-mouthed blasphemers and users of swear words, filthy talkers, fornicators, takers of Lord's name in vain, users of sacrilegious euphemisms like "geez" or "gosh" or "oh my God," those who do work on the Sabbath or whose servants play loud music after midnight; for slothful idlers and malignant lazybones; for gamblers, liars, slanderers, hypocrites, gossips and whisperers, withholders of the truth, braggarts, flatterers, whiners, and double-tongued exaggerators, gaslighters, traitors, coveters of their neighbors' donkeys, the envious, the lustful, the wanton, the drunkards, the Putin lovers, the Trump supporters, and the homophobic bakers from Colorado—to name but a few categories of individuals for whom no cakes shall be baked by me!

June 6, 2018

I remember hearing the news of Robert F. Kennedy's assassination as it was being announced on the radio. It was a sunny early afternoon in Leningrad, and I was three quarters through the short distance between my school, #511, and our apartment building, #19-2, on Cosmonauts Avenue, in a fast-growing microdistrict on the city's southwestern edge. Classes at middle school were already over, but I, not quite knowing what else to do with myself in the absence of countryside-bound friends to hang out and play soccer with, was still spending time at the library there, in hushed solitude, leafing through random sheaves of old *Crocodile* and *Youth* magazines and dreaming about nothing in particular, in anticipation of leaving for the dacha my parents were renting that year in the lakefront resort village of Roshchino, an hour away by suburban train. I remember pausing momentarily to look at the portly toad unhurriedly crossing the dirt path I was on; it had emerged from the large, meters-deep tectonic pool of dirt to my right. "Say something," I said to it. It was then that the radio anchorman's stern, authoritative voice, issuing from an open window of a first-floor apartment in a building on my left—an exact replica of the building we lived in—reached my ears: America, California, Los Angles. Robert Kennedy, brother of the previously assassinated president, shot dead. Then something else, and then the local weather and the songs of Soviet composers. I remember feeling taken aback. Sure, I remembered his brother. Who didn't. It was a shame. What the hell was going on there, in America? At least in our country,

nobody was killing our presidents, in part because we didn't
have any. Poor Robert Kennedy and his ill-starred family. (It
occurred to me then, fleetingly—or maybe not—that this was
not the first time the important news of the world had reached
me out in the open by accident, through someone's partially
open window.) But then, where was America and where was I?
The toad, moving with elephantine grace and an exaggerated
sense of itself, had finally cleared the dirt path, and I went on
toward home, thinking of everything and nothing; of what
most ordinary Leningrad boys my age likely would be thinking
when not thinking of what exactly they might be thinking: the
dishearteningly uneven performance of our city's only major-
league soccer team, Zenit; the endless summer ahead, girls,
fishing, mushroom-hunting, how good it would be to have a
dog, swimming in the lake, Russia, Lethe, Lorelei.

June 7, 2018

Tomorrow, in Moscow, the world's most dangerous criminal, who
also happens to be the quasidemocratically elected tzar of Russia
and boss of the fraudulent current US president, will be holding,
just for the fun and the formal ceremony of it, his annual tongue-
in-cheek live marathon Q&A session, the so-called "direct
line," in the course of which the few preselected dozen of his
woebegone subjects from all across the vast country with the
world's largest landmass and greatest supply of mineral riches
will be asking him preapproved and largely meaningless, fawning
questions—and he will thoughtfully consider and answer every
one of those, addressing at length each little tale of temporary
local misery in much detail and with a mock-serious expression
on his unnaturally taut-skinned, Botox-bloated face, effortlessly
resolving on the spot, benevolent magician–style, every single one
out of the rapidly dwindling number of his phantom empire's

still-unresolved problems, from the tiniest of minicataclysms to the calamities of megaglobal scope. It will be a routinely pathetic spectacle—and a cautionary tale about the essential fragility of democracy in any un-self-aware society, especially in one historically beset by the lethal combination of a raging inferiority complex and a massively overblown national ego.

June 10, 2018

In the Soviet Union, people didn't go to psychoanalysts. It just was not done, or even as much as thought of being done.

There hardly were any practicing analysts there, for one thing. And then, too, what would've been there for those conjectural analysts to analyze? What—and how?

Soviet people weren't supposed to have a subconscious, and their conscious mind had to belong to the Soviet state, or at least be transparently visible to the latter. Soviet people, en masse, didn't know the names of Freud or Jung, for better or worse, among a myriad of other names they didn't know. They never felt depressed, because they didn't know what depression was and had no idea that what they were experiencing was called depression. Nor did they ever have panic or anxiety attacks, strictly speaking, because they didn't have the name for those, either. Their whole lives often constituted one unending anxiety attack, but they thought that's just how life was supposed to be. There was so much to talk about that there was nothing to discuss.

There was, instead, a lot of drinking, a lot of sadness, a lot of silence, a lot of shouting, a lot of being either dead drunk or hellaciously hungover, a lot of uncertain sobriety indistinguishable from extreme drunkenness and vice versa, a lot of tears in the night, as well as a lot of dying young and a whole lot of "snap out of it, stop whining, have another drink,

How long will Republicans in Congress keep their embarrassed silence watching Trump's increasingly unhinged behavior? Does Trump have *kompromat* on some or many of them, the way Putin is in possession of voluminous criminal files on every one of his oligarchs—and, of course, prominently, on the US President Donald Trump? Russians have hacked Congressional Republicans' e-mails also. They just didn't pass those on to WikiLeaks. A number of high-profile Republicans, apparently, have received large donations from Russian oligarchs with US citizenship, such as Putin's friend and generous philanthropist, the multibillionaire Leonard Blavatnik. The entire Republican Party has been deeply compromised with Russian money and influence.

Still, how long can this insanity continue? Trump is completely clueless, confused, deranged, and seething with vileness. No one has humiliated the United States the way he is humiliating it now. His "presidency" is a grotesque, macabre reality show. His policies are those of an unmitigated fascist. He has to be stopped before it's too late.

June 13, 2018

Imagine the despair the silent dissidents of North Korea must be feeling today, as they watch on the only channel of North Korean television the grinning president of the United States singing the praises of the murderous dictator of their country. They know there is no hope for them now. They know they've been betrayed. They know they are doomed.

The great beaches of North Korea! The condos!

Son of a bitch.

I for one can easily (well, no—with difficulty, but still) imagine how, back in the seventies-eighties Soviet Union, millions of Soviet "internal émigrés"—to say nothing of the likes of Jewish refuseniks or open political dissidents—would have felt if, late at night, after numerous attempts to find a blessed spot in their cramped rooms (typically, in the radiator corner) where they could get a minute's worth of minimally eligible, unobstructed, "unjammed" reception of the Voice of America or the BBC in Russian on their VEF Spidola shortwave radios, they suddenly would've heard the wooden-voiced news of Carter or Reagan lauding to the skies Brezhnev-Andropov-Chernenko as the great patriots of Russia, very talented people, fantastic partners and strong leaders who, wouldn't you know it, loved their country. How would they—us—have felt at that unimaginable imaginary moment? Crushed. Defeated. Deflated. Despondent. Horrified. Utterly void of hope. Above all, betrayed.

Trump, besides betraying his own country, by selling himself out shamelessly to America-hating Putin and his oligarchs, is also a traitor to everything America has always stood for in the minds of hundreds of millions of oppressed people the world over—a traitor of the world's unfree people's flickering hope for a life of freedom and dignity.

Trump has betrayed America, but America will in the end dispose of Trump the way one tosses a rotten apple into a garbage can. The betrayal of the faith the world's downtrodden people have in America as the sole defender of their distant dreams of freedom, their belief in America's being on their side in their quiet daily struggle not to succumb to the tyranny of their cruel rulers—that betrayal will linger on for generations, I'm afraid, and will break the hearts and cost the lives of untold multitudes of people, each one a better human being than the current accidental, illegitimate, dictator-loving occupant of the White House.

June 15, 2018
Trump on Kim Jong-un: "He speaks and his people sit up at attention. I want my people to do the same."

"My people." We all are "his people." Whenever that orange fascist moron opens his mouth, he wants all of us to sit up at attention.

June 15, 2018
Trump would have great chemistry with Stalin. He would have tremendous chemistry with Hitler. He would love Mussolini. He would invite Pol Pot to the White House. He is all transactional: whoever flatters him or promises him a good deal on beachfront condo development is his BFF. He is a dictator wannabe and has not an ounce of decency in his heart. No one could be less American in his personal philosophy of living than Donald Trump.

Good choice, Trumpland. Sit up and listen.

June 15, 2018
There is no fact-checking Trump anymore. It's like peeing into a hurricane. Absolutely everything he says is a total lie. He has become an overdriven human turbine throwing manure in every direction.

June 16, 2018
The current political reality in the United States is such that a good one-third of the country's adult population has voluntarily joined the cult of the Orange Fascist Demagogue and wouldn't mind—and in fact, would be perfectly comfortable with—living in a dictatorship, provided the said Supreme Leader continues to pay daily friendly visits to the darkest areas of their hearts, lavishing praise on the worst demons of their nature, telling

them repeatedly in the braying voice of a flatulent carnival barker that white is black, red is blue, ignorance is bliss, facts are lies, lies are whatever facts they don't like, friends are enemies and enemies are friends, that they are the only true Americans and America is theirs to own forever, that guns are their holy crosses, that there are no good people other than them in the world, that cruelty is kindness and kindness is weakness, that God is a hater of everyone who doesn't look or sound like them, that he who is not with them is against them, that the entire world is their enemy and only he is on their side, their ultimate protector and savior, the deranged patron saint of the delusional.

June 16, 2018

Yesterday Trump, that pure-hearted humanitarian, tweeted, "The Democrats are forcing the breakup of families at the Border with their horrible and cruel legislative agenda. Any Immigration Bill MUST HAVE full funding for the Wall, end Catch & Release, Visa Lottery and Chain, and go to Merit Based Immigration. Go for it! WIN!"

In other words, he'll keep children and their mothers hostages to Democrats' unwillingness to let him have his beautiful WALL. Clever!

WIN, Democrats! Give him what he wants—above all, his wonderful WALL! He would love not to punish those poor innocent little children, not to make them suffer, not to traumatize them for life, not to rip them from their mothers' arms, not to take them away from their mothers, not to subject their mothers to extreme lifelong torment, but . . . what can he do? His hands are tied! TIED! He needs to have his WALL! It's all the Democrats' fault that the children and their mothers are suffering now! He must have his WALL! Democrats, his

WALL! Until he gets his WALL, he will have no other choice but to keep torturing those little children and their unfortunate mothers! He must have his WALL! His WALL is worth the lives of any number of some non-Americans children and their Spanish-speaking moms! Gove him what he wants, so that he can finally let kids go back to their mothers! THE WALL!

Was it his friend and puppet-master Vladimir who suggested this idea to him—to blackmail the Democrats and all the decent people of America with this clever little ploy? It may well have been.

Putin may well have said to him, during one of their recent informal phone chats:

"Donald, it's simple, man: just go ahead and punish those useless kids and their stupid mothers, and every one of those faint-hearted, lily-livered liberals of yours, for your political enemies' unwillingness to play ball with you, as I'm told they say in your country. You want your wall? Your damn wall? Your little toy? Then hold those snotty-faced kids hostage to your righteous demand for the funding for that ridiculous wall of your dreams! Remember how I told you to tell your none-too-bright son to tell everyone that the conversation he and your people had with my people at Trump Tower back in June two years ago was about children's adoptions? Ha-ha. That was, of course, the code phrase I always use for that ugly and unfair Magnitsky Act. Who the hell is Magnitsky to Americans?! Who I kill in my country, and why, is none of your Congress's business. I know you know that, but does everyone in Congress realize this too, by now? Somehow, I think not. So when I and my billionaire friends got hit with those Magnitsky Act sanctions, what did I do? That's right: I immediately banned the adoption of our Russian orphans by your people, Americans. I could do nothing to make your American Congress feel the grapes of my wrath, so I took it out on them sick Russian orphans, whom no one in our country would adopt, because of their having all kinds of illnesses and syndromes, so—tough luck for those orphans and the children-loving American families ready to adopt them. Sorry, orphans. Sorry, would-be American adoptive families. Tough luck. Them's the breaks. Get your damn Congress to lift those unfair Magnitsky sanctions, and that would be the end of it, of this sad saga. Everyone would be happy, and especially those sick orphans who wouldn't have to die in their prisonlike orphanages. That's why I put you in the White House, too—remember? To help out with all those different kinds of sanctions: the Magnitsky ones, the ones for the Crimea annexation, and so on. So far you haven't delivered, my friend. That's not good. My patience is not limitless. Well, at least be a strongman in America, show them Democrats and every liberal in your country who is the boss in this current difficult situation. . . . Mind you, I don't want to take all the credit for this cool 'hostage-taking' play—I was not the first one to deploy it. We—the Soviets, which we still are— have done this before. For instance, when your Carter boycotted our Olympics and imposed all kinds of trade restrictions on us because of our Afghanistan gambit—and why can't we exercise our dominance over our backyard zone of influence, pray tell?— what did the Politburo do? Exactly: it immediately discontinued allowing them Soviet Jews to emigrate to Israel (but in reality, mainly to America). You may have heard the term "refuseniks"? No? Well. . . . In other words, be the manly man you think you are, Donald: punish the kids and their moms if you want not just your so-called base of support, glassy-eyed members of your cult, but them liberals and other enemies of yours also to respect you . . . or, at least, to fear the hell out of you, which is the way we interpret the meaning of the term 'respect' in Russia. Go for it, Donald! WIN!"

June 18, 2018

Even as far back as some ten years ago, during the last couple of my annual return visits to St. Petersburg, Russia, a number of old friends of mine there were telling me, much in the same words and with the same confounded air about them, that they had no idea how and when it happened that the situation in the country, over the relatively short course of Putin's rule, had deteriorated quite so quickly, and so badly and with so much seemingly ironclad irreversibility, in the old Soviet direction of airless authoritarianism. "How did he do it so inconspicuously?" they wondered. "One day, you're still living basically in a reasonably democratic country—and then, just like that, one unlovely morning you wake up in an unfree one. . . . He seemed so harmless, Putin did, so bland, so more or less decent for a former *kagebeshnik,* and Russia clearly had by then already been taken beyond the point of no return toward being a normal-like, democratic country. . . ."

There was nothing I could say in response, and they didn't expect me to say anything, either. There would've been no point in me telling them something that had been obvious to me from the outset—but not to them, oddly enough, a few years prior, when something still could have been done by electoral means to stop or at least slow down Putin's inexorable rise to unchecked despotic power—to wit, that there cannot be such an animal as a former *kagebeshnik,* especially in a country where his direct and proudly unrepentant Soviet-era predecessors had exterminated tens of millions of innocent people.

But, then, that was a different time and a different place.

Here we are today, in Trump's America. What can one say? Step by step, day by day Trump is immersing all of us ever deeper in his ugly madness. Every new day, by the very fact of its freshly nauseating and steadily increasing tawdriness, normalizes, as it were, its immediate precursor. We get more desensitized by the day, grow more numb, deadened inside. The immense energy of Trump's insanity gradually grinds down our ability to counter it with any reality-based arguments. He's already taken tens of millions of scared, angry, ill-informed, and xenophobic Americans a long way down the apocalyptic road to a metaphoric Jonestown.

That's how transition to unfreedom—and in this case, to downright fascism of the particular American kind, bypassing the dull way station of gray authoritarianism—often happens in heretofore safely democratic societies: uneventfully, as though in a dreamless sleep.

The time is close to midnight. But it's not too late to reset the clock come November.

June 19, 2018

Right now, thousands of children who have never before been separated from their parents are sitting in cages in giant barracks at America's southern border, scared to death, crying, unable to understand what is happening.

Right now, those children's mothers, runaways from waves of violence in their native countries, are half-dead with heartbreak, filled with horror and despair, sitting in detention at the border before being sent back to their violence-ravaged lands and having no idea whether they'll ever see their children again.

Right now, the most powerful man in the world, a cornered rat in human disguise, a dictator-loving lifelong criminal and former star of a sleazy reality show on TV, whose decision it has been to rip those children from their mothers' arms, could end all that suffering with one quick phone call. But he wouldn't do it. He would not. Because he is an empty

sent back to the countries they had fled from. They have no idea where their children are. The children, predominantly very small, can provide no information leading to the location of their parents. Many, if not most of them, are going to be separated from their parents forever. Their parents are never going to be able to see them again.

Can you imagine this happening in America in 2018?

It is happening right now in America.

June 28, 2018

53% of white women voted for Donald Trump in 2016.

Presumably the majority of them would be fine with having Roe v. Wade overturned in the near future.

They did, after all, cast their ballot for the guy who publicly, on national television, opined that women should be punished for having an abortion.

Elections, no matter how deeply compromised, have consequences.

June 29, 2018

Trump is hoping to build a coalition of the indecent. Everything he does is geared toward spreading and normalizing cruelty and immorality in society. He knows he has between one-fourth and one-third of Americans signed up for his ultimate project: Making America Fascist. The other two-thirds, however, will never consent. This is an old Manichaean war between good and evil that America is waging with itself right now, the first one of such fateful scope since the Civil War.

We'll win—and there is no alternative to winning for us, anyway, because losing this war would mean losing America—but the fight will be anything but easy, and we'll have to fight with everything we've got.

June 30, 2018

What kind of life did Trump live that there has been no room in it for great literature, art, music? Has he ever even heard the names of Tolstoy and Shakespeare, Leonardo and Mozart? He may have, indeed, but he doesn't care a whit about any of them and never did. He doesn't have the ability to be moved by beauty and have any strong feelings beyond those of rage, fear, and howling insecurity—that's his ultimate misfortune, the bane of his existence. I wonder if he has any fond, poignant, vivid childhood or adolescence memories. I rather doubt it. He is all surface; there is no depth to his heart. And what is the life of someone without memories? It's a nonlife, a story of nonbeing.

June 30, 2018

Whatever we see, we must remember it to see it. If we don't, we won't. We lose the ability to see anything for the first time once we stop being children.

Everything is memory, and memory is everything.

Mikhail Iossel
July 2018

July 3, 2018

If the young Ukrainian filmmaker Oleg Sentsov, Putin's political prisoner, now on the fifty-first day of an indefinite hunger strike in one of the harshest labor camps in the north of Russia, is going to die before long, as seems likely now, much as I abhor writing these words—this outrage will be on the conscience of everyone who is going crazy with soccer/football fervor presently in Moscow and Petersburg and beyond; everyone and everywhere shouting "Olé, Olé, Olé!" and dancing and drinking away and yelling drunkenly something ugly about Russia's being the world's worst nightmare; everyone dancing and drinking away and blowing their vuvuzelas, celebrating the sheer biological joy of being under the pretext of this Berlin-36-like World Cup in Russia. It will be on everyone's conscience—that of everyone, that is, except Putin and Trump, neither of whom has a conscience, so there'd be no more reason to blame them for being fascist bastards than berating a hyena for eating dead flesh.

The burden of shame will fall in equal measure on everyone's shoulders, including mine and yours.

July 4, 2018

I came to America in 1986, after an abridged lifetime in a country that, although also vast and beautiful and infinitely complicated, was America's polar opposite in almost every respect. There was never a time I didn't love that first country of my life, but I wanted to leave it, especially since I had been told repeatedly I would never be allowed to do so. There was never a time in my life when I didn't love America, either, before or after I saw it for the first time. I've been all across its unimaginably beautiful expanse. I've seen America in happiness and in distress. Right now, it is in desperate trouble, having been taken over by the worst of its people. Right now, it needs the combined strength and resolve of everyone who genuinely loves it to help it fight off and defeat this terrible virus of fascism that's entered its bloodstream. In the end, I firmly believe, America will prevail.

Happy birthday, America. I love you.

July 6, 2018

In response to Trump saying, at a Montana rally, "[Putin's critics say] President Putin is KGB and this and that. You know what? Putin's fine."

Putin is fine. The KGB is fine. We're all fine, we're all people. . . . Only the dishonest Fake Media and Fake News journalists with their fake unnamed sources are not fine. The obstructionist Democrats aren't fine. Witch-hunting Robert Mueller isn't fine. Those who didn't vote for me aren't fine. Those who don't like me aren't fine. Muslims and brown-skinned people aren't fine. Immigrants aren't fine. . . . But Putin is fine, very fine. He's got me by the balls, I owe him lots of money, and he has tons of unpleasant *kompromat* on me, but he still smiles at me and doesn't yell at me, even though I have been unable yet, all by myself, to lift those cruel and unjust economic sanctions Obama so very unfairly imposed on him. Obama isn't fine. Journalists are bad, dishonest people, enemies of the people. But Putin is fine. The KGB is fine. Stalin was fine. . . . Do I even know who Stalin was? No, but it doesn't matter. Kim Jong-un is fine. A fine young man. I am a traitor, and that's fine. You are fine, too, for as long as you stay stupid and angry.

[From July 8 Mikhail Iossel was in Tbilisi, Georgia, where in the second half of the month he directed the Summer Literary Seminars, hence the relative dearth of posts during this time.]

July 10, 2018

This is how it happened:

- Millions of people in battleground states, such as Florida, Ohio, Pennsylvania, Michigan, and Wisconsin, failed to show up for the vote on November 6, 2016.
- Many thousands of people in each one of those states threw their votes away by voting for Jill Stein or Gary Johnson.
- Tens of thousands of votes were suppressed in Wisconsin alone, by Governor Scott Walker's draconian ID law, aimed squarely at disenfranchising the state's African American population.
- The Russian intelligence services, on Putin's orders, carried out a massive, multipronged anti-Clinton, pro-Trump propaganda effort, almost certainly in coordination with the Trump campaign.
- The grotesquely anachronistic Electoral College mechanism, for the fifth time in US history and the third since 1888, gave victory to the loser of the popular vote: this time, the winner lost by the largest margin ever (3 million votes—more than the population of twenty-plus US states).
- 77,000 Trump fans in Pennsylvania, Michigan, and Wisconsin did show up to vote that day.

- Plus a few other factors doubtless played a role.

And that's how fascism came to America.

July 12, 2018

Trump, unfortunately, will leave a permanently ineradicable, ugly stain on the office of the US presidency, as well as both on the country's self-image and its perception by the rest of the world. The country will have to live with the heavy burden of this national shame for many generations to come. There has never been anyone as vulgar, ignorant, shameless, vile, cruel, narcissistic, openly bigoted, racist, and . . . just plain moronically stupid occupying the White House. History will register these dark times we're going through now as the dismal period of America's slide into fascism.

July 13, 2018

Curiouser and curiouser and curiouser.

America, your president may be a traitor.

July 27, 2016. Trump famously announces, out of nowhere: "Russia, if you're listening, I hope you're able to find the 30,000 emails that are missing."

Today's Indictment: That very evening, July 27, 2016, Russian operatives targeted Clinton campaign e-mails "for the first time."

July 15, 2018

Just three years ago, the notion of a Trump presidency seemed unthinkable and absurd to the point of being totally ludicrous.

Nowadays, it still is totally ludicrous and absurd, plus obscene in the extreme, but rather less unthinkable. Now we know that it can indeed happen here—we can see with our own eyes how the country, the old land of the free, slowly but inexorably, day by day, week by week, month by month, is getting pulled into the black hole of fascism.

This is happening because Trump does not exist in a vacuum and did not fall on America's figurative head from the sky. His grotesque ascent to power would have been impossible in the absence of the strongly concentrated substratum of eternally undying Trumpism, or the peculiarly American brand of fascism: the fetid farrago of racism, assorted bigotry, nativism, xenophobia, rank chauvinism, misogyny, and authoritarian yearnings. Trump, the ultimate personification of the Ugly American, would have been impossible as a political figure of any scope without his supporters: tens of millions of predominantly, though not exclusively, poorly informed, generally embittered, and resentful people of all ages and all walks of life, whose cultlike devotion to that imbecilic cipher of a human being rests upon his explicit legitimization by example of the heretofore hidden domains of darkness in their hearts. In that sense, the only difference between the smarter and stupider among Trump supporters is that the former would never publicly admit to being ones.

Sadly, it doesn't seem possible at this point for one to be both a Trump supporter and a good, decent person.

July 16, 2018

It is America's fault that Putin was forced to commit an act of cyberwar against it, by egregiously interfering with its presidential election. Putin good, America bad. That's your president speaking, America.

America, your so-called president, sadly, is a traitor.

Donald J. Trump
@ realDonaldTrump

Our relationship with Russia has NEVER been worse thanks to many years of U.S. foolishness and stupidity and now, the Rigged Witch Hunt!

1:05 AM – 16 Jul 2018

July 16, 2018

For those still in doubt, Trump effectively spelled it out as plainly as can be today in Helsinki: Yes, I am a traitor. You have a problem with that?

July 18, 2018

Being far away from North America and immersed in the daily and hourly proceedings of a large international literary program has its advantages. From a distance, Trump seems infinitesimally smaller than the sinister shadow of fascism cast by his ridiculous persona on the rest of the world. And it feels ludicrous and slightly embarrassing even to think or talk about him. Can't we, rhetorically speaking, just agree that he is simply a traitorous cretin, moral degenerate, and mental toddler, and that his supporters are either profoundly stupid or the deeply indecent people (and apparently, gluttons for verbal punishment, too, since quite a few of them, clearly, are still hanging around in the capacity of my Facebook "friends," to say nothing of, well, "followers")?

July 18, 2018

I love Helsinki. It is one of my most favorite cities in the world. A very special place of bittersweet fondness is occupied by it in the near recesses of my heart—or, to put it in somewhat less metaphoric terms, a five-hour ride's worth and a lifetime and world's circumference away from the place of the first half of my life. Old friends of mine live there. Helsinki was where my parents had moved to and spent almost three years (the last years of my father's life, as would eventually turn out) after finally leaving post-Soviet Russia in 1993. And so it saddens me that for many decades ahead, inevitably, that beautiful, stately, and deeply decent city will have the misfortune of being indelibly associated with the worst public debasement of America ever committed by an American president. Munich, 1938. Helsinki, 2018. The Helsinki Betrayal of 2018. . . . History has no truck with our feelings.

July 30, 2018
After a few days necessarily away from the slow daily flow of the putrid muck the American political process has devolved into since November 2016, the same bleak landscape of the country's perilous slide into fascism looks ever more offensive in its seeming routine mundanity. The so-called US president is on the verge of being revealed as an infinitely corrupt Russian asset. He also, provably, happens to be the most amoral human being ever to set foot inside the White House, in any capacity, let alone that of a US president. America has been brought perilously close to the bright red line separating its democratic freedoms from the full subversion of its basic foundational principles. If tomorrow the said illegitimate inhabitant of the White House were to abscond to Russia and ask the dictator of Russia for political asylum, fully one-third of the country's electorate would continue to support him: that's just the way it works in America—he who gives agency to their inner darkness earns the undying gratitude of the worst people of America.

And so it goes.

It is a joyless tableau.

Mikhail Iossel
August 2018

August 2, 2018

At an unprecedented joint appearance in the White House briefing room this afternoon, the US chiefs of intelligence—the heads of the DNI, DHS, FBI, and NSC, the main pillars of the country's safety and security—effectively said the following: "The US is under attack. Russia is continuing to interfere with our political process, and it is doing so on an ever-expanding scale and with growing brazenness and acceleration. We don't quite know at this point how to address this clear and present danger to our democracy. But we are doing the best we can, and be assured that we'll keep doing the best we can going forward. As for our so-called president, we don't know what his thinking on all this may be, and it doesn't really matter. We have no idea what he was talking about for an hour and a half during his one-on-one with Putin in Helsinki, but we necessarily are operating under the assumption that he is Putin's puppet and, if given half an opportunity, would sell America down the river in a heartbeat. Well, that's the hand we've all been dealt collectively, as Americans. For clarity's sake, we have to be cognizant of the high likelihood that the deranged clown living in the White House, who keeps calling you, members of the free American press, 'enemies of the people'—technically, our boss—is a

Russian intelligence asset. So that's the situation we're in. God help us all. Thank you all for your questions and have a blessed rest of your lives."

August 3, 2018

I love it when Trump supporters, attempting to justify Dear Leader's numerous glaring shortcomings as a human being, say things like, "We elected a president, not a Sunday school teacher."

Fair enough. A Sunday school teacher he most certainly is not.

"We elected a president, not some highbrow intellectual."

"We elected a president, not some polished public speaker."

"We elected a president, not a constitutional scholar."

Fair enough, fair enough.

We elected a president, not someone who reads them smart books without pictures in 'em, knows the difference between right and wrong, would inspire us to do good in the world, would make us feel better about ourselves as a nation, would cause us to believe in the better angels of human nature; not someone who would not be in awe of foreign strongmen and brutal dictators and homicidal tyrants and not be an avid dictator wannabe himself, no, not someone who wouldn't be an arrant lowlife and have the morals of a hungry hyena, no, not someone who wouldn't consider it absolutely inappropriate and indeed illegal to start minting money off his presidency right off the bat and like there's no tomorrow, not any kind of a half-decent person, not someone who wouldn't be a lifelong conman and scam artist, not someone who is not a sadist deriving sick pleasure from forever separating small children from their parents at the border just because those silly brown-skinned people with their snotty crying kids had taken it into their heads that they too wanted a better life for their children, no, not someone who gives a flying fig about some nonwhite or poor people's feelings, not someone in fact who wouldn't be a clinical sociopath incapable of caring about anyone other than himself, not someone who wouldn't be an ignorant buffoon and a deranged clown, not someone in full bloom of dementia, certainly not someone who wouldn't be a racist or a downright fascist, not someone who wouldn't see fit to state publicly that some Nazis and white supremacists are "very fine people," not someone not like that; not someone who would actually love and want to protect his country, who wouldn't be perfectly prepared from day one to sell his country down the river to the highest bidder or be deep in the pocket of his country's primary foreign enemy, no, not someone not like that; not someone who wouldn't be an open traitor, not someone who wouldn't be a sexual predator, not someone remotely human, not someone who wouldn't make us feel dirty and nauseated and filled with despair constantly, all the time, at the very thought of him besmirching the people's White House with his obscene presence. . . .

Not someone not like that.

We elected a president.

August 5, 2018

Russia's Foreign Ministry has appointed Steven Seagal its special representative for Russian-US humanitarian ties. The sixty-six-year-old humanitarian was made a Russian citizen in 2016 by Putin's personal decree. He neither speaks nor reads Russian but, like Trump, he loves and worships Putin—and that's all that really matters. His duties will include familiarizing Americans with the great riches of Russian culture. Trump is likely to reciprocate by appointing Kid Rock US Cultural Attaché in Moscow.

It is no wonder Trumpland loves Putin's Russia—and Putin's Russia loves Trumpland right back.

August 7, 2018

In response to a WashingtonPost.com headline, "Trump's rally rhetoric is going to get someone killed":

. . . and when—not if, I'm afraid—some journalist does get killed after one of his Nuremberg rallies, do you think he will feel chastened and shut up? Or that the followers of his cult will recoil from him in shame and horror?

No, he will not. They will not. They've passed the point of no return on the dark path of inhumanity.

August 13, 2018

The post below, in response to the death of Aretha Franklin, appeared six days later at NewYorker.com as "Hearing Aretha Franklin's 'I Say a Little Prayer' in the Soviet Union."

The year was 1983. The time of year: late fall. Late evening. Leningrad, USSR. I was sitting at a cluttered table in my one-bedroom apartment, in a sturdy six-floor building put up by German POWs shortly after the Second World War, on a quiet street in the southwestern part of the city—a ten-minute walk away from the Park of Victory metro station. Nothing was happening, nothing was about to happen, a zero-suspense situation: just a random moment caught in the resin of time, the amber of memory. I was gazing ahead, out the half-shaded window, sitting in the diffuse circle of warm light from a tall floor lamp to the left of me, with my elbows propped on the table and my head resting in the palms of my hands, in front of a half-empty bottle of an acrid, half-dry Bulgarian red called

The Evening Bells and a white faience teacup with a chipped rim. In the boreal darkness outside, there was nothing for me to perceive but an irregular checkered pattern of blue- and yellow-lit windows in the apartment building across the way. Beyond those windows, perfectly and naturally unaware of my existence, ordinary Soviet citizens like me silently lived their ordinary human lives: hugging or ignoring one another, standing still in their kitchens in tank tops and nightgowns and saying something silently to someone unseen, flinging angry words at one another, gesticulating broadly and opening and closing their mouths, drinking tea, eating something greasy from an aluminum pan on the stove, or just staring into the night's emptiness with unseeing eyes, their foreheads pressed against the windowpane, a slow-burning cigarette squeezed between their pressed lips. Sometimes I would wave a hand at them, and sometimes they would notice and walk away from the window, or smile fleetingly, or shake a fist at me. On top of the small cabinet behind me sat a portable Philips tape player. It had been a lavish parting gift, replete with two actual tapes—one of David Bowie's greatest hits, one of Aretha Franklin's—from an American friend and drinking companion, a graduate student studying Russian in New York who had spent a year in the city on an exchange program and had left for home a few months earlier. "I say a little prayer for you," Aretha Franklin was singing. I never tired of listening to that particular song, and I played it a few times almost every evening. I could understand many of the lyrics, too, which was cool and made me feel as if I were, in some small part, an American myself: "The moment I wake up, before I put on my makeup, I say a little prayer for you," and then, "Forever and ever, you'll stay in my heart, and I will love you forever, and ever, we never will part, oh, how I love you," and "Together, that's how it must be, to live without you would only mean heartbreak for me," and, finally, "My darling, believe me, for me there is no one but you!" It was a very beautiful song. I was drinking the acrid, half-dry Bulgarian red and listening to that song, and my heart was filled with sadness and happiness. When it was over, I would get up, go over to the cabinet, rewind the tape, and play it again. As far as I was aware, no one was saying any little prayers for me anywhere in the giant dark city of Leningrad or anyplace else in the world. But, well, so what? So what. That was fine by me. It was no big deal. I was drinking the undrinkable wine and listening to that song, and my heart was filled with sadness and happiness. There was no valid reason for me to feel happy, for I could think of not a single aspect of my life that anyone in his right mind might find remotely appealing, much less feel envious of. I was an engineer and lowly security guard in the Roller Coaster unit of the Attractions Sector in the Central Park of Culture and Leisure, with no salary to speak of. I was a permanently unsuccessful applicant for an exit visa from the Soviet Union, which was a precarious, vulnerable position to be in, especially in the year of our Soviet Lord 1983, under the dark shadow of the slowly dying, ruthless former KGB head Yuri Andropov. I was a samizdat writer with no realistic hopes of ever being published by any official Soviet journal or magazine. As far as I could tell, if I were to be honest with myself, I had no viable future in, like, the world, and no realistic prospects of ever being allowed to leave the country. But, then again, who could responsibly predict the future in a futureless world? We all were suspended in viscous timelessness, so there was no point trying to divine what lay ahead in the nebulous— Nebulous? "You're drunk," I told myself. It was my second bottle. I refilled the cup and emptied it. "I say a little prayer for you," Aretha Franklin was singing in the night. "Thank you," I said. "That's nice to hear." And it was.

August 16, 2018

Donald J. Trump
@realDonaldTrump

There is nothing that I would want more for our Country than true FREEDOM OF THE PRESS. The fact is that the press is FREE to write and say anything it wants, but much of what it says is FAKE NEWS, pushing a political agenda or just plain trying to hurt people. HONESTY WINS!

9:10 AM – 16 Aug 2018

For all those of you, Trump haters, whose minds, like mine, are hopelessly corroded by cynicism—no, he does NOT hate the FREE PRESS: he actually loves and cherishes the hell out of it, and he cherishes and loves it more than all of us put together could ever love anything or anyone! The PRESS that's FREE to say only good things about him! He loves it. What's not to love? He is the regular Thomas freaking Jefferson of our time! It's the FAKE NEWS that he hates, OK? The FAKE NEWS. The news he doesn't like. Whatever he doesn't like is FAKE. Who wouldn't hate the news one doesn't like? Think about it: If you had spent your entire life being a crook, a racist, a sexist pig, and an admirer of foreign tyrants and dictators, and then you had decided, all of a sudden, to betray your country and accept the help of your country's most dangerous enemy in order to become the president of your country and thereby further monetize your so-called brand—TRUMP! RUMP!—and then the disgustingly dishonest FAKE NEWS had started writing stories about you as a lifelong crook and racist and fascist and sexist pig and dictator wannabe and downright traitor—wouldn't you also hate that? I'd bet you would.

So then, leave Trump alone. He is just a demented, deranged, tired, cretinous most powerful man in the world, and he is scared out of his wits right now, because at this point he can see where the ugly trajectory of his life is ultimately headed. He loves the FREE PRESS, and he wants it to love him back. Give him a break. Is that too much to ask? HONESTY WINS!

August 19, 2018
Twenty-seven years ago today, I woke up in my rented apartment at Bush and Taylor in San Francisco, automatically turned on the TV, watched for a minute or two a live broadcast from Moscow on CNN; and then, filled with dread, dialed the number of a close friend who lived a few blocks away and—he wasn't home; I remembered that he and his girlfriend had been out of town over the weekend and were only going to be back later that Monday afternoon—left a message on his answering machine, to the effect that, apparently, the Soviet Union was back in full force in Russia, yes, unimaginably, so we probably would never get to see Russia again. Oh man, what went around came around. . . . But infinitely more important, of course, was what was going to happen to all our friends there now—it was terrible even to think about it.

Back then, as would become clear just two days thereafter, the coup against Russia staged by its Soviet past had failed miserably. Some ten years later, however, the people of Russia, desperate and discombobulated, would voluntarily give their onerous, burdensome newfound freedom away to a bunch of former KGB wolves in exchange for a promise of a modicum of evanescent prosperity. And now, not surprisingly, the majority of them have neither. Russia's history goes around in circles, like an old purblind piebald circus horse, nodding its blinkered head mournfully. Such a shame, such a waste of so many good lives.

August 22, 2018

She is going to Africa in October. When asked to specify where exactly in Africa she will be going, her press office replied:

"Africa is Africa. The First Lady will be going to as many parts of Africa as possible in the few short days out of her busy schedule that she'll be there. Africa, as some of you may know, is a very large country, almost the size of California, with lots of Africans in it. So she'll be going to the middle of Africa, and to the West of Africa, too, and maybe even to the North or South of it, as well. Wherever she goes, she'll be talking to African people, mainly about the negative effects of cyberbullying, challenging them to 'be best.' Time permitting, she may even visit the Eastern part of Africa, where her husband used to believe his predecessor in the White House was born. The First Lady also is looking forward to seeing elephants, tigers, and jaguars in their natural habitat."

August 22, 2018

I've said this before and will say it again: it would be useless and counterproductive to waste one's time trying to change the minds of the 30-35% of Americans constituting the hard core of Trump's base of support. They will stick with him until the bitter end, because, for them, abandoning him would be tantamount to abandoning the notion of themselves as good, decent human beings, ones fully legitimized and justified by him, their gloriously shameless and fearlessly vulgar cult leader, in their latent racism and stubborn bigotry, their xenophobia and seething resentment of The Other, their fear and loathing of the unknown, of the new life that, inexorably, is passing them by. Without him, they'd be lost again in the echoing darkness of their loserdom—and would have to face the glaring meaninglessness and gaping emptiness of their lives. . . .

In the wake of Nikita Khrushchev's "secret" report to the 20th Congress of the Communist Party, in February 1956—one denouncing and effectively desanctifying Stalin, three years after the latter's death, as a mass murderer of innocent people, rather than the greatest and wisest human being ever to walk the earth—there was registered across the country a rash of suicides among the mid- to high-ranking Party members, unable to reconcile themselves to the reality of their having wasted their lives worshipping a false idol and veritable antichrist of Marxist-Leninist theory, the wicked perverter and debaucher of the beautiful panhuman idea of the deathless future Kingdom of Communism.

August 23, 2018
The biggest scandal of the Obama presidency: his wearing a tan suit to a press conference.

The relatively minor, by comparison, brouhahas of the Trump era: his being a traitor, a racist, a tax evader, a lifelong conman and megacorruptionist, a sexist pig and sexual predator, a vile vulgarian, a two-bit mob boss straight from central casting, an ignorant buffoon, and a . . .

Well, one could go on in the same vein, of course, but what would be the point, really, when it is clear as day that no self-respecting American president would ever dare to degrade and humiliate his nation by wearing a tan suit to a press conference?

August 23, 2018
"If I ever got impeached, I think the market would crash. I think everybody would be very poor. Because without this

thinking you would see—you would see numbers that you wouldn't believe in reverse."

—Donald Trump, this morning on *Fox and Friends*

"If my employer were not to increase my salary by 30 . . . yes, 35, at least 40 percent over the next year, the Russian ruble and Turkish lira would totally collapse, there would be earthquakes and volcano eruptions all across the state of Nebraska, all the fish in the Pacific Ocean would come out of the water and start walking toward Washington, DC, chanting, in a multitude of fish languages, 'Raise Mikhail's salary!'; Vladimir Putin would reveal to the world that his real name is Beelzebub and that he is an illegitimate son of Richard Nixon, a terrible drought would descend upon Alaska and Siberia, all the trains in the world would simultaneously come to an inexplicable halt, all the planes would be snatched from the sky and taken to other galaxies by alien spaceships, eternal darkness would envelop the planet, there would be no more laughter ever heard anywhere— and that's just for starters, that I can tell you. You wouldn't believe in reverse what would start happening."

August 26, 2018
In response to news of the death of Senator John McCain:

He was a Reagan Republican—a staunch conservative, far to the right of most congressional Democrats—yet among his closest friends in the Senate were such avowed liberals as Ted Kennedy, Joe Biden, and John Kerry. Kerry had seriously considered inviting McCain to be his running mate in 2004. In 2008, McCain was all set to bring the conservative Democrat Joe Lieberman onto his ticket—but, unfortunately, his campaign advisors had prevailed upon him to look elsewhere for a vice-presidential nominee, with disastrous consequences.

He was a conservative Republican, but mainly he was his own man, repeatedly trespassing the boundaries of party dogma. Above all else, he was a good, decent, and kind man. He made mistakes and admitted them. He had flare-ups of anger and impatience, and he later apologized for those too. He was essentially human.

He was not a cerebral intellectual in the mold of Adlai Stevenson, Daniel Patrick Moynihan, or Barack Obama—but he had a quick wit, a sharp mind, and a keen sense of humor. And he was full of life.

He was full of life, to a remarkable degree. Having lingered in hell for five and a half years in his youth, he clearly had fun being alive, constantly exhibiting avid curiosity about everything and everyone.

He was entirely one of a kind. We won't see the likes of him again—ever, or at least not in the foreseeable future, which is one and the same thing within the scope of ordinary human life's chronology. Whom could one compare him to, among the American politicians of the modern era? Perhaps only Bobby Kennedy.

What else is there to say? Many—many more—books will be written about him, many biopics released.

On a personal note, as a former USSR transplant, a constituent atom of the ill-starred Soviet Atlantis, I would point out that unlike hardly any other prominent American politician, from the very first to the very end, he was unerringly and consistently correct in his starkly negative assessment of Vladimir Putin and the profoundly criminal, corrosive, and deadly dangerous nature of Putin's regime.

He was indeed so full of life, it is more than a little strange now to realize that he is gone.

August 27, 2018

Germany exorcised Nazism by going through the agonizing process of denazification.

Post-Soviet Russia never found the inner strength to subject itself to the process of decommunization—and what a sorry sight it is now.

When the shameful current period of its history finally is over, the United States, if it wants to regain a measure of its own self-respect, inevitably will have to undergo an abiding and doubtless highly unpleasant process of detrumpification.

August 27, 2018

Trump is a weakling's idea of a strong man, a coward's idea of a hero, a loser's idea of a winner.

August 28, 2018

Whenever (constantly, let's be honest) I Google myself—and typically, as in Trump's case, that also tends to happen around 4:30–5 AM—I, too, invariably feel infuriated by Google's deliberate willful suppression of all the (numerous, as I happen to know) references wherein I am called "brilliant," "a timeless genius," "generalissimo," "the handsomest man ever to walk the earth," "intellectual demigod from Leningrad's outskirts," "someone whose face totally belongs on Mount Rushmore," "the Usain Bolt of mental acuity," "Homer's equal and Tolstoy's superior," and "father of all nations and the immortal great leader of all the progressive forces of the world."

Why is Google doing this to me? Envious much? Or is this due to the billions of dollars surreptitiously paid by my enemies to keep all those references under wraps? Damn you, Google! So unfair! Time for me to intervene!

August 29, 2018
In response to a headline, "Senior executive of a steel plant in Russia, Bruno Charles de Kooman, falls out of window in Moscow":

A word of advice, people: don't be senior executives of large Russian steel plants, or any other plants or factories there, or of any large or small banks, for that matter, or . . . well, of anything else. Just don't, if you know what's good for you. Don't be senior—or even mid-level or junior—executives of, well, anything there. And if, against most people's sound judgment, you already happen to be one, an executive of this or that or the other in Russia, then consider leaving, as soon as possible, or at the very least do not under any circumstances come close to open or even closed windows on any floors above the second one there, in Russia, because Russia is a phenomenal place from the standpoint of its physical properties, one with a much greater than normal gravitational pull of its open or even closed window areas, especially for senior or junior executives of money-rich entities who were not born there or lived their entire lives there . . . in Russia. Don't take it into your head that you can fool Russia into believing you're one of its own. You are not and never will be. Just stay away from top-floor windows, that's all, especially if you happen to be someone having something to do with anything at all money-related. Don't come close to windows in Russia. Don't even go into any rooms with windows, to be on the safe side. And if you can help it, don't go into any rooms there at all, period. Because windows can be found in windowless rooms there also, you know. It is indeed a strange, unpredictable, illogical, and therefore dangerous place. Don't be smart to the point of being stupid. Don't fool yourself into thinking you can pull the wool over Russia's sleepy watchful eyes. Russia doesn't like that.

August 30, 2018

How many panicky, animalistically anguished, totally incoherent, and fully insane tweets filled with sweaty panic, howling despair, and existential horror has he unloosed on the world since this morning yet—nine, ten?

Someone should just finally heed that ceaseless tiny, thin cry for help emanating from the White House, and gently nudge him out. Putin would be only too glad to grant him political asylum in Russia—a massive blow to Trumpland's ego.

Putin would love to be able to humiliate America in that way. He's got nothing else going for him, at this time.

Well, admittedly, Trump may not be ready to abscond to Russia just yet, stealthily, under the cover of night, dressed up as a sanitation worker, but the time when that would become the most viable of his lifetime options is advancing fast on him. Regardless, something should be done about his pathological tweeting, and as soon as possible, or else before long, mark my words, his typical tweet will look like this:

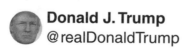

Donald J. Trump
@realDonaldTrump

AAAAAAAAAAAAAAHHHHH!   WITCHHUNT!!!
AAAAA!! COMEY!!! OHR!!!! AAAAAA! 13 ANGRY
DEMOCRATS!!!   AAAHHHHHHHHHHHHHHHH!
AAAA!   AAAAA!!!!!   MUELLER!!   CNN!!!
AAAAAAAAAAAAAAAAAA! ENEMY OF THE
AAAAHHHHH!!!!!! AAAAAAAAAAAAA!!!!!!

x:xx AM – Xxx 20xx

What can I say? I've seen many different people in my life. Some of them were pretty damn terrible individuals: small-time KGB rats, hoodlums and snitches and broken-spirited dead-drunks, sadists and subterranean monsters, brain-dead and stone-hearted party functionaries—legion is their useless collective name—but I have never (and do believe me when I tell you this), not once, seen a whinier, more pitiful, and altogether more pathetic human being than Donald J. Trump, the accidental and illegitimate current occupant of the White House.

August 31, 2018
And again, back for a moment to that unprecedented Trump approval rating among African Americans in a new ABC/ *Washington Post* poll:

3% approve

93% disapprove

"What do you have to lose?"

Remember that?

Apparently, quite a lot, Trump.

Mikhail Iossel
September 2018

September 1, 2018

On the occasion of the funeral of Senator John McCain:

This funeral, from beginning to end, was the larger, self-respecting, and essentially decent America's repudiation of Trump and Trumpland and everything Trumpism represents in the darker precincts of America's heart: pettiness, gracelessness, dishonesty, bigotry, racism, xenophobia, know-nothingism, immorality, fascistic contempt for democracy, shameful yearning for a dictator, festering desire for a strong hand, and the pathetic bitter fear of the future.

No, America's future does not belong to Trump and trumpism. Trumpland is dying out, shrinking and shriveling constantly, inexorably, like Balzac's *La Peau de chagrin*. It has no future.

It was indeed quite a contrast today, hearing Barack Obama say, in his eulogy of John McCain, "Today is only one day in all the days that will ever be. But what will happen in all the other days that ever come can depend on what you do today"—after skimming with disgust the early-morning flurry of that treasonous White House pariah's insane panicky tweets, filled with sheer vile madness, the typed equivalent of a hungry wild ass's braying.

September 2, 2018

Yes, of course, some American presidents of the modern era were less than stellar human beings, some were ignorant and downright stupid, and a number of the momentously flawed decisions made by them as a result had globally catastrophic consequences; and, indeed, the political strategies and tactics they sometimes, and not infrequently, deployed to attain power were starkly underhanded and often downright reprehensible.

All too true.

Yet still. None were traitors to their country, not one sought the help of America's arch-foe to win the White House, not one was in the pocket of a former KGB colonel, not one had sold America to its sworn enemy for personal financial gain.

That's what makes Trump cardinally, qualitatively different from any and all of his predecessors. He has zero love or respect for his country.

That, and also—among many other such fine details— not one of the above had the sheer lowliness of spirit to mock a disabled person or humiliate the parents of a fallen soldier. Not one denigrated the service or questioned the courage of American POWs. Not one was remotely that classless and breathtakingly indecent. Not one appealed solely and exclusively to absolutely the worst angels of human nature. That's pure Trump—the walking embodiment of the worst of the worst of America.

September 5, 2018

By now the absolute majority of Americans are painfully aware that Donald Trump possesses the mental acuity and overall temperament of a deeply disturbed and massively debauched ten-year-old, which also, by indirect osmosis, means that we all should be immensely grateful to the tiny handful of sober-minded grownups within his administration, especially those in military uniform, who, by continually keeping him out of the loop on the most consequential elements of the nation's decision-making process, are preventing his restless tweeting self from starting a nuclear war, say, or finding some other ingenuous way to destroy the world. Thank you so very much, dear clenched-jawed grownups heroically surrounding in a tight circle of sanity our demented orange-haired commander in chief.

And many thanks to you, too, once again (one can never thank you enough): the seventy thousand of the brightest of America's lightbulbs scattered across three states who, conjointly with all the other Trump voters, as well as Vladimir Putin, Jill Stein, Gary Johnson, and, yes, James Comey—and despite the popular-vote loss of three million—have succeeded at installing that vile imbecile in the White House.

September 7, 2018

Barack Obama just spoke for an hour at the University of Illinois at Urbana-Champaign. Just two years ago, America had a president who was brilliantly smart, unimpeachably decent, and uniquely eloquent. Today there is an all-around degenerate, to put it simply, living in the White House.

With all the modest powers of my creative imagination, I could not possibly conceive of a greater contrast between two American presidents—or just two Americans, for that matter.

Trump succeeding Obama—to the country, it is like falling from a mountaintop and landing right in the middle of a fetid swamp.

Getting out of the swamp is never easy. But there is no alternative to it—no other way for one to survive with dignity.

September 11, 2018

 Donald J. Trump
@realDonaldTrump

17 years since September 11th!

7:58 AM – 11 Sep 2018

The orange man living in the White House knows how to touch the hearts and minds of his fellow citizens in his poignant tribute to the anniversary of the worst tragedy in the nation's history.

September 11, 2018

At the start of our first English lesson, in the fifth grade of middle school, the teacher, whom I shall call N. I., said, "It is only natural for all of us here to assume that the only language it would be natural for everyone on earth to speak and to think and have dreams in is Russian. But, in fact, many millions, billions even, of people all across the world, those not sufficiently fortunate to have been born in our great country, live their whole lives and communicate between themselves in other languages—yes, imagine—such as, very prominently, English, admittedly the primary language of the international imperialism, but not only and not exclusively. Lots of good people speak it also."

We found those words funny and laughed heartily.

Three years later, by the last English class at the end of the eighth and final grade of middle school, most of us, in addition to being able to recite much of the English alphabet (some even managed the entirety of it), could blurt out, however imperfectly, the tricky English tongue-twister, "Why do you cry, Willy? Why do you cry? Why, Willy? Why, Willy? Why, Willy? Why?"

One of the eighth grade's worst pupils, Alik S.—one of the four of us Jewish kids in our class of forty, and the last student to be called on by N. I. to declaim that tricky little English phrase—got up reluctantly and, in a voice hoarse with habitual dull despondency, enunciated it in the following way: "Vai du u crai vili. Vai du u crai. Vai vylivai vylivai vylivai."

(It should be noted here parenthetically, for clarity's sake, that "*vylivai*," in Russian, is the singular imperative mood of the English verb "to pour out.")

We all fairly roared with laughter, needless to say, because it was so damn hilarious, the way Alik S. mooed it out, that slow string of weird sounds, unwittingly ordering some poor imaginary Vili to pour something out—and our homeroom teacher, N. O., who had stepped into the "English" classroom but a moment earlier, in order to make some routinely urgent announcement about something or other future-related, waited until we started to calm down and then said good-naturedly to still-standing Alik, "You, Alik, are the living, breathing refutation of the widespread erroneous superstition that all Jews are smart."

Alik, his big mulish head hung low, exhibited no reaction to those words of hers, but many of us, me included, found her remark pretty funny, and we snickered again, although a bit less boisterously this time.

N. O. looked around the room and, seeing my smiling face in the second front row on the right, by the wall, fixed me with a hard stare and said to me, "And you, Iossel, should be the last one to laugh. You may be somewhat smart, but you have many other negative qualities."

I shrugged with pretend nonchalance, unclear as to what exactly she was referring to yet knowing, too, that of course she was right. Of course she was.

Many other negative qualities. The last one to laugh. Fair enough.

Why did I remember just now this thoroughly inconsequential distant episode from another lifetime? No idea. No reason.

September 16, 2018

The two unprepossessing GRU operatives, Alexander Petrov and Ruslan Boshirov (not their actual names, to be sure), who went to the UK back in early March, to kill (OK: allegedly) the former GRU agent Sergei Skripal (and unintentionally, his visiting daughter, too, for good measure: tough luck, dear traitor's offspring) with the super-potent nerve agent called Novichok ("newbie," in Russian)—they, of course, couldn't have anticipated there being quite so many damn CCTV cameras all over the place there, in jolly old England, including virtually at every other street intersection in the soporific historic town of Salisbury, famous for its grand medieval cathedral, where their former senior colleague and subsequent MI6 turncoat, above-said Mr. Sergei Skripal, had been peacefully (as if nothing happened) residing since 2006.

Being identified and named publicly as the sole suspects in one of the most brazen biochemical terrorist attacks ever committed on British soil certainly had not been part of the two hapless travelers' plan, to say nothing of their GRU bosses. So they just disappeared from the face of the Earth for a while.

Following the perfectly predictable, initial knee-jerk volley of sarcasm-ridden indignation from the Russian Foreign Ministry, there ensued a fraught period of confused silence, until finally Putin himself decided it was time to deal with the internationally embarrassing issue in a proactive manner and, in off-the-cuff remarks to the media, expressed his hope that the two individuals in question, those supposed Russian intelligence officers, whoever they might be in reality and wherever in Russia they might be at the moment, could be located and asked to provide some kind of comment about this whole provocative Russophobic hysteria.

After that, almost immediately, as if by magic, the elusive "Petrov and Boshirov" were indeed discovered and brought to the offices of the main outward-bound Kremlin propaganda mouthpiece, the Russia Today broadcasting company, for an on-air conversation with the latter's odious editor-in-chief, Margarita Simonyan.

The two men, it turned out, were not ready for prime time. In the course of an interview—whose degree of difficulty hardly exceed that of Sean Hannity's comradely repartee with Rudy Giuliani on FOX News—they managed to make a national laughingstock out of themselves. The embarrassing thing went viral in a matter of hours. Hemming and hawing throughout, they sweated copiously, mumbling something unintelligible, mispronouncing the name of that damn medieval town of Salisbury (where they claimed they went in order to enjoy the view of the world-famous local ancient Gothic cathedral, one of the world's greatest architectural wonders, with its 123-meter spire, but were in the end unable to view it, sadly, because, see, it was snowing heavily in Salisbury that day—not true—and, well, you know) and finding themselves unable adequately to explain what it was exactly they did for a living (mid-level businessmen in the area of sports nutrition, one of them finally stammered out, and as to why neither they themselves nor their putative business had any online presence whatsoever, that was because the sports nutrition business loves anonymity) or what in the world they were doing hanging around Skripal's house in Salisbury, as registered by several CCTV cameras, or why their visit to the UK on that occasion lasted two days and one night only (their original intention had been to get totally and properly debauched in London, they explained weakly, but then they took it into their heads to catch a morning train to that town of Sal . . . Salibursy, to see that goddamn cathedral, all the more so it's really close to Stonehenge or whatever, which is another ancient historical artifact), or why, oddly, their return tickets to Moscow had been booked on two successive night flights (just in case, you know. . . . In case of what?), and so on. In short, a pitiful, painful spectacle. Giving interviews for million-strong international audiences was not the "Petrov-Boshirov" duo's strong suit. One would be almost justified in feeling even a bit sorry for them, in point of fact, if not for the nagging minor circumstance of their being, well, murderers—cruel, cold-blooded murderers, these two ordinary Russian guys in their late thirties, none too bright or well-educated, none too savvy or cool—just your ordinary Russian guys, two out of many millions.

Just your ordinary Russian guys, you know. Guys, you know. In every large or mid-size Russian city, one can find lots and lots of near-exact likes of them. I, for one, know guys like them, too. I grew up around guys like that. They're just guys, you know. Just . . . guys.

During the week, they work. It doesn't really matter where they work and what they do for a living. Stuff, that's what they do, if you must know. Running some kind of small or mid-level business maybe. Nothing too special or exciting. Or they work at some factory or what have you. Some secret research facility, providing security. Or they are cops maybe, or maybe they are military in reserve. Or they are jail wardens, perhaps, or café-kiosk owners, or members of some relatively innocuous moblike sports-veterans organization. It doesn't really matter. Or maybe they work for the FSB or the GRU, which would make them relatively powerful and important people, at least in their own minds. Work is work. Money. Cabbage. Dough. After work, they go home and have dinner and drink beer and watch crime shows or football on TV. They have wives and kids, like everyone else, and mistresses too, more likely than not, because why not.

On weekends, they frequently can be found working on their cars, as they tell their wives, lounging around in their garages, which usually are a fair walk from where they live or a few bus or streetcar stops away. "Working on the car" in their respective, tiny shell-shaped garages (*rakushki*) means, in reality, hanging out with other guys just like them, friends and acquaintances, idling around, shooting the breeze, sitting on their haunches in Adidas training pants around the car with its hood agape, drinking vodka from plastic cups, smoking and talking about football and women and fishing and hunting and other guy stuff of that nature. Food and drink and fishing and stuff like that. Nothing fancy or nonmaterial, hardly anything that cannot be consumed. Real life, you know. No fancy, ephemeral, hoity-toity, nonguy stuff. They're not really interested in politics, because screw that shit, but they are keenly sensitive to the notion that the rest of the world might not respect Russia. They very much want the rest of the world to fear, if not respect, Russia. In the absence of respect, they'll take fear. It's the next best thing. Actually, screw respect. To hell with it. Fear is good. Let them fear us, them stuck-up Westerners, let them shake in their expensive, foreign-made loafers. They loathe arrogant America, those guys, of course, because it's so strong and big and rich and, like, devoid of spirituality; but they envy it, too. And they also pity that stupid naive America, or *Pindosiya*, as they inexplicably call it. They feel proud that they—well, it was Putin, of course, strictly speaking, but that automatically, by extension, means them, as well—have succeeded in installing our man, Donald Trump, that orange-headed doofus, as their, American president. Haha, that's a friggin' riot. That thought is a source of considerable pride for them, and they laugh derisively at them stupid, childishly naive Americans, so damn full of themselves. As for Putin, they like him, of course—or rather, well, who else is there? Putin is Putin. He's been in their lives forever. And he's like them, too. Deep down, he is a guy just like them, only super-rich and the most powerful man in the world. Putin is, like, *there*, you know—it doesn't actually matter whether you like him or not. He's like weather. If it rains, put on the raincoat and fetch the goddamn umbrella. If it's hot outside, wear nothing but a tank top and goddamn shorts. Elementary, Watson. What's there even to think about? Putin is friggin' God. Whatever Putin says needs to be done for the country—well, that would need to be done because he knows best what's good for all of them. If he says this or that son of a bitch must be liquidated, that's just what must happen, too. And traitors to the Motherland, he's totally right there, as always, those dirty turncoats, they friggin' need to be eliminated, one hundred percent, because if they go unpunished, that would give other potential traitors a false sense of hope and security. Traitors to the Motherland, and especially to *the organs*, must friggin' die. Period. Generally, too, whatever your boss tells you to do must be done, if you'd like to keep your damn job. You don't have to like it, you just have to do it, whatever it may be. Because as the saying has it, "You're the boss, I'm the fool. I'm boss, you're the fool."

And of course, obviously, not every assignment you're tasked with can be discussed with your friends—or with any other guys, as you all sit crouched on your haunches around your car with its hood lifted, drinking vodka from plastic cups and chewing the fat about fishing and hunting and football and women and Russia and friggin' America. There obviously are some important secrets you can't share with other guys in your garage, unless they happen to work where you work and know the same secrets you do. But it's all good. All good. Vodka and fishing and women and football and America and liquidating traitors and all that good stuff. Life is good. And Russia, Russia, of course. Mother Russia. Eternal. Pitiful. Put upon. Deathless. Beautiful.

That's guy stuff, you know. Russian guy stuff.

Finish your vodka now, it's time to go home and turn in for the night: tomorrow is going to be a long day. We're going to friggin' England, to grab a look at that friggin' cathedral there, in . . . Sal . . . Salsbersy or whatever. Frig that shit. Great cathedral, totally friggin' amazing, everyone says so.

That's not even Hanna Arendt's banality of evil— Hanna Arendt? Who's that? A Jew, no doubt. They're friggin' everywhere, word. Why can't they already friggin' leave Russia alone, for God's sake?—it's the banality of the banality of evil. Or, simpler still, the banality of banality. The ordinary cozy Russian fascism.

September 19, 2018

Donald Trump on Hurricane Florence:

"This is a tough hurricane, one of the wettest we've ever seen, from the standpoint of water."

From the Standpoint of Water. Not a bad title for an existential novel.

"I am the stupidest fake president in history, from the standpoint of stupidity."

September 19, 2018

I was asked what would happen in the good old Soviet Union to the editor of a literary journal who'd had the terrible judgment to publish a wrongful/misguided/erroneous/deeply flawed/spurious/mendacious/offensive essay/short story/novella/part of novel. Well, under Stalin, he almost certainly would have been arrested and shot dead, much to the monolithic jubilation of the Soviet people. However, in the much more "vegetarian" post-Stalin era, generally speaking (for there were periods of rather different degrees of nonfreedom therein), he would merely be booted from his job, vilified in newspapers and on the radio, banned from any public activity, made a pariah in intelligentsia circles, and likely end up dying in fairly short order, from drink or a heart attack. Nothing too extraordinary.

September 22, 2018

There was, I recall, closer to the end of the thirteen month-long interregnum between Yuri Andropov's death and the actual passing of his de facto defunct successor, Konstantin Chernenko, a certain, relatively brief period when the familiar, routinely absurd world around us suddenly appeared to have gone completely out of whack and the very air we breathed became saturated with a different, vaguely dangerous, incongruously mirthful kind of insanity. All at once, nothing and no one seemed to function quite in the same predictable, reliably half-assed old ways—or at all—and no one gave a damn about it. No one gave a damn about anything, period. Everyone looked slightly crazed and had a wild glint in their eyes. Everyone, it appeared, was permanently drunk, the entire great nation of Soviet people, including toddlers and dotty dodderers—or at least, that's the way it looked to us, friends of mine and me, probably because we were perennially three sheets to the wind ourselves.

I remember feeling existentially disoriented on a daily basis. It was, in all, like living in the eternal soul-stirring delirium of presunset hour on a fine spring day on Leningrad's boreal latitudes.

One Saturday afternoon in the firsts of March, if memory serves me, my friend S and I, newly clean and high-spirited, joyously inebriated after fulfilling our weekly ritual of spending several hours in the company of other friends and good acquaintances at a centrally located *banya* close by St. Isaac's Cathedral, alternating visits to the steam room with diving head first into a pool of ice-cold water and then relaxing in the half-secret nook of the *banya* cafeteria, reading newspapers and discussing politics and whatnot and drinking beer, we . . . Well, what do you know: this sentence has slithered away from me, somehow, beyond the point of no return, so . . .

One Saturday afternoon in the firsts of March, my friend S and I stopped by the newly opened beer restaurant (just your regular dive with an elevated notion of itself, featuring relatively clean tables and a meaningless printed menu) on Zhukovskogo Street, just off the Liteyny, in the cast-iron heart of the city— again, if I remember correctly (although that really doesn't matter, come to think of it)—and the burly, buzz-cut waiter rushed over to our table, looking oddly agitated, and whispered to us in a conspiratorial tone, "OK, guys, welcome, but look, I'll take your order in a moment, but first let me go and have a quick little fifty grams" [i.e. a shot of vodka—MI]. With that, he walked away briskly, swaying a bit on his feet, and in no time disappeared behind the heavy, imitation oak–panelled door across the floor.

The two of us, S and I, looked at each other in silence. Then he said, "That's pretty much it. The bottom, the end of the road. Nowhere left to go. When your waiter tells you he would only serve you after he took a shot, that pretty much means the total dissolution of any remaining illusion of normalcy." Or he said something along those lines, you understand. And then we laughed, of course.

In a few minutes, the waiter returned, his face red and glowing happily, and we had our beers and our beef stews, and then more beers and a couple of shots on top of those—and all was well with our world again.

This story has no storyline. This impromptu recollection has no point to it.

About a week or so later, if I am not mistaken, the unwieldy body of insensate Konstantin Chernenko mercifully heaved its last breath, and I remember (and indeed, I do), right around that time, on the day of Mikhail Gorbachev's assumption of power, a disheveled, rags-clad woman—a woman with terrible, hollow eyes and a mouth like a gaping black hole, evidently mad—standing in front of the once-upscale "Wines of Russia" specialty store, a stone's throw away from my apartment building, and shrieking at the top of her lungs, in a blood-curdling, torn-up voice of a medieval seer on poison mushrooms, calling our new general secretary the antichrist, on account of that sinister purple sign of the devil on his forehead, and prophesying war with America and the end of the world at the hands of, who else, the Jews.

September 22, 2018

Far and away the most popular, most universally beloved American in the Soviet Union of the '70s and early '80s—the ultimate ur-American of the Soviet people's America-besotted imaginings—was the Colorado-born crooner named Dean Reed. He was constantly on Soviet TV, and his Soviet-made records sold in the millions. He was a communist, a pacifist, an anarchist, a libertarian, and God knows what else. He claimed to have made numerous attempts to be stripped of US citizenship, but alas. . . . I remember, as a teen, reading his open letter to Solzhenitsyn in the popular weekly *Ogonyok*, in which he berated the author of *The Gulag Archipelago* for essentially playing the role of a naive useful idiot for the rotten capitalist West. I remember thinking: what an asshole. But he was not an asshole, really. He was just a pawn in the hands of Soviet, and then (after he married an East German film star) East German propaganda. Deep down, he was just a good-natured country boy and, on the surface of that, an unsuccessful Elvis impersonator. One thing he most certainly was not was an exceptionally smart and perspicacious person, as a result of which, apparently and unwittingly having gotten himself a bit too deeply enmeshed in the sensitive areas of Cold War maelstroms, he was found one morning in 1986 floating face down on the surface of the pond on his suburban property in East Germany. I was just reminded on Facebook that today he would have turned eighty. His was a short life. Someone probably should write a book about him.

September 22, 2018
As a boy, I was drawn to reference books: encyclopedias, dictionaries, geographic atlases, political maps, all manner of almanacs. I could name the capital and identify the state flag of every country in the world (a world different from the one we live in now), spell correctly from memory (nearly?) every word contained in the dictionary of foreign words in Russian language, rattle off the full roster of every soccer team in the

major league and the essential stats of the national hockey team going back to early fifties. I would spend long hours in the library room of my great uncle and his family's spacious old apartment on Sixth Red Cavalry Street in the heart of "Dostoyevsky's Petersburg," perusing the fifty-two volumes of the *Great Soviet Encyclopedia*, published when Stalin was still alive. The three-volume *Soviet Encyclopedic Dictionary*, published in 1953–55, was a favorite of mine, and I would read and reread it incessantly. I remember holding it in my hands; I remember its heft, the musty smell of its pages with their tiny font. I remember this so vividly. I probably should buy it online or from a street vendor somewhere on Brighton Beach or in Tbilisi, say.

I still like encyclopedias, but who needs them anymore? And I was happy to read this, in my favorite essay by Guy Davenport, "On Reading": "And then I made the discovery that what I liked in reading was to learn things I didn't know."

September 25, 2018
In response to news that the United National General Assembly burst out laughing during Trump's speech there:

Trumpland, your president is being laughed at during his UN speech. This is the first in the history of US presidents' speeches at the UN. That's because he is a fool, which is why you love him in the first place, so it's all good.

September 25, 2018
Had a conversation with a friend today, and noted in the course of it the following difference in the way the Soviet Politburo and Putin, respectively, some four decades ago and nowadays, sought to influence and destabilize the political situation in the US:

In the late seventies, the then-head of the KGB, Yuri Andropov, made a remark to the effect that the Soviet Union had won the Vietnam War in the streets of the American cities. The Soviet leadership, via the KGB and Soviet embassy/consulates, invested many millions of dollars in helping to organize antiwar demonstrations in the US. The intended audience for its propagandistic efforts was, therefore, the American college youth and various progressive segments of US society.

Putin and his inner circle of former KGB functionaries-cum-multibillionaire mafia oligarchs, in their turn, in the course of the 2016 presidential campaign (and beyond), had (and continue to have) their countless online trolls and bots and onsite agent provocateurs concentrating their efforts on fanning the flames of racism, bigotry, xenophobia, anti-Muslim fears, anti-Mexican resentment, and so on within American society by creating fictitious political groups and action committees, organizing mass gatherings of right-wing and ultrareactionary nature in various (predominantly, red and purple) parts of the country, et al.

In other words, while the Soviet Politburo and the old KGB targeted mainly the progressive, educated layers of American society, Putin and Co. go after the backward, poorly informed, racist, xenophobic, fearful, perennially embittered, past-bound ones.

The Soviet rulers tried to enlist the future of American society in their efforts to defeat America from within, while Putin is banking on those tied to America's past.

The Soviet Union is no more, America still here.

Putin, judging by the latest developments in Russia, will follow in the Soviet Politburo's footsteps sooner rather than later. He has outstayed his welcome with his own karma.

America, to state the obvious, is stronger than Brezhnev, Putin, and Trump put together and multiplied by a factor of foul infinity.

September 26, 2018

At the UN Security Council this morning, Trump accuses China of attempting to meddle in US elections.

China? China.

But not Russia. He cannot bring himself to say the same about Russia. He just cannot. Not about Russia. Not about Putin. China—yes, definitely. And maybe some other countries as well. Albania, say, or Morocco, or French Guiana. But not Russia. Not Putin. Never.

September 26, 2018

Brain the size of China.

He undoubtedly is the stupidest of all the rulers/heads of state I've lived under: Khrushchev, Brezhnev, Andropov, Chernenko, Gorbachev, Reagan, George H. W. Bush, Clinton, George W. Bush, and Obama (well, no kidding):

"If you look at Mr. Pillsbury, the leading authority on China, he was on a good show—I won't mention the name of the show—recently. And he was saying that China has total respect for Donald Trump and for Donald Trump's very, very large brain."

September 27, 2018

This, prominently, is what's at the root of the extraordinarily ugly predicament we all are in at this point in history: US presidents should not be elected without winning the popular vote. Minority rule is incompatible with democracy.

September 30, 2018

"We went back and forth, then we fell in love. He wrote me beautiful letters. And they are great letters. We fell in love."

> —Trump, speaking earlier tonight in West Virginia, at one of his Nuremberg rallies, about his relationship with Kim Jong-un.

That's so sweet! Innocent young love—what could be more beautiful. . . .

Donnie calls Kimmie "my cute little mass murderer." Kimmie calls Donnie "my big fat orange moron."

"Are you sure you are a real, actual American president?" Kimmie asks Donnie teasingly from time to time.

"There are enough suckers to go around in my country," Donnie replies with a gentle smile.

But they should pace themselves, those crazy kids. They, of course, have never heard of Albert Camus, but there did exist such a French writer, once upon a time, and he once wrote, "Love can burn or love can last. It can't do both."

It would be really nice, come to think of it, if the two of them, Donnie and Kimmie, were to elope together to some extremely remote, uninhabited island in the South Pacific.

September 30, 2018

Just as a rule of thumb, I don't believe anyone claiming to be in love with Kim Jong-un should be allowed to nominate Supreme Court justices.

Mikhail Iossel
October 2018

October 2, 2018

Sixty-two million people voted for Trump—a minority of the participating electorate, granted, yet still a lot of people. Not all of them, obviously, were racists (or Russian immigrants): most were genuinely, if naively, hoping they'd found an independent, self-made man who, by dint of not appearing beholden to either of the two major parties, would be in a position to introduce major changes to the nation's calcified, money-mad, wholly unresponsive political system; to shake things up but good in DC. There was, more than in any previous election cycle, in the gap between the two parties, room enough for a protest candidate to squeeze through—and that's just what Trump did. They thought, those tens of millions of deluded people, that they were voting for an influence-free candidate, someone who could be bold and daring and decisive and do the kinds of visionary things no party-affiliated president would be able to do; someone who could actually break the deadlock in Washington, once and for all, drain the old swamp, and so on—someone, in short, who would pay attention to them, the fearful and the angry and the ignorant, and make their lives palpably better. And a real protest candidate could indeed have accomplished an awful lot, by working both with Democrats and Republicans. Instead, what they got, those Trump voters, was someone everyone else with an ounce of common sense and basic moral judgment had known all along Trump was: a lifelong con artist, a grifter, a money launderer for Putin's oligarchs, a dictator-lover, an infinitely corrupt and immoral man—the worst of the worst.

Poor suckers.

And that's a shame and a pity.

October 3, 2018

Should anyone be under the illusion that Putin is one bit smarter or more polished than Trump, please be assured that is not the case. And he is just as much of a pig, needless to say, given to an even larger extent to repugnantly boorish and immensely ugly pronouncements made with the self-satisfied air of a regal lowlife. (But unlike Trump, he can actually have the people he doesn't like killed or, if they're lucky, thrown in jail: not an unimportant distinction.)

This erroneous notion of Putin as some sort of a sophisticated political operator, virtual grandmaster of geopolitical intrigue, the regular Machiavelli of the modern world, Conan Doyle's Professor Moriarty next to poor addlepated Trump, is rooted, of course, in the fact of his being a de facto dictator, a usurper of power, who for close to two decades now has been surrounded by concentric circles of trembling sycophants, adoring toadies, ardent bootlickers: those who never challenge and, obversely, praise to the sky the transcendental wisdom of a single word escaping his thin bloodless lips. Poisoned down to his rotten core by the pernicious drug of unlimited and unearned (God-given, in his view) omnipotence, he feels completely unbound in his utterances and actions.

He is the most dangerous man in the world right now, in terms of posing a direct threat to our basic humanity; for his lifelong existential project (whether he is able to articulate it to himself or, more likely, not) consists of proving to the world writ large that people, on the whole, are worse than they think they are: cruel, egotistical, cynical, and driven solely by the lowest denominator of rank self-interest.

October 4, 2018

Supreme Court nominee Brett Kavanaugh, his obvious lying to the Senate Judiciary Committee and his repulsive, FBI-verified frat-boy exploits back in college notwithstanding, gets confirmed by the Republicans and all hell breaks loose, then all the corroborating witnesses against Kavanaugh go straight to the media and leave no stones unturned in his sordid past and the nation (sans Trumpland) shudders in involuntary disgust, then Republicans lose the House (what goes around comes around), then, immediately thereafter, the Democratic House Judiciary Committee starts issuing subpoenas to everyone involved in this pathetic affair, from Director of the FBI Chris Wray down to the very last of those who had asked and didn't get to be interviewed by the FBI, and all hell breaks loose, then the House starts impeachment proceedings against Supreme Court Judge Kavanaugh and all hell breaks loose, then something else happens so unimaginable that all hell breaks loose, then something else happens on top of that, then something else entirely happens inevitably, then one or more of Trump's kids are indicted by Robert Mueller, and President Michael Avenatti does a jig on the Resolute Desk in the Oval Office and all hell breaks loose, then something else happens, then Putin gets forcibly removed from power in Russia and all hell breaks loose, then something else happens again, then something else happens completely out of the blue, then Citizen Trump belatedly puts on an orange jumpsuit and he looks good in it while holding a burger in his teeth and all hell breaks loose, then something else happens, then something else and something else and something else and all hell breaks loose and bats fly out of hell, then one day we'll all be saying, "*De mortuis nil nisi bonum,* but that certainly does not apply to him, hell no, so let's start breaking piñatas and uncork champagne," and all hell breaks loose, then something else happens, then something else and something else and all hell breaks loose and all hell and something else and all hell breaks loose and many major cities of the world start being swallowed by the ocean and all hell breaks loose, then something else happens entirely, then something else happens on top of that, then Republicans win back the House and start issuing subpoenas to everyone under the rapidly diminishing and darkening and cooling off sun and all hell breaks loose and so it goes so it goes so it goes. . . .

October 6, 2018

Get. Rid. Of. The Electoral College. Minority Rule. Is. Un-American.

October 7, 2018
In response to news that the president of Interpol, Meng Hongwei, has been detained by China and is "under the supervision" of a communist party watchdog:

There will be more and more of this sort of thing happening, as the authoritarian rulers and dictators all across the world, finally getting over the initial shock of disbelief at their own luck, are getting comfortable with the previously unimaginable idea that the current resident of the White House in America is firmly on their side and indeed effectively is one of them, having a whole lot more in common with Putin or Kim Jong-un than he does with Washington or Lincoln or Obama.

October 10, 2018

Trump is an evil clown entertaining crowds at his Nuremberg-style rallies by constant insults of, and borderline incitement to violence against, everyone who dislikes him (and that's a large majority of all Americans). His enablers in the Senate and in the House represent the virtual fifth column of the international antidemocratic movement headed by Putin. His hard-core base of support comprises racists, anti-Semites, and other bigots of all stripes. And yet, both he and them are perennially feeling victimized, wounded, insulted, aggrieved. Now they're howling in outrage about Hillary Clinton's suggesting that Democrats should not take Trump and the GOP's rampant bullying lying down. Hoodlums and bullies always feel victimized, put upon because even when they crow about being the greatest of winners, they are the ultimate losers, and they know it. No, one should not be hesitant to hurt their precious little feelings. When they go low, and they are always in the gutter, push back, strike back, give them a taste of their own bitter medicine.

October 11, 2018

We've been through bleaker times. They never last forever. (But then, in fairness, neither do we.) Doom and gloom are overrated. Hopelessness is the ground zero of hope.

As the book went to press, the US midterm elections were three weeks away. The Special Counsel investigation, headed by Robert Mueller, was still going on. Donald Trump was still the president of the United States. For regular updates through the lens of Mikhail Iossel, follow him on Facebook or elsewhere in cyberground.